RELIGION AND ATHEISM IN DIALOGUE

The divide in our societies between those who are religious and those who are not is becoming increasingly apparent in many areas of contemporary life. This fascinating book, based on conversations between religious and non-religious participants, asks if societies divided on such fundamental questions can nonetheless find some common ground.

A rich array of topics is explored, including the linguistic complexities of using the concept of 'God', the relation between science and religion, the ethics of altruistic concern, sexuality and gender roles, and the possibility of shedding light on important positions often taken to be intractable or non-negotiable. In addition, topics of a more reflective nature, but also prone to polarise, are also examined, such as spiritual experience and practice, mindfulness, the arts, and the nature of human consciousness.

Religion and Atheism in Dialogue will interest anyone who is concerned about the current tensions and even conflicts exhibited between religious and secular positions on a range of key issues, and how it might be possible to move beyond them. It will also be of interest to students of ethics, philosophy of religion, and religious studies and all those who are concerned to explore how better dialogue across differences might be possible.

Anthony J. Carroll is a philosopher, theologian, and parish priest in Andalusia, Spain. His previous books include *Protestant Modernity: Weber, Secularisation and Protestantism*; *Il Giardiniere Invisibile: Credere, Non Credere, Cercare*; and most recently *A History of Philosophy: The Condensed Copleston*. He was co-editor with Richard Norman of *Religion and Atheism: Beyond the Divide* (Routledge, 2016).

Richard Norman is Emeritus Professor of Moral Philosophy at the University of Kent and a Patron of Humanists UK. His books include *On Humanism* (Routledge, second edition, 2012), *Understanding Humanism* (with Andrew Copson and Luke Donnellan; Routledge, 2022), and *What Is Humanism For?* (2025).

RELIGION AND ATHEISM IN DIALOGUE

Doing Difference Differently

Edited by Anthony Carroll and Richard Norman

LONDON AND NEW YORK

Cover: *Boats reflecting in the water at Lake Paprocany in Tychy, Poland.* By Robert Wygoda. Courtesy of Getty Images

First published 2025
by Routledge
4 Park Square, Milton Park, Abingdon, Oxon OX14 4RN

and by Routledge
605 Third Avenue, New York, NY 10158

Routledge is an imprint of the Taylor & Francis Group, an informa business

© 2025 selection and editorial matter Anthony Carroll and Richard Norman; individual chapters, the contributors

The right of Anthony Carroll and Richard Norman to be identified as the author of the editorial material, and of the authors for their individual chapters, has been asserted in accordance with sections 77 and 78 of the Copyright, Designs and Patents Act 1988.

All rights reserved. No part of this book may be reprinted or reproduced or utilised in any form or by any electronic, mechanical, or other means, now known or hereafter invented, including photocopying and recording, or in any information storage or retrieval system, without permission in writing from the publishers.

Trademark notice: Product or corporate names may be trademarks or registered trademarks, and are used only for identification and explanation without intent to infringe.

British Library Cataloguing-in-Publication Data
A catalogue record for this book is available from the British Library

ISBN: 978-1-032-88104-1 (hbk)
ISBN: 978-1-032-88102-7 (pbk)
ISBN: 978-1-003-53618-5 (ebk)

DOI: 10.4324/9781003536185

Typeset in Sabon
by KnowledgeWorks Global Ltd.

CONTENTS

Notes on Contributors	*viii*
Preface by Anthony Carroll and Richard Norman	*xii*

PART I
The 'God' Debate | **1**

1	The Religion and Atheism Project: Some Initial Reflections *Brian Pearce*	3
2	Beyond Transcendence *Julian Baggini*	12
3	Transcendence *Fiona Ellis*	20
4	Transcendence, Immanence and Panentheism *Michael W. Brierley*	25
5	God and Being: Resonance and Analogy *Richard Norman*	33
6	Personal Presence, Analogy and Resonance: A Dialogue *Robin Gill*	40

vi Contents

7 Postscript: Without Naming God 52
Brian Pearce

PART II
Opportunities for Convergence **55**

8 The Kindness of Strangers: Empathy, Altruism and the
Case for Convergence 57
John Saxbee

9 Can Humanists be Spiritual? 67
Jeremy Rodell

10 Understanding Spiritual Experience: Two Approaches
or One? 78
David Scott

11 The Spiritual and the Religious: Interlinked or Separable? 87
John Cottingham

12 Moral Failure and Spiritual Practice 97
Michael McGhee

13 Persons and Communities Transformed by Practices 106
George Guiver

14 Ritual for the Non-religious 115
Elizabeth Slade

15 Science, Humanism, and Religion 123
Raymond Tallis

16 Make Up a Story 133
Joanna Kavenna

17 Physics, Humanism, and Openness 144
Andrew Steane

Contents **vii**

PART III
Religion and Diversity **155**

18 Religion, Non-religion and Values: What Has Changed
and What Stays the Same? 157
Linda Woodhead and Andrew Copson

19 "The Wonder of Diversity": A Gift to Global Ethics 172
Alan Race

20 Catholicism and Atheism 182
Peter A. Huff

21 Atheism and Esoterism: A Muslim Perspective 192
Reza Shah-Kazemi

22 Faith, Sexuality and Gender: Navigating Difficult
Conversations 202
Christopher Lynch

23 Gender, Islam and Dialogue: A Muslim Feminist
Perspective on Navigating 'Hard-to-Have' Conversations 211
Sariya Cheruvallil-Contractor

PART IV
Conclusion **221**

24 Doing Difference Differently 223
Anthony J. Carroll and Richard Norman

Index *231*

CONTRIBUTORS

Julian Baggini is the author, co-author, or editor of over 20 books including *How the World Thinks*, *The Ego Trick*, *How to Think Like a Philosopher*, and, most recently, *How the World Eats: A Global Food Philosophy*. He has written for numerous newspapers, magazines, and think tanks and has served as Academic Director of the Royal Institute of Philosophy.

Michael W. Brierley taught liturgy, church history, and modern doctrine at Ripon College Cuddesdon, Oxford. He is the editor of *Public Life and the Place of the Church* (Ashgate Publishing, 2006), *Life after Tragedy* (with Georgina Byrne, Cascade Books, 2017), and *A Way of Putting It* (Sacristy Press, 2023).

Anthony J. Carroll is a philosopher, theologian, and parish priest in Andalusia, Spain. His previous books include *Protestant Modernity: Weber, Secularisation and Protestantism*; *Il Giardiniere Invisibile: Credere, Non Credere, Cercare*; and most recently *A History of Philosophy: The Condensed Copleston*. He was co-editor with Richard Norman of *Religion and Atheism: Beyond the Divide*.

Sariya Cheruvallil-Contractor is Professor in the Sociology of Islam at Coventry University and chairs the Muslims in Britain Research Network (2020–2025). She works within feminist-pragmatist frameworks to interrogate social hierarchies in knowledge production. Her publications include *Muslim Women in Britain: Demystifying the Muslimah* (Routledge, 2012) and *Muslim Women in Britain, 1850–1950: 100 Years of Hidden History* (Hurst, 2023).

Andrew Copson is the Chief Executive of Humanists UK, a charity founded in 1896, two of the purposes of which are promotion of humanism and the promotion of harmony between the religious and nonreligious. He is the author of *Secularism: A Very Short Introduction* (OUP, 2019) and the editor of several books on humanism.

John Cottingham is Professor Emeritus of Philosophy at the University of Reading and an Honorary Fellow of St John's College, Oxford University. His work has focused especially on the philosophy of religion, early-modern philosophy, and moral philosophy. He has published over 30 books, including 16 as sole author, of which the most recent is *The Humane Perspective: Philosophical Reflections on Human Nature, The Search for Meaning, and the Role of Religion* (OUP, 2024).

Fiona Ellis is Professor of Philosophy at the University of Nottingham. Her most recent monograph is *God, Value, and Nature* (OUP, 2014), and she has published on a variety of subjects including the philosophy of love and desire, the meaning of life, and the nature of religious understanding. She is writing a monograph entitled *The End of Desire: Meaning, Nihilism, and God*.

Robin Gill, Emeritus Professor of Applied Theology at the University of Kent, was the first holder of both the Michael Ramsey Chair at Kent and the William Leech Research Chair at Newcastle. His recent books include *Sociological Theology* (three volumes, Ashgate/Routledge, 2012–2013), *Moral Passion and Christian Ethics* (CUP, 2017), *Christian Ethics: The Basics* (Routledge, 2020), and *Human Perfection, Transfiguration and Christian Ethics* (CUP, 2024).

George Guiver was a parish priest for nine years and entered the Community of the Resurrection, an Anglican Benedictine monastery, in 1983. He has taught liturgy in the Community's College and also at Leeds University, was Superior of the Community for 15 years, and has published six books and edited others.

Peter A. Huff is Chief Mission Officer and Professor of Theology at Benedictine University in the USA. He has held endowed chairs at Xavier University and Centenary College of Louisiana. His books include *Allen Tate and the Catholic Revival*, *The Voice of Vatican II*, and *Atheism and Agnosticism: Exploring the Issues*.

Joanna Kavenna is a writer whose novels include *Zed*, *A Field Guide to Reality* and *Inglorious*. Her short stories and essays have appeared in the *New Yorker*, *Paris Review*, and *London Review of Books*, among other publications.

x Contributors

She was one of *Granta's Best of Young British Novelists*, has held the Alistair Horne Fellowship at St Antony's College Oxford, and was the 2024 Frankland Visitor at Brasenose College Oxford. Her forthcoming novels are *Seven* and *Soon We Will Know* (Faber).

Christopher Lynch is a teacher, trainer, Safeguarding Lead, and experienced Middle Leader who works at a secondary school in London and as a consultant for Humanists UK. A published writer in many journals and magazines, Chris led LGBT Humanists from 2021 to 2023 and currently sits on the SACRE for Sutton, London.

Michael McGhee is Honorary Senior Fellow in Philosophy at Liverpool University. He was educated at a Roman Catholic seminary and later became a practising Buddhist. He is the author of *Transformations of Mind* (CUP, 2000) and *Spirituality for the Godless* (CUP, 2021) and a founding editor of *Contemporary Buddhism*.

Richard Norman is Emeritus Professor of Moral Philosophy at the University of Kent, and a Patron of Humanists UK. His books include *On Humanism* (Routledge, 2004, Second edition 2012), *Understanding Humanism* (with Andrew Copson and Luke Donnellan, Routledge, 2022), and *What Is Humanism For?* (Bristol University Press, 2025).

Brian Pearce OBE served in the Civil Service for 25 years, then spent two years on a consultation on the development of inter-faith work, leading to his becoming the first Director of the Inter Faith Network for the UK in 1987 until 2007, then as its part-time Adviser on Faith and Public Life from 2007 to 2012. He now promotes 'religious/non-religious' dialogue and the development of 'progressive Christianity'.

Alan Race is a retired Anglican priest who has pursued a double vocation both as a Christian pastor and as a theological educator with a specialism in interreligious theology and dialogue. He is currently Chair of the World Congress of Faiths Executive Committee.

Jeremy Rodell is (volunteer) Dialogue Officer for Humanists UK, and among a number of other roles, humanist representative, and Vice Chair, of Richmond Faith and Belief Forum, and Chair of South West London Humanists.

John Saxbee is an Anglican minister with experience as a parish priest and theological educator and was Bishop of Lincoln from 2001 to 2011. His doctoral studies majored on Kierkegaard, and he has published books on liberal Christianity, biblical studies, and the philosophy of intercessory prayer.

David Scott teaches philosophy at the University of Victoria, British Columbia, Canada. He has written on themes in metaphysics (philosophy of mind) and epistemology in early modern philosophy, focusing on Descartes, Malebranche, and Leibniz. Recently he has written on philosophy of religion, particularly theodicy.

Reza Shah-Kazemi is an author of works in Islamic Studies and Comparative Religion. Currently, he is a Senior Research Associate at the Institute of Ismaili Studies, London, and Managing Editor of *Encyclopaedia Islamica*.

Elizabeth Slade is the Chief Officer of the General Assembly of Unitarian and Free Christian Churches, a coalition of free and inquiring congregations. Prior to this, she was the chief operating officer at Sunday Assembly, and devised secular pilgrimages based on beloved novels, after her background in healthcare led her to examine the role community plays in our collective well-being.

Andrew Steane is a Professor of Physics at Oxford University. He established the ion trap quantum computing work in Oxford. He discovered the *Steane code* and Quantum Error Correction. He is the author of several textbooks and *Faithful to Science*, *Science and Humanity* and *Liberating Science*. He received the Maxwell Medal (2000) and the Trotter Prize (2020).

Raymond Tallis is a retired physician, philosopher, poet, novelist, and cultural critic. For contributions to humanities, he has DLitt University of Hull (1997) and LittD University of Manchester (2001) and for contributions to medicine, he has DSc St George's Hospital Medical School (2015) and ScD University of East Anglia (2017).

Linda Woodhead MBE, FBA is F.D.Maurice Professor in the Department of Theology and Religious Studies at King's College London. She is a sociologist of religion whose books and articles explore the decline of churches, the rise of spirituality and nonreligion, and the values and beliefs of Gen Z. She co-organised the Westminster Faith Debates with the Rt Hon Charles Clarke.

PREFACE

This book is a successor to *Religion and Atheism: Beyond the Divide*, which we also co-edited and which was published by Routledge in 2017. That earlier book was prompted by an awareness of the growing diversity in religion and belief, particularly in the UK. Most striking is the increasing number of people describing themselves as 'not religious' or as having 'no religion'. But as our subtitle reflected, this does not represent a divide into two clearly demarcated opposed camps. There has also been a growth in the diversity of religious traditions in this country, and within particular religions there are great differences in the ways in which their adherents understand their beliefs and commitments. Likewise among the non-religious there are not only atheists, agnostics, and humanists but also, for instance, those who see themselves as 'spiritual but not religious' and those who believe in 'supernatural' entities or forces of some kind. The aim of that book was to assemble a range of contributors to explore the nature of the disagreements between the religious and the non-religious and to probe the extent to which there is common ground between them.

After the publication of that book, some of us who had contributed to it carried on meeting, mostly online, to continue the conversations around those themes. New people joined the group, and we found the discussions immensely rewarding. Talking directly to one another has led to deeper understanding, and it has also been a reminder that good dialogue is possible if the participants take seriously the challenge of trying to achieve it. We came increasingly to think that we wanted to share that experience and what we had gained from it, and we discussed how another book might serve that purpose. This new collection is the fruit of those discussions.

The chapters in Parts I and II have all been written by participants in our continuing dialogues. Some of the chapters describe our exchanges, some of them reflect the substance of our discussions, and some of them directly reproduce the dialogue format either within or between the chapters. In Part III, we take some initial steps towards broadening the conversation, with the aim of locating our dialogues in a wider context, of extending the range of religious traditions represented, and also of looking at how dialogue can best address difficult issues such as disagreements about sexuality and gender. In our own Conclusion, looking back at the preceding chapters, we offer some thoughts on what we have learned from these dialogues and on what makes for good dialogue.

We are very grateful to everyone who has agreed to contribute to the collection. Special thanks go to Brian Pearce and John Saxbee, who played an important part in the initial planning of the book, providing suggestions on what topics should be covered, who should be asked to contribute, and what form the contributions should take. We hope that we have done justice to their vision for the book.

Our world is one in which good dialogue is hard to find, and where disagreements too often take the form of dismissal, abuse, and vituperation. We would like to think that this book might make a small contribution to the promotion of better dialogue.

Anthony Carroll
Richard Norman

PART I

The 'God' Debate

1

THE RELIGION AND ATHEISM PROJECT

Some Initial Reflections

Brian Pearce

> After the publication in 2017 of the book *Religion and Atheism: Beyond the Divide*, a number of the contributors began to meet and to engage in discussions on how to take forward the project of the book. This paper by Brian Pearce was written in late 2019 and set the scene for many of the discussions, in which other participants subsequently joined.[1]

Introduction

The Religion and Atheism project seeks to increase mutual understanding and respect between those who have a religious commitment and those who do not. The purpose of this note is to explore (from a Christian perspective) some key issues which arise in the dialogue across this divide. It focuses primarily on issues of a metaphysical and theological character but also offers some reflections on the search for common ground.

For most followers of a religious tradition, the desire to live well in accordance with its ethical imperatives is likely to be of more importance than questions of dogma and belief. Nonetheless, hostile critiques of religion, such as the 'New Atheism', often focus on a perceived lack of credibility in its foundational beliefs. Dialogue about the conceptual framework of those beliefs is therefore an important element in the agenda of the Religion and Atheism project, including how the term 'God' may be understood, whether the concept is accepted or rejected. After all, the key feature of atheism is by definition a rejection of theism – of the validity of the very idea of God. What is at stake in discussion of that term is nothing less than our understanding of the characteristics of the universe we inhabit – of the 'totality of what is' – and the need for an adequate and plausible way of describing this. Inevitably,

DOI: 10.4324/9781003536185-2

4 Religion and Atheism in Dialogue

issues arise in this endeavour over the language we use, with different understandings of terminology and differences in usage between science, philosophy, theology and religious liturgy. However, metaphysical issues confront us all in the context of comprehending a reality we all share. It is important for us to explore them as best we can with mutual interrogation and clarification of each other's positions. This should help us to develop, refine and, perhaps, improve upon some of the views which we currently hold, even if our beliefs are ultimately matters of trust rather than assured certainty.

Christian theology and New Testament scholarship

Our religious traditions offer a great variety of concepts of God, and there are important non-theistic religious traditions as well. It would be desirable in due course to have broader participation in our project from other religious traditions, but this note has in mind mainly the concepts of God to be found in the Christian tradition, as this is the one most familiar in the United Kingdom and most under challenge from atheism.

Christianity has developed, of course, from within the Jewish tradition and Greek philosophical concepts also had a major impact on it from early in its history. From the outset, there has been a multiplicity of metaphysical frameworks which have continued to develop and be revised in the light of contemporary thought, scientific understanding and recent scholarship. There are many different Christian denominations, and often a range of divergences *within* denominations on the interpretation of scripture and on core doctrines, with differences between 'conservatives' and 'liberals', for example, in Christological understandings of the person of Jesus of Nazareth, on the physical or otherwise nature of his resurrection and on issues of human sexuality.

Many people who have been exposed to Christianity in their childhood have rejected it in later life, having encountered only a simplistic understanding of it, based for the most part on literalist understandings of the Bible and a strongly anthropomorphic concept of God. They are therefore likely to be unaware of the shifts which have taken place in more recent years in both Christian theology and New Testament scholarship. Today there are many Christians, including eminent theologians and New Testament scholars, who reject an unreflective literalist approach to scriptural texts, even though they will make varying judgements on their historicity, and similarly will have more nuanced understandings of God. Current scholarship has helped to emphasise the significant place in scripture of symbol, imagery and metaphor, as well as the important role of narrative, in various forms of storytelling, including parables, in conveying religious, as distinct from historical, truths. There is also now a greater awareness of the riches to be found in other religious traditions and a resulting development of more pluralist theologies.

It can legitimately be claimed that these more nuanced approaches are well grounded within the mainstream Christian tradition.

Simply to ask 'Does God exist?' is to assume – wrongly – that there is collective agreement on a definitive concept of God. A conversation about 'God' needs to explore whether there is a disjunction between, on the one hand, our understanding of the characteristics of the universe of which we find ourselves a part and, on the other, what our concept of God entails, regardless of whether we accept or reject its reality. This note suggests some possible elements of a plausible concept of 'God' as these manifest themselves within contemporary Christianity. Arguably, they are not wholly incompatible with secular understandings of the universe in which we live and might well demonstrate a degree of overlap between the beliefs of those who are theists and those who are not.

The character of our universe

Religious traditions began with the attempt to make sense of the world in which people found themselves and to respond appropriately to what they encountered in it. The experience which we have all had of this encounter may, of course, be described in either religious or secular terms. We need a metaphysics which makes sense of the existence of a universe long before the appearance of life or ourselves on the scene. There is indeed 'more than' us to it. We humans did not invent the universe or make the 'stuff' of which we are made. Any thoughtful person experiences awe and wonder at the extraordinary scale, intricacy, variety and interconnectedness of the universe and at its ordered reliability. These can be recognised and appreciated by the religious and non-religious alike. While both 'creationism' and so-called 'Intelligent Design' have been discredited, there is nonetheless a dynamism to be found in the workings of the universe, with what some will see as a purposive movement, evident in the processes of evolution, towards complexification and the development of consciousness and self-consciousness.

We learn about ourselves and the universe through a whole variety of disciplines within both the natural and social sciences, from our own experiences and from the reported experiences of others. There is much common ground to be found in the wide acceptance of the findings of the physical sciences (and it is important to note the extent to which science, like religion, has to make use of metaphor to describe what it finds). Despite attempts to set science and religion against one another, many religious scientists affirm a complementarity and compatibility between them. However, many philosophers – and scientists as well – reject 'scientism', the overambitious claim that the methodology of science can by itself provide a sufficient explanation of all that is. 'Scientism' is not in itself a scientific proposition, but rather a philosophical one, grounded in a reductionist materialism. But most of us believe there is a need to find room in our metaphysics for the 'non-physical' aspects

6 Religion and Atheism in Dialogue

of what we encounter, such as mind, values, emotions and artistic creation. We are embodied creatures but do not appear to comprise just 'stuff'.

It is crucial to be clear how narrow or broad is the content being attributed to 'matter'. For some, physical matter is all that there is. For others, the nature of 'matter' can be understood in a more 'expansive' way. The 'New Materialisms' movement points to 'matter' having a broader range of properties and capacities than is commonly assumed; and the radical philosophical concept of panpsychism suggests that all matter has a 'mental' aspect to it. Alternative concepts of 'emergence' seek to explain how the physical might have given rise to the phenomenon of mind. Accounting in a satisfactory way for the co-existence of 'mind' and 'matter', and working out an encompassing relationship in place of an unbridgeable dualism, is a difficult task, arguably *the* most significant problem facing science and philosophy.

We all live in the same world, but we 'see' and understand it differently. What might a non-reductionist understanding of the world look like? New concepts of 'naturalism' are emerging which embrace all that we find within the world – all that is 'natural' – including that which goes beyond a physicalist reductionism, and which can in consequence accommodate both the conscious 'mind' and concepts of value and meaning. And perhaps 'God' too, depending on how that word is understood! The terms 'liberal naturalism' or, better, 'expansive naturalism', which reject as inadequate any narrow concept of the natural, have been used to describe this position. Positing a universe of interconnected relationships beyond the purely physical, it rejects as inadequate the picture of a crudely mechanical universe and leaves room for a concept of the 'spiritual'.

This more expansive concept of 'naturalism' sits better with an understanding of the human which is not deterministic but allows for free will as a genuine reality. While the existence of free will is a matter of philosophical debate, we do *feel* that we can make genuine choices. Indeed, those who favour a deterministic metaphysics do not appear to live their lives as if they believe it to be true, but rather to operate on the basis that their actions and decisions have genuine meaning.

God as 'Being itself'

Christian theology has always argued that God cannot be confined within human thought and concepts. Indeed, it suggests that God is unknowable in Himself/Herself/Itself as distinct from the effects of the 'Divine' we encounter; and that we can only describe God – inadequately – through analogy and by studying what God has created. That having been said, within mainstream contemporary theology (but in line with authoritative figures of the past, if not with 'folk' religion), God is now frequently seen not as *a* being among other beings, but rather as 'Being itself'. God is not an entity or an addition to the universe, which is to be found there or not. God is not to be seen as an item of furniture in it, present or absent. Nor is God relegated to some 'supernatural' realm. As is often said by theologians, God and the world are one, not two; and the unsatisfactory historical concept of a two (or even three) decker universe has long been discarded. Rather, God is understood as being integral to the universe and omnipresent within it, holding it together as an interconnected reality, which is why it is a *uni*verse. Further, God is held to be what constitutes and sustains the existence of a *dynamic* – not inert – universe, providing 'the ground of our being' and the source of all that is. Perhaps God can be helpfully understood as a 'force field', or thought of as a verb or adjective than as a noun. It has been suggested that God should be seen not just as 'the ground of our being' but also as 'the ground of our becoming'. An approach of this kind avoids creating a dualistic framework of God and the world by emphasising instead a unity in the 'totality of all that is'.

A theological position which finds increasing favour today is that of panentheism, which sees the world as being *in* God – what might be described, in religious terms, as a God-soaked world. Panentheism – unlike pantheism which sees God and the world as being identical – also understands God as being *more* than the world. Although the term itself has only been widely used in recent times, the panentheist position is one with strong historical roots in a variety of religious traditions, combining as it does the traditional concepts of 'immanence' – to be found in the world – and 'transcendence' – that which lies beyond the world.

Sometimes the term 'transcendence' is used today in the same way as 'supernatural' has been used in the past, avoiding the latter term because of the associations of the 'spooky' it has collected over the years. 'Transcendence' is also often used in a secular way to describe experiences which go beyond the everyday, usually characterised by a sense of connection to something greater. There is scope for confusion here, with the term sometimes implying that there is more to reality than we humans can perceive – the 'more than' that lies 'beyond' – or alternatively covering the special moments when we have a 'transcendental' experience which breaks through our everyday experience of life, perhaps in the face of a stunning landscape or when hearing an uplifting piece of music. Are these different experiences, or similar experiences which are differently understood? There can be a knife edge's difference between a religious and a secular experience even though the two frameworks within which they are understood may appear to lie far apart conceptually.

An interventionist – or omnipresent – God?

Some of the imagery associated with God in the past has been of *a* being, in 'Heaven', external to the world but intervening in it from time to time – a view which panentheism counters. There is obviously great moral difficulty

8 Religion and Atheism in Dialogue

with the concept of a God who sporadically intervenes within the natural order, from the 'outside'. Why would God intervene to heal one child's cancer but not that of another? Why did God not intervene to stop the Holocaust? Arguably, it is more plausible to understand God as providing the dynamism which powers the evolutionary process, and offering resources, which are always and consistently available to all, of healing and what might – in terms of Christian theology – be called 'grace', a concept with parallels in a number of religious traditions and perhaps best understood as a proactive 'enablement'. This kind of God is not seen as an 'absentee' – as in deism – but rather is understood to be *omnipresent*, in an active way, while respecting the ordered nature of a universe which may offer resources and capacities we have yet to fully understand and appreciate.

The concept of an omnipresent, rather than intermittently interventionist, God does, however, put into question the status – within a variety of religious traditions – of accounts of exceptional 'miracles' which appear to 'break' the natural order. For many Christians the universe will be seen as miraculous in itself, and the notion of sporadic 'miracles', rupturing the orderedness of nature, will be found by them to be an obstacle to faith, rather than the reverse. While most Christians would probably accept the traditional understanding of some miracles as historical events, there has from early times been some unease about doing so (as in Judaism too). In the light of greater scientific understanding and developing New Testament scholarship, an increasing number of Christians today, while being committed members of a Christian community, would see miracles more in symbolic terms than as historical events, albeit in some cases related to them. Moreover, the boundaries of what is 'natural' – even if unusual – may have to be expanded in the light of greater knowledge.

A 'personal' God?

Understanding 'God' in a panentheistic way, not as *a* being among other beings but as Being itself and the omnipresent source of all that is, may offer a more plausible concept of God and one more congruent with the findings of science. But how does this fit with the traditional concept of a *personal* God, which is an important source of comfort to many people? Complementary strands of belief and imagery can be found in religious traditions which offer both a 'personal' God and the more abstract God of metaphysical reflection. We humans are 'persons' in relationship with others and with all that is, including therefore, in religious belief, the 'omnipresent' God. Indeed, relationship has been seen as being at the heart of God. In the Christian tradition God *is* love. Theological language has often spoken of God in terms of a *personal* relationship with the believer, whether in prayer or in religious experience.

The Religion and Atheism Project **9**

Seeing God in abstract terms as 'being itself' may therefore seem too sterile, particularly given that personal language about God has predominated in religious worship and devotion. Unnuanced concepts of a 'personal' God can run the risk of domesticating divinity and indeed trivialising it, but *not* using personal language, in a religious setting at least, risks inadequately expressing the experiences to which people have testified across many centuries. However, because personal experience *is* inevitably *personal*, it is difficult adequately to convey its content to others who have not themselves had such experiences, as is the case, of course, with other kinds of experience such as love and beauty.

For many people, personal religious language of the traditional kind will seem natural in prayer and worship, even if they do not, in theological terms, see God as *a* 'Person'. A basic religious experience described by many is a consciousness of absolute dependence on 'something' – *other* and beyond – that grounds our very existence and makes possible everything we experience and everything we do. And 'God', or some equivalent, is the name which has traditionally been given to this 'Other'.

What lies beyond – as well as within – oneself can be encountered as a presence in one's life, in a way which gives rise quite naturally to the use of personal language to describe what is experienced variously as support, care, or judgement by some 'higher power'. In consequence, religious belief and worship often express themselves in ways that suggest that God is, by analogy, in some ways like us – even though much greater and more powerful. However, religious traditions, as in the apophatic tradition in Christianity, in Judaism, which even refrains from the naming of God, and the Hindu injunction *neti neti* (which can be translated from the Sanskrit as 'not this, not that'), teach their followers that God is beyond human imagining. Indeed, we are warned against devoting too much time to speculation about the ultimate, the sacred or the divine, rather than focusing our attention on the needs of others. If religious experience is essentially a sense of being close to God, then this is arguably not at odds with the concept of God offered above.

Ethics and goodness

Goodness has been understood to be a key attribute of God, a source of value and a sense of 'oughtness' – the 'moral imperative' of our consciences which call for a response from us in a transformative experience which invites us to go beyond self-centredness in living fruitful lives. Religious traditions offer grounds for hope that the 'Totality of what is' is fundamentally on the side of goodness, linked to a belief that we too should be a source of goodness. Accompanying assumptions are that we possess free will in making moral choices, and that the universe is constructed in such a way that doing the 'right thing' leads to genuine human flourishing.

10 Religion and Atheism in Dialogue

On this understanding, a belief in God stands over against the sense of meaninglessness which can lead to a corroding cynicism, alienation and self-centred hedonism, undermining our capacity to have trust in the universe or others around us. But there are varying routes for the construction of a strong ethical framework and a sense of meaningfulness. Humanists act ethically, but without grounding a moral imperative in a religious belief as distinct from their experience of what kinds of actions lead to fruitful lives. Some people may see belief in an inherent goodness in the world as a false optimism flying in the face of reality. For others, both religious and non-religious traditions offer in their different ways a framework for their values, with much common ground in the virtues they seek to promote, the values they aim to uphold and their understanding of what constitutes human flourishing.

The 'Nones' and spirituality

In recent years sociological studies have shown a decline in the number of people in the United Kingdom who claim to be adherents of Christianity and a growth in the number who do not profess to follow any religious tradition – the so-called 'Nones'. However – as people search for meaning in their lives – alongside those who follow the historic religious traditions or belong to one of the multiplicity of 'New Religious Movements', surveys also show that a significant proportion of 'Nones' declare themselves to be 'spiritual', while not religious.

The concept of the 'spiritual' is a slippery one, encompassing a wide range of beliefs and practices. Some will overlap with those of 'religious' people. After all, historic religious traditions have developed their own spiritualities as one of their core elements. However, a considerable number of those who see themselves as 'not religious' seek to develop their own personal spirituality. And, more generally, there are many varieties of atheism, just as there are of religious practice and belief. The overall scene is therefore a very diverse and complex one.

Finding some common ground?

There is a need to encourage dialogue across boundaries between those who continue to follow historic religious traditions, those who are adopting newer forms of spirituality and those following a humanist or some other non-religious/philosophical tradition. There may well be more commonality between them than their different terminologies would suggest, but in exploring this we need to find a shared language with which those of different persuasions can feel comfortable. We also need to show humility in recognition that our current understandings and commitments, while held with integrity,

The Religion and Atheism Project **11**

are necessarily provisional, subject to revision in the light of further evidence, experience and reflection.

This note has focused primarily on issues of a metaphysical character. May some common ground emerge here? The following potential areas of overlap start from a very general base while moving towards more 'religious' positions.

a A sense of 'oneness' in the universe of which we find ourselves a part.
b A sense of awe and wonder at its order and beauty, perhaps accompanied by a sense of gratitude for our lives.
c A sense of a 'beyond' – of 'transcendence'.
d An awareness of a purposive dynamism driving the evolutionary process.
e Experience of that dynamism as an active power which is benign in intention.
f Experience of that power as a source of 'oughtness' – of an ethical imperative which can provide us with a broad consensus on what constitutes flourishing and wellbeing.
g A sense that this active power responds in some way to our engagement with it.

As recent experience with inter-faith dialogue has illustrated, there is scope for a fruitful engagement between all those who are interested in drawing on the wisdom of different traditions, both religious and secular; and in that process a need to be ready to discard our, possibly longstanding, misconceptions of 'the other'. On this basis, we can come together to seek common ground, hopefully encouraging what is valuable and fruitful; cultivating attitudes of awe and wonder, thankfulness and mutual respect; pursuing the shared goals of social and economic justice; recognising our interconnectedness and mutual interdependence; and shouldering the shared responsibility we have for the future of our planet. But we shall not be able to create and identify a broad consensus of this kind if we spend all our time sitting in our own different tents rather than talking with others! Dialogue, with goodwill and across boundaries, lies at the heart of the Religion and Atheism project.

The questions posed by Pearce's paper were taken up in discussions over the next five years, and the discussions were facilitated by the use of on-line meetings from 2020 onwards. The ideas explored in those dialogues are reflected in the following chapters in Part I and those in Part II of this book.

Note

1 A version of Pearce's paper was published in the journal *Theology* in 2020 with the title 'Towards a non-reductionist view of the universe: meeting points for open-minded theists and atheists'.

2

BEYOND TRANSCENDENCE

Julian Baggini

The search for common ground needs to steer a careful course between two opposite excesses. One is the desire to claim too much ground as common, which in practice turns into the demand for the other side to cede territory. The other is to be too satisfied with too little, celebrating common cause when the only points of agreement are so general or thin that it is no more than the common ground of all humanity, like agreeing that the world is round or that torturing kittens is wrong. The happy mean between the two is to find ground that is extensive and rich enough to provide a meaningful meeting point but which leaves both sides with enough equally good terrain to call their own.

In our theism/atheism dialogues, the transcendent has often been proposed as such a suitable common ground. It sounds substantive enough for agreement on its importance to provide a source of rich and meaningful accord. 'Transcendent' is after all a big abstract noun with intellectual heft. Most people don't really know what it means, while most philosophers think that they know what it means, but can actually mean very different things by it. Indeed, the fact that we may agree that it is in general important but we may have very different conceptions of what the transcendent ultimately is seems to make it a Goldilocks meeting point: we don't completely agree or disagree about it, but agree just enough. However, on closer inspection, our conceptions of the transcendent highlight what divides the theist and the atheist more than what brings them together.

Minimally, the transcendent is just a portentous way of referring to anything that is greater than ourselves. A sense of the transcendent in this sense is a human universal which has nothing especially to do with one's theist or atheist convictions. Everyone knows what it is like to be awed by nature, or

DOI: 10.4324/9781003536185-3

to feel a belonging with a cause or group of people. This is not the common ground of atheists and theists but the common ground of humanity. Agreeing that it matters is no more significant than agreeing that love of family matters, or that we should be kind to children.

However, if you try to get the concept to carry more weight, it soon ceases to provide a meeting point and instead becomes the bearer of disagreement. This is most obvious when the theist takes it in an ontological sense to refer to some kind of entity or power that transcends the material universe. Obviously, the atheist will deny the transcendent in this sense. (Interestingly, far from all atheists deny that moral values have some kind of independent existence.)

In our group, as is common among more philosophically minded theists, the theists tend to avoid making straightforward ontological claims about the divine. God, we are told, is not "a being among other beings". As Brian Pearce has said, many contemporary theists might be more comfortable talking of God "with a verb or an adjective, rather than a noun which implies that 'God' is an object". For example, Fiona Ellis quotes Stephen Mulhall saying that "Belief in God is best understood, not as the addition of one supernatural entity to the supposed furniture of the universe, but rather as an atmosphere or framework that orients us in everything we say, think, and do". Similarly, John Saxbee cites Paul Tillich and John Robinson to describe God as "the 'more'" which is "beneath rather than beyond". And Rowan Williams is also referenced by Ellis as someone who rejects the idea of God as a transcendent entity. Rather, as she summarises his Wittgensteinian view, "we should think of the existence of God in the way that we think of the existence of colour in the visual field. The question 'what difference does colour make?' cannot be answered with reference to some particular. Colour is all-pervasive in our discourse – and so too God".

These are all variations on a theme of describing the transcendent without recourse to an ontological transcendent realm. But while the atheist will find common cause with the rejection of such a realm, none of the ways in which God is otherwise conceptualised remotely resonate. These ways of talking only highlight how differently atheists and theists see transcendence. For the theists, it remains a pointer to something divine, whereas for atheists it is nothing of the sort.

It may even be that these theological conceptions reflect a more basic, experiential difference. John Saxbee has given the example of the theoretical physicist Alan Lightman looking at the stars from a small boat at sea, and being "overcome by the overwhelming sensation that he was merging with something larger than himself 'a grand and eternal unity, a hint of something absolute'". An atheist in such a position may also be overcome by feelings of awe, but I doubt any would describe that in terms of an 'absolute'. Both theist and atheist may have experiences of the transcendent but we bring our worldviews and conceptual frames to our experiences and so the ways in

14 Religion and Atheism in Dialogue

which such experiences differ may be as significant as the ways in which they are the same.

It also seems to me that however theists conceive the transcendent, there is almost inevitably an ontological claim that atheists could not accept. Even if 'transcendent' does not refer to some kind of separate, non-material realm, it always seems to refer to some feature of reality that is absent in any atheist metaphysics. For the theist, there will usually be more things in heaven and earth than are dreamed of in atheist philosophy.

This is true even if the theist is a kind of naturalist. Fiona Ellis argues for an 'expansive naturalism' which denies the dualism of naturalism/supernaturalism but which allows for God to exist within the naturalistic world. If this is correct, it would refute the idea that the atheist/theist divide is based on the naturalist/supernaturalist one. But it would not provide us with common ground because for the atheist, the natural world has no place for God. It presents a challenge, not a hand of peace to the atheist: you think that a commitment to naturalism rules out belief in God, but you are wrong!

Furthermore, theists who do not conceive of the transcendent in straightforward supernatural terms are probably not representative of ordinary believers, most of whom have more concrete notions of their God. So we're caught on the horns of a dilemma. If we accept the fact that most theists take God to be a really existing agent of some kind, their ontological conception of the transcendent is completely different to that of the atheist. If we take the theist to be making no such ontological claims, then that theist is representative of a minority intellectual cadre and so even if we are able to come close to agreement with them about the transcendent, that does not establish much shared ground between theists and atheists as a whole.

My hunch is that one way or another, theists and atheists will almost always disagree about metaphysics, and the only kinds of theists who are committed to the existence of nothing more than atheists are atypical of theists as a whole. It is helpful to understand that the gap between many theists and atheists may not be as absolute or as large as many presume, but that is to better understand the distance between our respective grounds, not to find common ones.

For all these reasons, I do not see a broad agreement that some sense can be made of the importance of transcendence in human experience as a significant meeting point for theists and atheists. If that is right, why does the transcendent seem to be so attractive as a common ground? The cynic may conclude that the reason is that it is easy to agree that it is important in one shared sense and gloss over the ways in which it is just as important in ways that are not shared at all. 'Transcendent' allows for just enough ambiguity to fudge the illusion of agreement.

Even if there is some truth in this, there also is a less cynical explanation. When theist and atheists talk about their shared experience of the transcendent, they are not so much talking about how they conceive of the object of their experience, but their attitudes towards it. What is shared is a sense of 'reverence' or 'awe' and with that an acceptance of the limits of our understanding and power. This corresponds with what is often thought to be a religious attitude or orientation towards life, but in dialogue, we discover that it is not the property of religion and at all but can be shared by atheists.

The first major caveat here is that, if this is true, it is not a meeting ground for all theists and atheists. An atheist humanist may resist this attitude, preferring instead to think of "man as the measure of all things", exalting human reason and agency rather than taking an attitude of humility. A theist might also not share this attitude exactly, by, for example, believing too confidently that they know God's will and through him have almost unlimited power, to conquer death, for example. Nonetheless, most theists and atheists should, arguably, adopt this attitude. That is enough: if our search for common ground requires that we find somewhere all theists and atheists can meet, our project is doomed, since atheists do not all agree with each other, and nor do theists. The common ground we seek is for theists and atheists with a common, serious and critical interest in finding the right existential and ethical attitudes towards life. To use an old-fashioned term, it is the common ground of 'seekers'.

What makes this common ground potentially fertile is that the attitude brings with it certain ethical obligations. To recognise one's limits and smallness is to recognise that living in the world brings with it responsibilities and the seriousness of mind to shoulder them. If you are not the sovereign of all you survey, then you should not act like one. Others and their needs have claims on you. Furthermore, the attitude also involves a kind of humility which speaks against certainty and dogmatism. The attitude thus implies a kind of existential attitude in which we recognise the seriousness and mystery of the world.

We can recognise this shared attitude in our responses to what is called transcendent, but because we often interpret transcendence very differently, that moment of agreement risks becoming very short. For the theist, it can be difficult or even impossible to separate out a feeling of the transcendent from the feeling of the presence of God. I suspect that a more natural expression of what they actually feel would be that they sense the divine and that by referring to this as something 'transcendent' they are already translating the experience into something a non-theist can relate to. Similarly, the atheist may, as Richard Dawkins has put it, feel an awe that has no hint of the divine, but by using the language of transcendence, the theist can have a sense of what they mean.

However, I believe this is a case of misdirection. It encourages us to misinterpret where our perspectives meet. When the atheist stands in awe of things greater than themselves, that awe is rooted in a sense that the 'greater than' is not 'separate from' or 'above' ordinary reality. Put simply, it is a recognition

16 Religion and Atheism in Dialogue

of the immensity of the immanent: this material world, the only one we have, has a vastness and complexity beyond comprehension, an extension in time and space immeasurably beyond the here and now. Similarly, when we feel a deep connection with nature or with a group, we are appreciating the richness and value of things that are very much material and present.

For the atheist, then, nothing is ontologically transcendent, everything is immanent. But for most theists, God is ontologically transcendent in some way, even if not as "a being among other beings". So on this point there is no common ground.

But, fortunately, even though the transcendent is important for theists, they also take a keen interest in the immanent world, which they see as God's creation, with value in itself, not just a waiting room for the place to come. Awe, reverence and humility can also be inspired by observing this creation. Atheists are similarly inspired by the wonder of nature. Nature is remarkable both when you zoom in and see how it operates in detail and when you zoom out and see the immensity of the universe. Nor is the immanent world a cold, mechanical one. The immanent is not reducible to discrete objects and individuals located in specific times and places. It gives rise to consciousness, art, love and intelligence. The immanent makes for a better shared ground than the transcendent, in part because it is literally our shared ground: whatever we may think about what else there is other than the material world, that world is the one we live in and share.

As with the transcendent, it is possible that this meeting ground becomes too thin. Of course, we all agree that we live in a physical universe. This is no more a rich meeting point than agreeing that the sun rises in the morning and water is essential for life. But for theist and atheist 'seekers' as I called them earlier, the immanent is more than just the quotidian stage for our lives. It is a primary source of existential and ethical insight. When we adopt the right attitude towards it, it inspires what I have called a kind of immanent religiosity, shared by theist and atheist seekers.

In my book on Gabriel Axel's 1987 film Babette's Feast, I argued that the film presented a form of this immanent religiosity which was more profound than a purely transcendent one. It showed how religion fails us when its focus is entirely on what is to come and is at its best when it makes us attend appropriately to the world as it is now. Furthermore, I argued that this pointed the way to a kind of immanent atheist religiosity and that there was a great deal of commonality between both theist and atheist forms of this religiosity. For the remainder of this contribution, I'd like to sketch some of the most important features of that argument in an attempt to make the case that immanence, rather than transcendence, is where the most fertile atheist/theist common ground lies.

Take the sense of our own smallness in the grand scheme of things. When we contemplate the vastness of the cosmos, many describe a feeling of transcendence. But many others interpret this in terms which are more suggestive of immanence. Think again of the example of Alan Lightman looking at the stars from a small boat at sea. Lightman said that he felt he was "merging with something larger than himself", "a grand and eternal unity". This sense of deep connection is also felt by many who take psychedelics as well as those having certain kinds of religious experience. Here, the key feelings are of connection, merging or dissolving. To me, this sounds more like being overcome by the immanent than becoming aware of a transcendent beyond or above.

Experiences of all kinds are altered by our prior beliefs, expectations and experiences. To minds primed by beliefs about an eternal, divine other, awe may be interpreted as being directed at something beyond ourselves. To minds primed to believe that we are fully part of nature, awe can be seen as directed at nothing more than the incredible immanent.

This might appear to suggest a divide rather than a meeting point: religious awe takes as its object the transcendent; atheist awe the immanent. But in reality, the religious can be awed by both the imminent and the transcendent. To marvel at God's creation is to take as one's focus both God (the transcendent) and creation (the immanent). So what I call immanent religiosity is the entirety of an atheist's religiosity but usually one part of theist religiosity.

The theist, however, might want to consider whether their focus is properly in balance. A lot of religious architecture, ritual and song directs believers towards awe at the transcendent, but many core teachings direct them to the world and the needs of its people. I believe that the cultivation of the best existential and ethical attitudes is helped by attending more carefully to the immanent world around us rather than anything above or beyond. The fragility of life is evident everywhere we look. Ruins and tombstones provide plentiful and concrete reminders of how we are but temporary occupants of the worlds we inhabit. To stand on the Jutland shore and look out to sea, as Babette does, is enough to put us in our place. Nothing in this requires us to imagine that there is anything plus ultra – more beyond – as John Saxbee characterised our sense of the transcendent. It simply requires a deep appreciation of how this – the material world – contains more than we can imagine.

I think this is part of what Fiona Ellis is trying to capture in her notion of expansive naturalism. The atheist, on her view, should not be so narrow-minded as to assume that the natural world's contents are exhausted by what science can describe. Even God might have a place in this natural world. Atheists struggle to understand what this kind of God is and are not persuaded by arguments for its existence. Still, there is a common ground here: both theist and atheist can agree that setting aside any disagreements about a transcendent realm, the immanent one defies complete capture by human understanding and so an attitude of reverence and awe towards it is appropriate.

18 Religion and Atheism in Dialogue

Seeing our smallness and limitations also suggests a need for humility. Communion and belonging are possible because we are threads in a tapestry, not isolated atoms in a void. Interestingly, this is what is suggested by the kind of awe inspired by certain kinds of religious and psychedelic experiences. In such states, many people do not experience the vastness of a transcendent other but feel themselves to be deeply at one with the entire cosmos. To put it another way, they feel the immanence of ultimate reality, understanding that there is no fundamental separation between our finite selves and the infinite totality.

Love is also central to the theist's conception of the universe, with God's unlimited love a model for frailer humans to emulate. Given the importance of this, it is striking how feelings of awe and wonder have little obvious connection with the fostering of love. Indeed, a sense of our smallness can actually reduce the sympathy we have for our fellow human beings. Nationalists like Hitler, Stalin and Putin were indifferent to the deaths of even their own citizens because they saw the historic destiny of the nation as more important than the lives of mere individuals.

To spread the gospel of love, it is more effective to turn one's attention to our fellow human beings in the here and now. That is what the most moral characters in Babette's Feast do and by their example, we are shown the true meaning of Christian love. And yet, by so doing, it also shows us that there is nothing exclusively Christian about it. Theist and atheist are united when they focus on the needs of imperfect human beings; they part company when the source of love is sought outside of the natural world.

Fortunately, however, few theists take a neat either/or position. Take the puritan sisters in Babette's Feast. When helping the poor, they say, "You who seek Christ, turn your eyes on the vault of heaven. There you will see the sign of his infinite kingdom". The eyes of those following the advice seem to be struggling to see anything. Yet by showing love in this world, the sisters also show how we can see what they would call God's love at work in this world too. This suggests that in calling for a focus on the immanent for the sake of finding shared ground, we do not need to ask anyone to give up any beliefs in the importance of the transcendent. To return to an earlier point, to share ground, you also have to leave some other ground to each party. We can agree on the importance of the immanent and disagree about the importance of the transcendent.

Conclusion

One of the most famous passages in the New Testament is the parable of the Good Samaritan (Luke, 10). The story is told because a lawyer asked Jesus how he could "inherit human life" and was told to "love the Lord thy God with all thy heart, and with all thy soul, and with all thy strength, and with all thy mind; and thy neighbour as thyself". To this, the lawyer replied, "And who is my neighbour?" Jesus gave his answer in the form of the now famous story of a man who was left for dead by robbers, ignored by a priest and a Levite (an assistant to the priests) but helped by a Samaritan, a gentile. This, the lawyer correctly identifies as his neighbour.

The story illustrates the importance and limitations of common ground. On the one hand, the lawyer is in search of eternal life, something transcendent. He is told that loving both God and his neighbour is necessary for this. And yet his neighbour turns out to be someone who has a very different view of ultimate reality, belonging to another religion, perhaps not loving the same God.

Those of us interested in theist/atheist dialogue are seeking to become better neighbours with those we have profound disagreements with. The story of the Good Samaritan suggests that such neighbourliness is best based not on conceptions of ultimate reality but on shared humanity. If that is correct, it would be perverse to seek common ground in a conception of the transcendent when more often than not, when we spell out what that means, we only reveal our disagreements more fully. Better to seek common ground in how we orient ourselves to the immanent world, the one that both parties agree exists and matters. If we do that, we can see how the immanent gives grounds for humility, awe and compassion that shape our existential attitudes and moral convictions. Furthermore, we will find that they shape them in very similar, if not identical ways.

3

TRANSCENDENCE

Fiona Ellis

How does one begin to talk sensibly about transcendence? The differing and often conflicting claims made within theology itself make it exceedingly difficult to determine what it means to defend the notion in theological terms, and this is before one factors in the positions and disagreements of those who operate for the most part beyond such a context – the atheists, the positivists, the phenomenologists and the existentialists, to name just some of the figures whose positions contain important implications for an understanding and assessment of this notion. Add to this that what is at issue here involves, at some level at least, a kind of speculation about ultimate reality, and it becomes compelling to agree with one recent thinker that '[t]he state of being unsettled on such matters must be accepted as an aspect of the human condition', and that '[i]nstead of vainly hoping to resolve such matters conclusively, we should hope for an ongoing conversation with a modest aim of gaining more clarity on differences that matter, and of perceiving significant convergences, analogies, and similarities'.[1]

The aim of engaging in an ongoing conversation along these lines has been central to our atheism/theism dialogues, and I agree with Baggini that some of the differences that matter have centred upon the notion of transcendence. I also agree that there is a conception of transcendence which has nothing especially to do with one's atheist or theist convictions, namely, when the transcendent is used to refer to anything greater than ourselves. Phenomenologists like Husserl and Sartre describe the physical things we perceive as transcendent in this sense. They also use the notion of transcendence to capture this sense of reaching beyond ourselves to a world of transcendent things. We are said to transcend ourselves in this respect, or as Heidegger puts it, we are a

DOI: 10.4324/9781003536185-4

'stepping-over' or 'surpassing'. Heidegger denies that this has anything to do with attaining some timeless realm of being.

The idea of a timeless realm of being takes us to a weightier conception of transcendence and to a clear source of dispute in the ongoing conversations of our group. The typical atheist associates the relevant realm of being with God and denies the existence of anything that is transcendent in this sense. We can note, however, that there are atheists who believe that values are transcendent in this sense (e.g. Iris Murdoch), and several contemporary moral philosophers – likewise atheists – have developed a Platonism along these lines to defend a form of moral realism.

What of the theists? Baggini claims that the theists within our group, being philosophically minded, 'tend to avoid making straightforward ontological claims about God'. It is certainly true that there are philosophically minded theists who fall into this category. A famous example is Don Cupitt – the Cambridge theologian who 'takes leave' of God to develop a non-realist theological framework in which God seems to be nothing more than a construction of language. As per Baggini's stress upon the rejection of a *straightforward* ontological claim about God, we should note Cupitt's insistence that it is 'religiously appropriate to think that there may be beyond the God of religion a transcendent divine mystery witnessed to in various ways by the faith of mankind'.[2]

Baggini's own examples of how to avoid making straightforward ontological claims about God are taken from the group's ongoing conversations and include talking of God 'with a verb or adjective, rather than a noun', rejecting the idea of God as a transcendent entity, and describing God as 'the more' which is 'beneath rather than beyond'. He takes these approaches to be 'variations on a theme of describing the transcendent without recourse to an ontologically transcendent realm', adding that the atheist will find common cause with the rejection of such a realm.

Things are rather more complex than this dialectic suggests. First, the idea that we should talk of God with a verb rather than a noun is not an expression of non-realism. The point is rather to say something about the nature of God's reality, namely, that the distinction between who God is and what God does cannot be made out. As the theologian Nicholas Lash puts it, 'the holy mystery of God simply *is* the giving, the uttering, the breathing that God is said to be and do'.[3] This is a straightforward ontological claim, although it does suggest that the relevant reality, being God's reality, is not itself particularly straightforward.

The denial that God is a transcendent entity offers a further variation upon this latter theme, for it lends emphasis to the radical ontological difference between God and everything else: God is not a part of the world (whether within it or beyond it) and is not any *kind* of being. The sensible theologian will say that this radical difference serves to capture what it really means for

22 Religion and Atheism in Dialogue

God to be transcendent and that it is fudged if God is reduced to an entity in the 'beyond'.

What of the idea that God is 'beneath' rather than 'beyond'? This can sound like a problematic concession to the offending framework. After all, if it is problematic to locate God out there in the 'beyond', then how can it be any better to re-locate God in the depths? The approach in question is familiar from theologians like Paul Tillich and John Robinson, both of whom are anxious to avoid a conception of God as inhabiting a transcendent world above nature – as if 'to call God transcendent [...] one must establish a "superworld" of divine objects', as Tillich puts it. The point is familiar from before, and according to the recommended alternative, God is to be found in the '"ecstatic" character of *this* world, as its transcendent depth and ground' (Robinson, *Honest to God*, p. 34). Robinson adds that 'this is not the abolition of the transcendent in pure naturalism; it is the apprehension of the transcendent as given in, with and under the immanent' (*Exploration into God*, p. 79).

We are back with the idea of transcendence as a reaching beyond or a surpassing, and the claim now is that this transcending is characteristic of the natural world itself – including the beings within it – and that it is to be understood in a theistically significant sense. This theistic or 'ecstatic' naturalism goes hand in hand with an appropriate reticence concerning how much can be said or known about the relevant transcendent depths. We are reminded of Cupitt's reference to the 'transcendent divine mystery' which lies behind the God of religion, and both Tillich and Robinson can be understood to be targeting and replacing a distinctive and problematic version of such a God – one according to which God is on a level with anything else.

None of this amounts to a rejection of an ontologically transcendent realm although it does suggest a corrective to certain problematic conceptions of such a realm. Nevertheless, Baggini is right to say that there remains a fundamental disagreement between the atheist and the theist, namely, that the theist takes the natural world to point towards the divine, whereas the atheist does not. This is a straightforwardly ontological disagreement.

My theistic naturalist – and it is the position that I myself take seriously – grants with Baggini the seriousness and the mystery of the world and she takes an attitude of humility and reverence towards it. So, she shares the common ground of Baggini's 'seeker', and she also agrees that when she stands in awe of things greater than herself, 'that awe is rooted in a sense that the "greater than" is not "separate from" or "above" ordinary reality'. She acknowledges 'the immensity of the immanent' in this respect, but she denies that this excludes the transcendent, and on this point, as Baggini rightly says, there is no common ground between the theist and the atheist, except in so far as the atheist accepts a conception of the transcendent that has been purged of anything theistic.

But what does such a purging exercise really amount to? This is where things become rather more complex and interesting, for if the anti-dualistic picture I am seeking to defend makes any sense at all, then this exercise cannot be a matter of lopping off a second, super-world and settling for the natural world. Now, the theologically informed atheist could accept the theist's anti-dualist agenda, grant her preference for talk of the world's transcendent depths, but insist that an atheistic viewpoint must involve their rejection. On this way of thinking then, rejecting a theistic conception of the transcendent is a matter of rejecting the idea that reality has the relevant depths. The theist will be quick to ask why such depths are not already implicit in the atheist's notion of an 'immense immanent', and if the response to this is that this immanent has been shorn of any reference to the 'ontologically transcendent', then the question, again, concerns how this exclusion is to be understood. It is worth noting that even the supposedly arch-immanentist Spinoza can be said to defend a conception of the transcendent which carries some ontological weight, for he distinguishes between God *or* nature, understood on the one hand as the creative and self-sufficient source of things (*natura naturans*), and on the other, as the framework of finite things that are dependent upon and conceived through this source (*natura naturata*). The doctrine of creation this involves is taken very seriously by theologians like Tillich and Robinson, and it allows us to uphold a distinction between the transcendent and the immanent, albeit within a non-dualistic framework.

Baggini ends his paper by outlining an immanent atheist religiosity through which to make the case that 'immanence, rather than transcendence, is where the most fertile atheist/theist common-ground lies'. The idea of an immanent religiosity would be taken seriously by all the theists I have mentioned, so Baggini is clearly onto something important here. Yet my theist would deny that the fertile common ground is to be found in immanence rather than transcendence if this is intended to imply that these concepts can be divided through in this manner. Rather, she will insist that they are irreducibly intertwined and must, therefore, reject the idea that 'immanent religiosity is the entirety of an atheist's religiosity but usually one part of a theist's religiosity'. As for the claim that 'the immanent [realm] defies complete capture by human understanding and so an attitude of reverence and awe towards it is appropriate', she will point out that this concession to humility provides further reason for taking seriously her own position, and that her own position offers a reason for viewing it with reverence which, from an explanatory point of view, seems more robust than the idea – suggested by Baggini – that such an attitude can be traced back to our failure to plumb the relevant depths.

Where do we go from here? Baggini concludes that, rather than seeking to resolve ineliminable metaphysical disagreements, we would do better to:

> seek common ground in how we orient ourselves to the immanent world, the one that both parties agree exists and matters. If we do that, we can see how the immanent gives grounds for humility, awe and compassion that shape our existential attitudes and moral convictions. Furthermore, we will find that they shape them in very similar, if not identical ways.

24 Religion and Atheism in Dialogue

The important idea that we should be seeking common ground in how we orient ourselves to the world reminds me of Heidegger's claim that our philosophical starting point should involve a description of the shape of human experience in all its aspects – our 'being-in-the-world' as he puts it. This, for Heidegger, is intended to lead eventually to a more profound understanding of self and world as we make explicit and scrutinise the shape of the relevant attitudes to uncover a more authentic mode of being in the world. The investigation here is intended to be ontological in the deepest sense with important implications for questions of both human and ultimate reality, and it is held to follow from all of this that there is something suspect about the idea that the world towards which we are oriented is a purely immanent realm. As Heidegger puts it, '"world" does not in any way imply earthly as opposed to heavenly being, nor the "worldly" as opposed to the "spiritual". For us "world"... [signifies] the openness of Being...[Man] stands out into the openness of Being' (*Letter on Humanism*, p. 228).

Does this mean that we can, after all, make progress about matters of ultimate reality? I have argued that there are important clarifications to be gained in this context, especially concerning what it means to conceive of transcendence in ontological terms. In short, talk of an ontologically transcendent realm need not imply dualism, and the theologians to whom I am indebted have sought to undermine such a framework. Couldn't the atheist come to acknowledge the relevant difficulties? I have tried to give a sense of how such a dialectic could unfold, and of how one might try to marry Baggini's preference for a more practical orientation with an interest in ontology. This is not to suggest that the disagreements can be resolved once and for all, but it does call into question the overly confident assertion that we are confined to the immanent and it is unclear to me that this notion, taken in itself, can sustain the kind of common ground Baggini is seeking to defend.

Notes

1 Chin-Tai Kim, 'Transcendence and Immanence', *Journal of the American Academy of Religion*, Vol. 55, No. 3 (Autumn 1987), p. 547.
2 Don Cupitt, *Taking Leave of God* (London: SCM Press, 2001), p. 104.
3 Nicholas Lash, 'The Impossibility of Atheism', in *Theology for Pilgrims* (London: Darton, Longman and Todd Ltd., 2008), p. 23.

4

TRANSCENDENCE, IMMANENCE AND PANENTHEISM

Michael W. Brierley

Introduction

The late American Episcopalian theologian Norman Pittenger once wrote that a vital question for any professed atheist is 'In what God do you not believe?'[1] By this, he meant that the Christian tradition presents a range of different options for the doctrine of God – effectively a multiplicity of divergent deities – and rejection of one particular variety of divinity did not necessarily entail that all possible alternatives were unviable as well. It was entirely conceivable that another strain of the doctrine of God might prove more congenial to the critic, and impervious to the objections levelled at the type in which the atheist expressed disbelief.

It is not the intention of this chapter to suggest that atheists are closet theists, and that as soon as the right doctrine of God is exposed to them, they will joyfully embrace belief. It is rather to claim that theists and atheists alike must exercise great caution and care in characterising the position from which they disassociate themselves, in case there are nuances in that stance which they have missed, and they end up distancing themselves from a belief which their dialogue partner does not in any case hold. The purpose of exploring nuances in the doctrine of God – the heart of difference between atheists and theists – is not to bring dialogue partners to a united view (despite routine references to the search for a common ground), for that is rarely the effect of dialogue. It is instead to illuminate difference with as much exactitude as possible, identifying where contrasts are key and so yielding greater understanding, appreciation and, indeed, friendship.

The two previous chapters in this section have explored nuances of the word 'transcendence' in an endeavour to clarify what is at stake between

DOI: 10.4324/9781003536185-5

26 Religion and Atheism in Dialogue

theists and atheists. I concur with Julian Baggini that consideration of the word 'transcendence' does not progress dialogue very far, because its meaning is determined by the standpoint from which it is used: does it refer, for example, to a transcendence outside the world, which intervenes immanently, as in classical theism? Or should it be interpreted, as for panentheists, in terms of transcendence 'within' immanence? Or does it involve humans surpassing themselves – what Raymond Tallis and existentialists have called self-transcendence? I also agree with Fiona Ellis that immanence is more complex than Baggini may credit, and that interpreting transcendence and immanence in a non-dualist way holds promise for insight into what theists might be claiming and accordingly what atheists might repudiate. Ellis herself advances 'expansive naturalism' as a helpful interpretation of transcendence and immanence in a non-dualist vein. I wish in this brief chapter to offer the concept of 'panentheism' – to which the discussion group represented in this volume has recurrently turned[2] – as an analogous and similarly useful tool for unpacking what (at least some) theists believe, in order productively to amplify for atheists a nuanced version of theistic belief, and assist in pinpointing the rubs of difference between atheists and theists. Panentheism is a view to which I myself subscribe, albeit as a theist who entertains the very real possibility of being thoroughly mistaken.[3]

Panentheism

Literature on panentheism has mushroomed over the last two decades.[4] Well-established panentheists such as Joseph Bracken, Anna Case-Winters, Philip Clayton, David Griffin, Catherine Keller and David Nikkel have continued to develop their positions; fresh defences of the subject have emerged on the scene; sceptical voices have correspondingly arisen to challenge adoption of the idea; and the question of how panentheism should be defined has provoked rigorous debate.[5] The 'coiner' of panentheism, Karl Krause, has been the subject of a first major study in English,[6] and particular interest has been taken in delineating panentheistic traits in different religions.[7] Meanwhile, the potential of panentheism for ecology, spirituality and dialogue with other disciplines continues to be explored, special issues of the journals *Sophia*, *Zygon* and *Modern Believing* have been devoted to explicating the word,[8] and multi-authored volumes have investigated 'alternative concepts of God'.[9] Panentheism is thus of considerable interest in theology today.

The word 'panentheism' derives from the Greek *pan en theos*, literally meaning 'all in God'. At its simplest, then, panentheism is the view that all things exist within the divine. Interpretation of the preposition 'in' is clearly crucial here: in what sense are all things 'in' God?[10] Panentheists wish to assert a closer relation between God and the cosmos than something existing within a larger realm as a foreign or alien entity, such as, for example, a cherry stone contained within the stomach of a person's body.[11] An analogy which more closely represents the claims of panentheism is that of an unborn child within its mother's womb: entirely dependent on its mother, even 'part' of its mother, yet beyond the mother's total 'control'.[12] Philip Clayton has accordingly suggested that panentheism has to supplement the notion of everything existing within God with the converse idea (which on its own might be little different from the classical doctrine of omnipresence) of God being in all things, pervading them simultaneously as they exist within the divine, in a mutual coinherence.[13]

A yet tighter definition of panentheism can be found in an essay of 2006, which, in my view, still holds.[14] According to this definition, panentheism has three hallmarks: God is not separate from the cosmos (distinguishing panentheism from classical theisms in which God is separate from the cosmos, although perhaps present to it and even affected by it); God is 'more than' the cosmos (distinguishing panentheism from pantheisms in which God is not so much 'in' the cosmos as identified with the cosmos); and God is affected by the cosmos, either in a 'basic' sense of God suffering what the cosmos suffers or in a more 'advanced' sense of God being dependent on the cosmos. These three premises are specific enough to be distinctive, and yet general enough to include most of the forms that panentheism has taken. It is not the case, therefore, that 'no one knows exactly' what panentheism means.[15]

This definition is significant, because it provides nuances in the doctrine of God which may be underappreciated by atheists in their dialogue with theists. At least four such nuances can be discerned. First, the panentheistic premise that God is not separate from the cosmos eliminates a feature of the doctrine of God that atheists sometimes attribute to theists. Baggini, for example, claims that under atheism, the dimension of 'greater than' in the experience of awe is not 'separate from' ordinary reality, implying that for theists, this is the case, whereas a separationist metaphysic of this kind is precisely what panentheism denies. The panentheistic analogy of a child within its mother's womb, not ever being delivered, is appropriate *precisely* because the child is never separate from its mother. Again, Baggini avers that atheist and theist 'part company when the source of love is sought outside of the natural world'; where again, this notion of externality is exactly what panentheistic interpretations of the doctrine of God refute. Once more, Baggini propounds that religious and psychedelic experiences involve 'no fundamental separation between our finite selves and the infinite totality', as though this were at odds with theological doctrine. Yet it is the very purpose of panentheism to codify or enshrine such a lack of 'fundamental separation'. Raymond Tallis himself may be in danger of misconceiving theism (even if it is a popular misconception) when he refers to 'a Being' that has been subject to humanity's spiritual projections.[16] Talk of 'a Being' involves objectification, externality and separation. Tillich, after Hegel, regarded externality and separation as

28 Religion and Atheism in Dialogue

characteristic of finitude. God, however, is infinite, and nothing can be external to the infinite, so the infinite *has* to include the finite; God has to include the cosmos; God is not 'a Being' but Being itself. A separationist ontology paradoxically blurs the distinction between God and cosmos, because it reduces God to a finite entity.

Second, atheists sometimes assume that theists hold that the divine and its values are independent of the cosmos. Baggini, for instance, suggests that some atheists disavow transcendence in the sense of values or purposes that are independent of humanity, implying that this is the notion of transcendence held by theists. However, advanced forms of panentheism (admittedly departing here from orthodoxy) would maintain that God is not independent of the cosmos but dependent on the cosmos or *a* cosmos to some extent.[17]

Third, Fiona Ellis states that under expansive naturalism, transcendence and immanence are 'irreducibly intertwined'. This language of 'inextricable intertwining' (or equivalent) is a feature of the writing of prominent panentheists.[18] In other words, panentheism exhibits nuances in its doctrine of God that are similar to those incorporated in the expansive naturalism advocated by Ellis.

Fourth, Ellis refers to the interpretation of transcendence outlined by John Robinson, as 'in, with and under the immanent'.[19] Robinson was keen on Bonhoeffer's phrase, 'the beyond in the midst',[20] and wrote of 'transcendence *within* immanence', an expression which he traced back through Harry Williams and A. C. Bouquet to the early twentieth-century theologian Alexander Nairne.[21] Both phrases articulate the closeness – the 'anti-separationism' – that panentheism seeks to encapsulate, being variations on the theme of 'in'. Indeed, use of the prepositions 'in, with and under' has, again, been recognised as characteristic of panentheism.[22]

Theists are not therefore bound to subscribe dualistically to two separate worlds. Robinson's rejection of the 'two-tier' universe was simply making popular a trend in theology and philosophy that stretched back to Hegel (who was a panentheist), if not Spinoza (who has also been claimed as a panentheist). Dialogue between atheists and theists needs to beware *a priori* assumptions about what constitutes theism, given the long and venerable stream of panentheistic positions in philosophical theology stretching from the Enlightenment to the present day. Such a stream affords subtleties within theism that those on the non-theist side may have yet fully to explore.

Isolating the difference between atheism and theism

If the difference between atheism and theism is not to be located in the dualism and separationism which expansive naturalist and panentheist interpretations of divinity resist, where does the difference between the two therefore lie? If part of the definition of panentheism is for God to be more than the cosmos, then in what does the 'more than' consist? In a paper to the discussion group, Fiona Ellis observed that God is more properly the subject into which we enter rather than the object which we identify. It is not so much that we love God, but that, as Christian scripture puts it, God 'first loved us'.[23] Ellis pointed to Simone Weil's view that we err when we try to relate to God as an object (as that would externalise and finitise God), for God has to be on the side of the subject; and also Levinas's talk of our 'giving expression' to the infinite, as opposed to trying to relate to it as an object, so that 'God is closer to me than I am to myself'.[24] Paul Fiddes has argued that God's reality is not something that could be known as an object of perception: God is related to by means of participation in God's reality rather than by objectification. 'God is not the *object* of desire but the one *in whom* we desire the good. God offers a movement of desire in which we can share'.[25]

For the same reason, many panentheists (and perhaps some other theists) would prefer to describe God not as 'a person' (for that would again turn God into an object) but as 'personal', that is to say, having some characteristics that are associated with personality. Perhaps the only ultimate distinction between theism and non-theism, given that both can detect goodness within the cosmos, is that theists ascribe personality to that goodness. As Andrew Steane wrote in a paper for the discussion group, 'Theism is, to a large extent, the willingness to adopt personal language'. Might it be that the 'only' difference between atheists and (panen)theists is a conviction that love is personal or 'responsive' in some way?

The reframing of the difference between God and cosmos in terms of participation within a movement of desire or love has the effect of shifting the difference between the two into moral territory, which itself is significant, given that ethical considerations are often a motive for abandoning classical theism in favour of panentheism.[26] If God is the subject of a relationship of love in which the cosmos participates, then the difference between the cosmos and God becomes one of imperfection and perfection. The cosmos is fallen, sinful and imperfect, whereas God is perfect; the cosmos exhibits love to a limited extent, whereas God is love. This seems to align with the notion of transcendence rendered by John Cottingham – a teleological transcendence rather than the 'experiential transcendence' that is encountered through art, music, nature or worship – in which transcendence is a yearning for the good, thus identifying the 'more' or 'beyond' with a moral perfection which we intuit and in which we participate, albeit in a finite and fractured way.[27]

Conclusion

Julian Baggini proposes that non-dualist tendencies in modern theology 'are probably not representative of ordinary believers', and the preserve of a 'minority intellectual cadre'. This, however, may be to underestimate how far

30 Religion and Atheism in Dialogue

panentheistic impulses have permeated Christian tradition. They are certainly discernible in scripture, and the mystical tradition has arguably been the chief carrier of panentheism through theological history. It does not negate the suggestion that 'full-blown' panentheism began in the Enlightenment to say that its seeds can be traced much earlier. Norman Pittenger (to return to the theologian with which this chapter began) had a penchant for expounding the theology of various figures, who turned out to be remarkably panentheistic and quite similar in their views to Pittenger himself: apologists of the early Church, Irenaeus, John Scotus Eriugena, Abelard, Hugh of St Victor, Bonaventure, Albertus Magnus (teacher of Aquinas and 'first Thomist') and Aquinas, Luther, John Donne, Ralph Cudworth and Kierkegaard, not to mention a variety of modernists and contemporaries.[28] These studies provided evidence for Pittenger's claim that the position which he championed was the one that was most faithful to the earliest Christian witness.

Furthermore, to style panentheism as elitist may also misconstrue the extent to which the doctrine of God has been in ferment over the last sixty years, and particularly the last twenty. Another category in the doctrine of God that has not featured in this chapter, for example, and remains to be explored, is pantheism and its potential consonance with atheism.[29] Many other 'isms' are currently being proffered in the landscape of the doctrine of God. Far from non-binary conceptions of God being elitist, it could be claimed that the hegemony of classical theism is finally being toppled, and that panentheism represents a 'post-colonial' doctrine of God that no longer has to be defined by certain emphases within the Western theological tradition. The doctrine of God, in short, is opening up and opening out, and dialogue between atheists and theists must take account of its increasing profusion and diversity.

Panentheism is perhaps the most venerable alternative to classical theism. Its nuances counter misconceptions and false binaries of theism, as this chapter has striven to show, and it thereby contributes to isolating genuine differences between atheism and theism, as this chapter has also attempted to demonstrate. In so doing, panentheism helps dialogue to be all the more informed, profound and constructive. It is no coincidence that panentheism has featured prominently in the discussions that lie behind this book. Like a Roman road that has ended up in the current day as a minor route, more direct than its contemporary busier counterparts, or a former train line that has become a valued cycle path, panentheism is a historic, if lesser-known, way which can enable atheists and theists who traverse it together to make considerable progress in their shared journey of 'doing difference differently'.

Notes

1 W. Norman Pittenger, *Goodness Distorted* (London: A. R. Mowbray and Co., 1970), p. 87; cf. p. 92, and Matthew Fox, *The Cosmic Christ: The Healing*

of Mother Earth and the Birth of a Global Renaissance (New York: Harper Collins Publishers, 1988), p. 57. For Pittenger, see Michael W. Brierley, 'Norman Pittenger (1905–1997) and Panentheism', *Theology* 109/6 (2006), pp. 430–8, and the recent assessment of his significance in Gary J. Dorrien, *Anglican Identities: Logos Idealism, Imperial Whiteness, Commonweal Ecumenism* (Waco, TX: Baylor University Press, 2024), pp. 33–6, 448–50, 457–75 and 478.

2 For an early approach, see John C. Saxbee, 'A Bishop's Foray into the Homeland of Humanism', *Church Times*, 7 February 2020, p. 14.

3 To quote Pittenger again (*The Christian Situation Today* [London: Epworth Press, 1969], p. 45): 'I may be mistaken about it all; life is a risk and I cannot claim absolute knowledge which would relieve me from the supreme venture of faith'. Cf. Andrew Steane on the resurrection: 'Some of us think Jesus was raised from death [...] but we know he might not have been, and we also know that we are not quite sure we know what we are talking about when we say that he was' (*Science and Humanity: A Humane Philosophy of Science and Religion* [Oxford: Oxford University Press, 2018], p. 212).

4 For literature to 2007, see Michael W. Brierley, *The Panentheist Revolution: Aspects of Change in the Doctrine of God in Twentieth-Century British Theology* (PhD thesis, University of Birmingham, 2007). For literature from 2007, see Michael W. Brierley, 'God's Relation to the World: Discovering Panentheism', *Modern Believing* 63/2 (2022), pp. 110–18.

5 For details, see Brierley, 'God's Relation to the World', p. 111.

6 Benedikt P. Göcke, *The Panentheism of Karl Christian Friedrich Krause (1781–1832): From Transcendental Philosophy to Metaphysics*, Berliner Bibliothek 5 (Berlin: Peter Lang, 2018).

7 The main contribution has been Loriliai Biernacki and Philip D. Clayton, eds, *Panentheism across the World's Traditions* (New York: Oxford University Press, 2014).

8 *Sophia* 49/2 (2010) (cf. *Sophia* 58/4 [2019]), *Zygon* 52/4 (2017) and *Modern Believing* 63/2 (2022).

9 Jeanine Diller and Asa Kasher, eds, *Models of God and Alternative Ultimate Realities* (Dordrecht: Springer, 2013); Thomas Schärtl, Christian Tapp and Veronika Wegener, eds, *Rethinking the Concept of a Personal God: Classical Theism, Personal Theism, and Alternative Concepts of God* (Münster: Aschendorff Verlag, 2016); and Andrei A. Buckareff and Yujin Nagasawa, eds, *Alternative Concepts of God: Essays on the Metaphysics of the Divine* (Oxford: Oxford University Press, 2016).

10 See the influential paper by Ryan T. Mullins, 'The Difficulty with Demarcating Panentheism', *Sophia* 55/3 (2016), pp. 325–46. See also Andrew M. Davis, 'Ambiguities in Panentheism: Definitions, Distinctions and Demarcations', on the author's academia.edu webpage.

11 Karl Pfeifer, 'Naïve Panentheism', in Godehard Brüntrup, Benedikt P. Göcke and Ludwig Jaskolla, eds, *Panentheism and Panpsychism: Philosophy of Religion Meets Philosophy of Mind*, Innsbruck Studies in Philosophy of Religion 2 (Leiden: Mentis Verlag, 2020), pp. 123–38 at 128–9; cf. Philip D. Clayton, 'Varieties of Panpsychism', in Brüntrup, Göcke and Jaskolla, eds, *Panentheism and Panpsychism*, pp. 191–203 at 198.

12 For references to this analogy in literature on panentheism, see Michael W. Brierley, 'The Potential of Panentheism for Dialogue between Science and Religion', in Philip D. Clayton and Zachary R. Simpson, eds, *The Oxford Handbook of Religion and Science* (Oxford: Oxford University Press, 2006), pp. 635–51 at 638–9.

13 Clayton, 'Varieties of Panpsychism', pp. 198–200.

14 Brierley, 'Potential of Panentheism', p. 640.

15 Joanna M. B. Leidenhag, 'Deploying Panpsychism for the Demarcation of Panentheism', in Brüntrup, Göcke and Jaskolla, eds, *Panentheism and Panpsychism*, pp. 65–90 at 65.

16 Raymond C. Tallis, 'Human Transcendence: The Possibility of Spiritual Irredentism', *Theology* 122/2 (2019), pp. 83–92 at 83.

17 Michael W. Brierley, 'Naming a Quiet Revolution: The Panentheistic Turn in Modern Theology', in Philip D. Clayton and Arthur R. Peacocke, eds, *In Whom We Live and Move and Have Our Being: Panentheistic Reflections on God's Presence in a Scientific World* (Grand Rapids, MI, and Cambridge: William B. Eerdmans Publishing Co., 2004), pp. 1–15 at 9–10.

18 Brierley, 'Naming a Quiet Revolution', pp. 8–9.

19 For Robinson's use of these prepositions, see further, Michael W. Brierley, 'Panentheism: The Abiding Significance of *Honest to God*', *Modern Believing* 54/2 (2013), pp. 112–24 at 116–7.

20 Dietrich Bonhoeffer, *Letters and Papers from Prison*, enlarged edn, ed. Eberhard Bethge (London: SCM Press, 1971), p. 282.

21 John A. T. Robinson, *Exploration into God* (London: SCM Press, 1967), p. 118 n. 1, and *The Human Face of God* (London: SCM Press, 1973), p. 241 n. 141.

22 Brierley, 'Naming a Quiet Revolution', pp. 7–8.

23 1 John 4.19 (New Revised Standard Version Updated Edition).

24 Cf. Augustine, *Confessions*, tr. Henry Chadwick (Oxford: Oxford University Press, 1991), p. 41; and Tennyson's poem 'The Higher Pantheism', with its talk of God being 'closer [to us] than breathing'. It is no coincidence that 'higher pantheism' was in fact a panentheistic movement of the late nineteenth and early twentieth centuries: see further, Brierley, 'Naming a Quiet Revolution', p. 2 n. 10.

25 Paul S. Fiddes, 'The Quest for a Place Which Is "Not-a-Place": The Hiddenness of God and the Presence of God', in A. Oliver Davies and Denys A. Turner, eds, *Silence and the Word: Negative Theology and Incarnation* (Cambridge: Cambridge University Press, 2002), pp. 35–60 at 55 (original emphasis). See, too, his larger work, *Participating in God: A Pastoral Doctrine of the Trinity* (London: Darton, Longman and Todd, 2000).

26 'Classical theism is fatally mired in imagery of divine aloofness and detachment' (Scott Cowdell, *A God for This World* [London and New York: Mowbray, 2000], p. 21). 'Conceiving of God as independent or separate from the cosmos has a moral cost. Panentheism is able to say that whatever the situation in the cosmos, however small or large, however catastrophic or morally [ambiguous], God is "in" it and inseparable from it. The "within" of panentheism is required if only (and perhaps only) to avoid the negative [moral] connotations of having God "without".' (Brierley, 'Panentheism', p. 115).

27 John G. Cottingham, *The Humane Perspective: Philosophical Reflections on Human Nature, the Search for Meaning, and the Role of Religion* (Oxford: Oxford University Press, 2024), pp. 200–11.

28 For the details, see Brierley, *Panentheist Revolution*, p. 391.

29 For pantheism, see Andrei A. Buckareff, *Pantheism* (Cambridge: Cambridge University Press, 2022), and the work of W. J. Mander.

5

GOD AND BEING

Resonance and Analogy

Richard Norman

What should we say about God? Acceptance or rejection of a belief in a deity would seem to be the fundamental divide between the religious and the non-religious. Of course, not all religions are theistic. The Buddhist tradition, for instance, is not build around belief in a god, at least not in the manner of the monotheistic religions. And surveys in societies such as the United Kingdom indicate that a significant number of people who describe themselves as 'not religious' or have no religion say that they nevertheless believe in some kind of god or 'life force'. Nevertheless, the main currents of thought such as humanism which have emerged historically from the criticism of traditional religious affiliation would see themselves as atheist or agnostic.

The aims of the dialogue pursued by contributors to this book have been both to achieve a better understanding of the differences and disagreements between the religious and the non-religious, and to explore how much common ground there is between us. It may help us to understand, perhaps, what kind of 'god' it is that others do or do not believe in, and why. But is there a space for common ground on the matter of belief in a deity, or is this the point at which we simply agree to differ?

In the dialogues which we have engaged in since the publication of the previous book, valuable discussion was generated by a paper which Brian Pearce circulated in 2020.[1] He drew attention to the fact that many contemporary Christians hold to a more nuanced theism than what is attacked by the more strident atheists. Within mainstream contemporary theology, he said,

> God is now frequently seen not as *a* being among other beings, but rather as 'Being itself'. God is not an entity or an addition to the universe, which is to be found there or not. God is not to be seen as an item of furniture in

DOI: 10.4324/9781003536185-6

it, present or absent. Nor is God relegated to some 'supernatural' realm. As is often said by theologians, God and the world are one, not two; and the unsatisfactory historical concept of a two (or even three) decker universe has long been discarded. Rather, God is understood as being integral to the universe and omnipresent within it.

On this view, then, God is not a supernatural being 'out there', somewhere outside the natural universe, who pops in from time to time, intervening to effect miracles or answer prayers or, on a grander scale, to create living things and give the evolutionary process the pushes which it needs. Talk of 'God' is to be understood not as talk about 'a being' but as a way of talking about and thinking about Being itself. This kind of theism does not rest on a dualist metaphysics. It does not require a division between two realms of existence, the 'natural' and the 'supernatural'. It is consistent with what has been referred to as an 'expansive naturalism'. It can acknowledge that this world is the one world there is, whilst eschewing a reductionist approach which supposes that the natural sciences can tell us all that there is to know about the world.

Pearce recognises, of course, that belief in a god can take many forms, and that it can often be much more simplistic – anthropomorphic, dualistic, thinking of God as a powerful supernatural figure who talks to people, watches over them, intervenes in their lives, and rewards and punishes them as they deserve. But good dialogue between the religious and the non-religious should foster the recognition that theism also takes much more nuanced forms, and should counter the propensity of some atheists to dismiss belief in God as on a par with belief in Santa Claus or the Tooth Fairy.

In this way, then, greater mutual understanding and respect, including mutual intellectual respect, can be the fruit of dialogue. But what about the scope for finding common ground?

Much of our subsequent dialogue, building on Pearce's paper, was conducted in the vocabulary of 'transcendence' and 'immanence', and this is reflected in the contributions by Julian Baggini, Fiona Ellis and Michael Brierley to this volume. The concept of 'transcendence' is one which has been used in the Christian theological tradition to refer to the human relation to God as that which surpasses us and at the same time fulfils us. If, as Pearce's paper suggests and as Fiona Ellis argues, we should reject a dualistic contrast between the 'transcendent' and the 'immanent', and should see transcendence as manifested in the immanent and as accommodated by an 'expansive naturalism', is there then room for common ground here between theists and atheists? Maybe the idea of 'transcendence in immanence' can capture the experience shared by the non-religious of a deep relationship to something larger than ourselves. The theology of 'panentheism' mentioned in Pearce's paper and discussed at greater length by Michael Brierley aims to do justice to the idea of God as both transcendent and immanent in a non-oppositional way – God as the Being which pervades the world, 'in whom we live and move and have our being', and who is at the same time, in a relevant sense, 'more than' the world. Might there be a convergence here with a dimension of human experience which can also be important for the non-religious, a sense of there being something greater than ourselves but with which we can aspire to be at one?

Doubts remain. As Baggini asks in his chapter, is 'transcendence' the right word to capture that experience of 'connection' and 'merging'? More fundamentally, is the language of 'God' actually helpful here? To the sceptical among us, panentheism can look like an unsuccessful attempt to have it both ways. If the emphasis is on 'God as immanent', as 'Being' in general, the distinctiveness of theistic language may seem to evaporate. Talk of God may begin to look like just another, perhaps, poetic, way of talking about the one world which we all experience. On the other hand, the insistence that God should also been seen as transcendent, as something 'more than', even if not separate from, the natural world, may seem to return us to the difficulties of classical theism – the need to justify ontological claims about the existence of that which is 'more'.

The question, then, is whether there can be a plausible version of theism which regards talk about God as talk about the nature of Being itself rather than a hypothesis about the existence of a particular being or entity, and which is sufficiently distinctive in what it says about the nature of Being to avoid collapsing into vacuity. It is not enough simply to define God as 'the Ground of our Being', say, or 'the whole of which we are a part'. What is it about a certain way of experiencing reality which might make the language of theism appropriate?

The most plausible suggestion, I find, is the one which, as Brierley says, was put forward a number of times in our discussions – that to talk of God as 'more than' the cosmos is to say that there is an irreducibly *personal* dimension to the nature of reality. This is how Robin Gill put it in one of our discussions:

> The nearest I can get to finding what I mean by God is 'personal presence'…. That's probably where we divide most. At our deepest moments, if we have a sense of personal presence, this is radically different from getting to our deepest moments and deciding there is nothing. But it isn't *a person…* Our language is deeply analogical…. When we use a term like 'person', we have to be very careful. But to say that, at our deepest moments, we have a sense of personal presence seems to me to get nearest to what I mean by God.

When pressed on what he meant by 'personal presence', he linked it with the language of *purpose*. This sense of a personal presence, he said, is "the

36 Religion and Atheism in Dialogue

sense that, finally, reality isn't something purposeless, isn't something meaningless. Reality really does involve a personal and purposive presence".

Theistic language, then, on this account, is a way of describing the deepest moments of our experience. Why might one see the theistic description as the appropriate one? Here Gill introduces another idea which I find helpful. It is that the description *resonates* with some people and not with others. It is not a matter of proof or argument, or of an inference to the best explanation. It is a matter of resonance.

On this view, then, the difference between the atheist and a theist such as Gill is between different ways of seeing our one world, different ways of experiencing it. And we experience it and describe it in one way rather than another because that way of seeing things resonates with us. To elucidate the idea of 'resonance', Gill makes a comparison with the nature of personal relationships. For most of us, a friend or a life partner is not someone whom one has chosen after weighing up the arguments and concluding that there are good reasons for entering into such a relationship. Maybe there are some who do it that way, but typically, it is that we resonate with the person, we 'click'. Gill also employs a comparison with our responses to art or music. Where some people will see nothing in a painting or hear nothing that grabs them in a piece of music, for others it will resonate.

If this is the way in which some theists and some atheists differ, then the difference between them becomes a much narrower divide. As an atheist, this is something I can welcome. It does not, of course, apply to all theistic belief. For many who believe in the existence of a God, that belief is an inference, the conclusion to a train of argument, and though I can respect the commitment to reasoned argument, the conclusion to which it is supposed to lead is an ambitious metaphysical claim about a supernatural being, of a kind which I struggle to see as plausible. Again, there are some theists whose belief is grounded in direct experience rather than reasoned argument, but the experiential claims are ones which I find inescapably alien. "How can I doubt that there is a god", some will say, "since he has saved me and he speaks to me constantly". In such cases, sincere though they may be, and though the experience clearly plays a vital role in their lives, I struggle even to imagine what it might be like. But if talk of God is a way of talking about what is at some level a shared experience of a shared world, seen in different ways, then we are, if not on common ground, at any rate on the same wavelength.

Having said that, I want to add two comments. First, we should resist too easy a slide to a relativist conclusion – that one way of seeing things resonates with me, another way resonates with you, that this is all there is to it and we can only agree to differ. I think we should hang on to the idea that what we are looking for is *truth*. There is a God or there isn't. It makes a vital difference which is the *right* way of seeing the world. And there are things in our experience which we can point to in order to bring out the appropriateness of seeing it in one way rather than the other.

Gill's comparison with music is helpful here. That there is something in the music which is there to be heard cannot be demonstrated by a logical argument, but we can draw attention to features which support a certain way of hearing it, and there may be such a thing as 'getting it right'. Consider this spectrum of cases:

"The theme of the allegro reappears, slightly altered, in the slow movement – listen, there it is, can you hear it?" Here it may be right to say that someone who cannot hear it is missing something which is there to be heard.

"The symphony ends on a note of despair" (Tchaikovsky's Pathétique, perhaps). "Why do you say that?" "Listen to the way it sinks into silence and inertia." In this case too it can reasonably be said that someone who cannot hear the despair is missing something.

"The symphony is a triumphant celebration." "No, it's ironic, can't you hear it? The triumph is exaggerated to the point of being a caricature." (It might be a symphony by Mahler, or Shostakovich.) Maybe in the end we have to acknowledge that it can be heard in either way. But that conclusion is itself open to debate, and we can still go on drawing attention to the features which seem to make one way of hearing it more appropriate than the other.

Likewise I want to suggest that if the sense of "a personal and purposive presence in the world" resonates for some but not for others of us, there may be more to be said. Someone for whom that description resonates may be able to point to features of our personal experience which support it – the awe-inspiring life of the natural world, perhaps – and may feel that those of us who cannot see it that way are missing something. We in turn may feel that the language of 'purposive' and 'personal' is being over-extended. And both of us may want to hang on to the idea that we are trying to 'get it right', even if we cannot conclusively demonstrate which of us is doing so.

My second comment picks up on something else which Gill has emphasised, both in that discussion and in his contribution to this book, that much theological language, and indeed much of our language in general, is deeply analogical. I take it that that is why he wants to talk about 'a sense of a personal presence' rather than saying that God is literally 'a person'. Ascribing personal qualities to God is making a comparison with human qualities, but they are not the same qualities: if God is 'wise', his wisdom is analogous to but not the same as human wisdom. To talk of God's 'love' is to employ an analogy with human love. And to find something analogous to those qualities

38 Religion and Atheism in Dialogue

exhibited in the world as we experience it is to make a claim about the nature of reality but is using analogies in order to do so.

Emphasising the use of analogy serves to distance such a position from a simplistic anthropomorphism. It helps to identify a theism of a kind which a sympathetic atheist can see as plausible. Does it point to common ground? It points in that direction, I think, but not all the way.

Here is one way of describing the persisting difference. The atheist, I suggest, can recognise the 'sense of personal presence' not as analogy but as *metaphor*. It is the kind of metaphor characteristic of poetry, and we can find the clearest and most illuminating examples in the Romantic poets. Think of Keats' Ode to Autumn:

> Season of mists and mellow fruitfulness,
> Close bosom-friend of the maturing sun;
> Conspiring with him how to load and bless
> With fruit the vines that round the thatch-eves run;
> To bend with apples the moss'd cottage-trees,
> And fill all fruit with ripeness to the core....

That personification of autumn as a beneficent spirit is not a factual claim about the nature of ultimate reality. The metaphor serves not to express a *belief* about the world but to express a human *response*, a feeling of delight in the abundant fruitfulness of a time of year. Compare Shelley's Ode to the West Wind:

> O wild West Wind, thou breath of Autumn's being,
> Thou, from whose unseen presence the leaves dead
> Are driven, like ghosts from an enchanter fleeing,
> Yellow, and black, and pale, and hectic red,
> Pestilence-stricken multitudes: O thou,
> Who chariotest to their dark wintry bed
> The winged seeds, where they lie cold and low,
> Each like a corpse within its grave...

Here we have a different human response, to autumn as the time when nature is dying off, and the scattered seeds are a reminder that life will revive – "If Winter comes, can Spring be far behind?" We do not have to ask: what is the truth here, which of these is the right picture? The metaphorical personification is the projection of a human mood onto its object.

In the same way, then, we might say that where theism uses the analogy of a personal presence to make a tentative statement about the nature of reality, for the atheist this can be at most a metaphor. The distinction between *analogy* and *metaphor* may look like a thin dividing line – perhaps it is – but the difference comes out if we consider the practical implications of the two ways of putting it.

One of the human responses which we have talked about in our discussions is the sense of *gratitude* – *cosmic* gratitude, the feeling which believers and non-believers can share, of being grateful to be alive and grateful for the 'blessings' of a world in which we delight. For the atheist, the gratitude belongs with the language of metaphor. It is *as though* there were someone or something to be grateful to. For the theist, however halting and hesitant the language may be in which to describe it, and for all the dependence on imperfect analogies, there *really is* someone or something to whom to express the gratitude. Likewise, for all the religious responses of prayer and ritual, of worship, praise, contrition or petition. For the theist they are possible. The atheist can understand them but cannot share in them.

By exploring these lines of thought, then, we may be able to reach a better mutual understanding, but as long as we employ the language of 'God', the common ground remains elusive. There are certain kinds of experience which at one level are shared but which the theist and the atheist characterise in differing ways. A certain description of it resonates with the one but not with the other. The valuable common ground, I suggest, is the experience itself – what we feel, as Gill puts it, "at our deepest moments".

Note

1 Included in this book as Chapter 1 earlier.

6

PERSONAL PRESENCE, ANALOGY AND RESONANCE

A Dialogue

Robin Gill

In a recent review, my colleague Richard Norman argues that debates about theism can be either too simplistic for well-informed theists and atheists alike or, when more sophisticated (say, in the work of Richard Swinburne), too prone to 'patronising anthropomorphism'. Instead, he calls for a better-informed dialogue among those 'who see the language of "God" as a groping and hesitant, largely metaphorical attempt to articulate a sense of the mystery of existence'.[1] I agree. These points are not remotely new to either of us, although they are overlooked in many recent debates.

Rediscovering medieval Abrahamic perspectives on theism

They were standard fare in the medieval Spanish flourishing of intellectual thought of key Jewish, Muslim and Christian scholars – a flourishing that profoundly influenced Western culture in ways that are slowly being rediscovered today. The pioneering work of the late María Rosa Menocal regarded them as 'ornaments of the world' offering, for a quarter of a millennium, 'a culture of tolerance in medieval Spain',[2] that is, until Jews and Muslims were, shamefully, expelled from Iberia by Catholic monarchists in 1492.

Twelfth-century Córdoba is crucial. There the Muslim Averroes (Ibn Rushd) was born in 1126 and the Jewish Moses Maimonides (Musa ibn Maymun) in 1135. Both read and wrote in Arabic and made extensive use of the works of Aristotle that had been preserved in an Arabic translation, but had been largely forgotten within non-Arabic speaking Western culture. In turn, a century later, Thomas Aquinas also made extensive and innovative use of Aristotle (by then translated into Latin) and repeatedly used, and argued with, the ideas of Averroes and Maimonides.[3]

DOI: 10.4324/9781003536185-7

Two works by Maimonides were especially important, his commentary on the Torah/Pentateuch *Mishneh Torah* and his philosophical treatise *The Guide of the Perplexed* (written about 1200 CE). The *Mishneh Torah* has long been used as an influential source of Rabbinic guidance by Orthodox Jews, while *The Guide* has been, until recently, a more significant influence upon non-Jewish thought, as has *The Incoherence of the Incoherence* by Averroes (who died in 1198 CE). There is debate about whether Maimonides read *The Incoherence* before he wrote *The Guide*, but there is wider agreement that he admired Averroes and that both scholars drew upon the earlier Islamic works of Avicenna and, earlier still, al-Farabi.[4]

What is striking about both *The Guide* and *The Incoherence* is their attachment to Aristotle's naturalism (sometimes conflated with Plotinus) and to a non-literalistic approach to Scripture (i.e. The Hebrew Bible/*Tanakh* for Maimonides and the Qur'an for Averroes). Indeed, for both, if naturalistic knowledge conflicted with a scriptural text, then the latter was to be interpreted and not to be taken literally.

The Guide offers an extensive critique of anthropomorphic biblical language about God, especially language that implies that God has 'a physical body'. For example, Maimonides writes that 'it behoves us to explain why hearing, sight, and the sense of smell are figuratively ascribed to Him, may He be exalted'.[5]

Brought up in the overwhelmingly Islamic culture of medieval Córdoba (where the recently discovered synagogue could fit many-times-over into the spectacular, albeit now Christianised, Great Mosque), Maimonides shared a reluctance to depict God and even adopted a very Islamic 'may He be exalted'.

Similarly, in his extended rebuttal of the influential 11th-century Sunni Persian al-Ghazali's *The Incoherence of the Philosophers*, Averroes, in his sarcastically titled *The Incoherence of the Incoherence*, insists that virtues ascribed to God in the Qur'an must be stripped of anthropomorphisms:

> When it is said that He is living, nothing is meant but that He is conscious of the knowledge through which the existent which is called His act emanates from Him... His life is His very existence... When it is said that He is the lover and the beloved, the enjoyer and the enjoyed, it means that He is every beauty and splendour and perfection.[6]

Aquinas was later to build upon this foundation in his extensive and complex discussion of the analogical nature of religious language. With few exceptions (notably the words 'holy', 'divine' and 'sacred'), attributes ascribed to God are attributes detected initially, and often partially, within human beings that are then deployed analogically, and with considerable difficulty, to depict God, if God is properly understood as God (regardless of whether God is thought to be a reality or not), despite the numerous anthropomorphisms in the Jewish and Christian Bible (and, indeed, in the Qur'an).

42 Religion and Atheism in Dialogue

It might be noted in passing that within quantum and cosmological physics, there is nothing unusual about such an analogical deployment of language. Terms derived from everyday human observations need to be considerably stretched to depict the curious worlds at the largest and smallest physical levels. So, electrons are depicted as simultaneously and paradoxically both waves and particles when manifestly they are finally neither. Or again, depictions of infinite time or space defy the everyday experience of humans who are bound by both. Equivocal poetry rather than univocal prose may work best for such depictions. For theologians educated in the 1960s work on science and religion by the late, great Ian Barbour, this, once again, is standard fare.

Maimonides is helpful also in depicting God equivocally and apophatically as 'presence':

> *Face [panim]* is an equivocal term, its equivocality being mostly with respect to its figurative use... In this sense it is said: *and the Lord spoke unto Moses face to face* – which means, as a presence to another presence without an intermediary... In this sense it is also said: *But my face shall not be seen*, meaning that the true reality of My existence, as it veritably is, cannot be grasped.[7]

Maimonides, Averroes and Aquinas, unsurprisingly, were all regarded with suspicion by some of their contemporary co-religionists for introducing the pagan Aristotle's alien concepts, for challenging the scriptural literalism of traditionalists, and, doubtless, for simply being too clever. Yet they continue to resonate across faith traditions today, not least in the recent books of the Catholic Janet Soskice and the Jewish Raphael Zarum.

Two recent Catholic and Jewish perspectives

Janet Soskice's *Naming God: Addressing the Divine in Philosophy, Theology and Scripture* builds upon her well-regarded *Metaphor and Religious Language*. She now addresses the historic problem of 'naming' God, let alone of 'defining' who God is thought to be (by either believers or non-believers), given that almost all human language about God is metaphorical/analogical. In the process she turns not only to Dionysius, Gregory of Nyssa, Augustine and Aquinas but also (significantly) to the Jewish Philo and, indeed, Maimonides, before moving on to Locke, Descartes and, finally, Ricoeur. In ethical terms, what emerges for a theologian is that (to coin a new cliché): *while God making humans in God's image considerably enhances their value, humans making God in their own image considerably devalues God.*

Soskice explains early that 'In the hands of great theologians like Gregory of Nyssa, Augustine and Dionysius the "ever-being" and eternal God of hidden silence is also *and always* the God of intimate presence'.[8]

For many Jewish and Christian theologians, she argues, actually naming God is problematic because, for them, God goes beyond language. She is tempted by Aquinas' *Qui est* ('He who is') following the epiphany to Moses at the burning bush ('I am who I am') and, with that, 'Being', but (probably trying to avoid Hegel) prefers 'intimate presence': 'God is, at every moment, the source and cause of all our being, of all that is' and 'God is not distant from creation but wholly present to them in every moment, creating and sustaining them'.[9] Philosophers following Locke and Descartes, she argues, are a serious distraction since God is not to be defined, nor to be thought of, as 'a thing' or 'person' who might or might not be 'proved' to exist,[10] but as intimate presence in an otherwise dispassionate world. The physicist Andrew Steane's conclusion is very similar, namely, that what might be termed 'God' is not some 'supernatural accessory', but rather 'a unity and creativity which is able to encourage, mould, forgive, require, aspire and affirm'.[11]

Soskice is also sceptical about the manner Aquinas' 'Five Ways' (again following Maimonides) is used today, either to prove or disprove the existence of God for A-level students:

> It is often remarked that, for all the attention they have subsequently received, the 'Five Ways' take up little space in the *Summa Theologiae*. Here... God's existence is taken as given, and indeed there is some debate as to whether Aquinas intended them as proofs.[12]

What was in the mind of Aquinas is probably beside the point and unknowable. Context is more telling. In the context of a sceptical 21st-century Western society, the Five Ways are easily dismissed as 'proofs' of the existence of anything except, possibly, the theoretical, but distant, God of deism, whereas in the context of 13th-century Christendom, they might rather have been seen as 'confirmations' of a widespread, deeply held, trust in God as a ubiquitous, creative, presence.

As seen by the latter, trust in God gave (and still gives) believers across Abrahamic faiths a very distinct take both on their own lives and on the world around them. It differs significantly, say, from Richard Dawkins' oft-repeated, bleak verdict that the world has 'precisely the properties we should expect if there is, at bottom, no design, no purpose, no evil, no good, nothing but pitiless indifference' (even if he sometimes, and confusingly, offsets this with statements about how lucky we are to be alive). On this polarised basis at least, the cosmic choice is between 'pitiless indifference' and 'creative, compassionate presence'.

Theologians might find it quite difficult to see why anyone should find resonance in 'pitiless indifference'. In addition, Pope Francis' encyclical *Fratelli Tutti* offers the pertinent warning that, in an increasingly dangerous world,

44 Religion and Atheism in Dialogue

'relativism always brings the risk that some or other alleged truth will be imposed by the powerful or the clever'.[13] Secular humanists more typically claim that in rejecting theistic belief, they are freed to choose their own creative values. Yet what Pope Francis warns is that in a world now engaging in, potentially nuclear, warfare and dictatorships, sinister values could well be imposed rather than chosen freely.

The Orthodox rabbi, with a doctorate in theoretical physics, Raphael Zarum raises similar issues frequently using Maimonides in *Questioning Belief: Torah and Tradition in an Age of Doubt*. For example, comparing Genesis' two accounts of creation with current scientific cosmology, Zarum states repeatedly that the former are 'not to be understood completely literally', especially when they clash with the latter.[14] Citing both Jewish and Islamic medieval sources as precedents, he argues against biblical literalism, setting out at some length the way that, in the past, it gave support to slavery, while also continuing to contribute to racism and exclusivism.

In addition, he consciously writes for intelligent fellow Jews in an 'age of doubt':

We tend to expect people to either believe in God or not, or just to say they don't know. We might ask them: 'Do you believe in God or are you an atheist or an agnostic?' But the truth is that we are not any of these consistently. They are not hard and fast categories. In life we move within and between them, traversing shades of devotion and skepticism, disillusionment and acceptance. And so religious doubt and despondency are not supressed in Judaism. On the contrary, the book of Psalms gives them a compelling voice.[15]

He might well have cited James Hinton's analysis of the 1990s transcripts stored by the authoritative British Mass Observation. As a self-confessed 'lifelong atheist who had never previously, as a historian (or otherwise), shown the slightest interest in religion',[16] Hinton reaches the surprising conclusion that similarly fluid theist/atheist/agnostic categories also typified most respondents, whether they self-identified as religious or not.

At another point, Zarum explores Paul Tillich's concept of God as the 'Depth of our Being', while opting, in the end, for the more specifically Jewish idea of God as *Shekina*, that is, cloudy presence.[17] He also admits doubts about the effectiveness/credibility of prayer, concluding that, whatever else it does, regular corporate prayer moulds characters:

It is faith spoken out loud, and it serves to focus our thoughts and fills out our days with purpose... In our prayers, we articulate our ideals. We give voice to our national hopes and aspirations. We express who we are as a people.[18]

A framework for a more fruitful dialogue

To summarise:

- Most theistic language is necessarily analogical, drawing from human, contextual experience.
- Anthropomorphisms in sacred texts (or in polemical debates – such as 'Easter Bunny' or 'Big Daddy in the Sky') should not be taken literally.
- God is better depicted (by theists and atheists alike) as Being or Presence rather than *a* being or *a* person.
- Logical proofs of the existence of God fail to convince not just atheists but also thoughtful theists because at most they deliver only deism.
- Resonance rather than logical proof might depict ongoing differences between *and among* theists and atheists.

This final point needs some elaboration.

'Resonance' is a term used in both music and modern physics. In music (as the theologian and musician, Jonathan Arnold, explains), three terms are often used in contrast to each other– dissonance, consonance and resonance. Each can be used helpfully within many disciplines, including science, and also within some of our most profound, personal experiences.

Following Stravinsky, dissonance occurs often, but not exclusively, within 20th- and 21st-century classical music, when notes are either too close or never resolve:

In music the interrupted cadence is a harmonic sequence that brings a phrase or a piece to an end. Rather than finishing with a feeling of homecoming, however, it ends with a sense of unease, that the work is not yet complete, and that there is a need for another ending that will help the listener to feel a sense of satisfaction.[19]

The Jewish Psalms and Job abound with such dissonance as a profound human/spiritual expression of lamentation.

In contrast, consonance is about harmony, when two notes played together not only do not clash but enrich each other, or when a cadence resolves safely back to the home key. Consonant music can have a positive function:

Music has often been used as a source of healing; from comforting the unquiet heart, or unlocking memories and melodies from a mind troubled with dementia, it has long been known to help soothe pain and release creativity. Music touches every aspect of our humanity, mind and soul.[20]

Resonance, Arnold argues, is the most fruitful metaphor for both social action and theology. In musical terms, resonance is about both projection

46 Religion and Atheism in Dialogue

and working attentively with others. To perform satisfactorily in public, a musician obviously needs to learn how to project a sound that is both heard by, and appreciated by, the listener. Yet as a member of a choir (or dance group), a performer also needs to blend in with others, as does an instrumentalist in a small ensemble. Likewise, organists, playing, say, a Bach Fugue, need to balance the different voices that they play alternately with their hands and feet, bringing out now one voice and now another.

In addition:

> There are the human relationships involved in music, between composer and the music composed, between the creator and the created; between the composer, who imagines the music, and the performer, who enables the music to come to life; and between the composer, performer and recipient, the audience or listener...We hear the resonance between singers and players, an understanding between violinist and cellist, between soprano and baritone... reciprocity, a mutual give and take with each musician within a group ... If there is not, then music cannot happen.[21]

Arnold finds similar resonance in both effective social action, as do some sociologists,[22] and in well-structured worship. It might also be found in an enduring and happy marriage. In the early, romantic phase of an intimate attachment, it is common for both parties to experience a bewildering, hormonal mixture of dissonance and consonance as they explore their differences from each other as well as their mutual passions, discerning whether they can trust each other. However, over decades of a happy marriage and beyond the joys and trials of bringing up children, they can, as I have found, reach greater resonance – sharing memories, family stories, anniversary celebrations, grandchildren and jokes. This resonance can, it seems, even continue strongly in the later stages of bereavement once shock and anger become less intense.

A very similar pattern can be seen in faith development, understanding 'faith' as trust rather than cognitive belief, especially if this faith development is grounded in a worshipping community. Actual beliefs among active participants in these communities – about, say, after-life, the existence of God, the divinity of Christ or the propriety of same-sex unions – can be very varied (as Hinton's analysis and Zarum confirm) and at odds with the prescribed beliefs of a particular denomination. Worshippers can, nevertheless, live with these differences once they learn to trust both each other and the act of worship itself, especially if this worship sustains a shared sense of purpose and meaning beyond the confusions of everyday life and 'the mystery of existence'.

Worship understood in these terms of resonance has features in common with resonance in quantum physics and chemistry (following Schrödinger), especially in the molecular bonding that constructs matter within both animate and inanimate subjects and objects. The elusive and short-lived Higgs boson particle, for example, is now known to be the agent that enables this resonance to happen across the universe. Although the highly mathematical Peter Higgs was not a theist himself (he hated the boson particle being called, tellingly, 'the God particle'), he was, nevertheless, well known for his passionate, non-mathematical commitments to justice and peace, generous to his scientific collaborators, and (as I witnessed at first hand while at Edinburgh University) commendably frugal and humble as a person. Within Christian worship, as understood by Arnold, such passionate commitments to social justice, generosity and humility are supported and enhanced by theistic prayer and trust and by repeatedly hearing Gospel accounts of Jesus' earthly ministry.

What this might suggest is that resonance is crucial to understanding how many people reach their most profound personal and moral commitments – whom to marry, what cause to support, what to worship, what music, words or rituals to feed their soul. Logical proofs may have little role in these profound, everyday commitments and may even be a serious distraction.

The challenge

If this framework is accepted (and, of course, it may not be), my challenge is simply: Which is more resonant, theism or secular humanism, especially given Ray Tallis' frank (Pascalian) admission, again in *Theology*, that: 'Irredentist humanism seemingly has nothing to match religions – at least not those which offer salvation. It has to live with the certainty of total extinction'?[23] Less concerned about my own personal extinction (which, if it happens, I will know nothing about), I feel only limited resonance (and cannot even imagine why anyone else should find any more resonance) with Dawkins' cosmic 'pitiless indifference' compared with the sustaining resonance of actively held theism.

Dialogue with Richard Norman

Norman: We agree on the value of the idea of 'resonance', Robin, but I think there is an ambiguity in your use of it. Sometimes you use it to refer to something essentially positive, as when you apply it to personal relationships, but you also use it in a more neutral sense to refer to how a particular view of the world may strike one as appropriate. In the second sense, but not in the first, I can see how Dawkins' view of the world as one of 'pitiless indifference' could resonate. Dawkins' problem is that he gets carried away by his metaphors, but a better example is Thomas Hardy. He is often

48 Religion and Atheism in Dialogue

seen as an unremitting pessimist, and *Tess of the d'Urbevilles* famously ends 'The President of the Immortals had ended his sport with Tess'. But there is also the wonderful passage earlier in the novel when Tess is walking over the hills in search of work as a dairy-maid and, struggling to express her delight in the sunbathed landscape, she lights on the words of the Benedicite, 'Bless ye the Lord'. I find that both these views of the world resonate. It is a world of senseless suffering, but also a world in which one is grateful to be alive. I don't see a contradiction; I think the world has both these aspects. Perhaps I can say that because I see both ways of putting it as metaphorical. Do I take it that you think only one view can resonate?

Gill: Perhaps it is only resolute Christian Fundamentalists and resolute Secular Materialists who would disagree with the ambivalence that you (and Thomas Hardy) rightly express. I have long been persuaded that the opposite to 'faith' is not 'doubt' but 'certainty', since mature faith takes doubt seriously. Resolute Fundamentalists and Materialists might be seen as far too monolithic, rigid and certain about their positions – similar, possibly, to tone-deaf people who express no appreciation of music in any form. In contrast, the secular Hinton and the Orthodox Jew Zarum (quoted earlier) conclude that most thoughtful theists and atheists have moments of both senselessness/pitiless indifference and gratitude/exaltation. So, at a descriptive level, both senselessness and gratitude can be said to resonate with the personal experience of many people, including ourselves. Zarum argues that both forms of experience are articulated in the Psalms which is perhaps why many Jews and Christians have found Psalms to be so resonant when, say, facing life-threatening surgery (as I did). At an evaluative level, however, the Psalmists finally find gratitude/exaltation to be more resonant than senselessness or, indeed, 'pitiless indifference'. To be provocative, I am puzzled about why anyone who is not morbidly depressed should conclude otherwise.

Norman: Yes, the willingness to doubt is important. So we agree about the value of the idea of resonance, and we agree that the world can wear the aspect of a benign personal presence and also that of pitiless indifference. And yes, I think that I too would ultimately "find gratitude/exaltation to be more resonant than senselessness or, indeed, 'pitiless indifference'". But now I want to ask where it is that we *differ*. You are religious, a theist and a Christian, and I am not religious, I'm an atheist and a Humanist. Most people would see that as a fundamental difference. But the problem with the language of 'resonance', and talk of 'a personal presence' as a way of apprehending reality as a whole, rather than the literal existence of 'a person', is that the idea of 'God' becomes attenuated and is in danger of becoming empty. So what is it that you accept and I don't? I appreciate the elusiveness of 'God'-talk, and the need to employ analogy. But when you speak of 'doubt', that implies that you want to believe that in the end there *really is* this personal presence; it's not, as it is for me, a poetic metaphor. So what is it, in the end, that that means, for you? What is it, do you think, that marks the real difference between us?

Gill: We have now come to a fundamental difference between us. We both experience moments of exaltation (I hope that everyone does), but I think you can only embrace the term 'gratitude' figuratively. I find much exaltation, say, in climbing the Rock of Gibraltar every week, while there, or walking to Canterbury Cathedral for the 8 am Eucharist most mornings, when not. But I don't thank the Rock or the Cathedral for this and, if I were to do so, I would give thanks only in terms of the common, but figurative, expression 'I am just grateful to have lived fairly healthily for so long'. This figurative language might work more accurately for secular humanists if you use, instead, the language of 'luck' or 'chance' (with a bit of personal effort to stay fit and to keep taking the pills). In contrast, I am grateful to God (who, for me, is always and obviously beyond univocal, straightforward language) for being responsible for, and present within, this life-abundant world and I sense God's presence both in such exalted experience and in moments of profound contemplation/prayer (I don't distinguish between the two). Sheer gratitude is my overwhelmingly resonant practice of corporate/eucharistic and private prayer (rather than petition, even when I faced serious surgery), accompanied by a frank acknowledgement of my fallible commissions and omissions (i.e. confession) and bringing before God those in particular need (i.e. intercession). In specifically Christian terms, this amounts – despite moments of intellectual doubt (which any thoughtful person surely has whatever their faith) – to a resonant sense of life-changing and enhancing grace, that is sustained by the Eucharist and by the example of Jesus, especially as he is depicted within the Synoptic Gospels (as I argue in *Human Perfection, Transfiguration and Christian Ethics*, CUP, 2024). My challenge to you, Richard, is what do you find in secular humanism that matches such resonance?

Norman: Good question. Two things in response. First the wonder of the natural world – the majesty of a mountain peak, the burbling of a stream, the peace of a woodland walk, the abundance of other

50 Religion and Atheism in Dialogue

living things, incomprehensibly alien and yet intimately connected with us. These are not just moments of exaltation, for me they are life-enhancing, sustaining and inspiring. In our discussions, I have quoted Wordsworth: 'One impulse from a vernal wood/ May teach you more of man,/Of moral evil and of good,/Than all the sages can'. When I first read this, I was puzzled. How can a wood be *morally* enriching? The answer is that it takes us out of ourselves, puts our immediate petty preoccupations into perspective and draws us into connection with a larger world. As Iris Murdoch says, it can 'clear our minds of selfish care'. Secondly, I am sustained by the human spirit. That can sound like a vacuous abstraction, but it becomes real. As I write, there have been violent hate-fuelled riots in some cities, after the murder of three young children. The vision of human evil can induce despair, and as you say, we all have times of doubt and despair. But in response, communities have come together, to mourn their loss, to clear the streets after the rioters, and to say 'We are better than this'. Ordinary people coming together, with compassion and courage, to rise above adversity and affirm their solidarity – for this I'm grateful and by this hope I'm sustained.

Gill: I think it is quite a short step from enchantment over the natural world and a commitment to moral objectivity – which we both share – to some notion of the sacred, whether or not the latter is framed in terms of theism. Of the previous generation of philosophers, Iris Murdoch, Mary Midgley, Mary Warnock and Richard Hare all avoided theistic claims (as did the coenobitic Wittgenstein), while expressing considerable enchantment and moral commitment. To me at least, they were all key, spiritually shaped ethicists – with Warnock and Hare remaining communicant Anglicans and Murdoch and Midgley attracted also to Buddhism. These philosophers represent an experience that many (perhaps most) thoughtful practitioners of a faith tradition will know only too well (as Zarum acknowledges frankly) – sometimes we regard the words we use as referring to a sacred reality, but at other times to just a useful fiction. And perhaps those who seldom or never take an active part in a faith tradition experience similar ambivalence in moments of personal crisis. We are all fallible human beings searching for meaning. In addition, just as some theistic Christian and non-theistic Buddhist monastics in India have discovered that they can learn from each other, so might theistic and non-theistic humanists, once we refrain from 'grabbing the default position' (Anthony Kenny's memorable phrase). And the world might be a better place if we did.

Notes

1 Richard Norman, 'Review of *Philosophers on God*', in *Theology*, July 2024, 127/4.
2 Maria Rosa Menocal, *The Ornament of the World: How Muslims, Jews, and Christians Created a Culture of Tolerance in Medieval Spain* (Boston: Little, Brown and Co., 2002).
3 Mercedes Rubio, *Aquinas and Maimonides on the Possibility of the Knowledge of God* (Amsterdam, NL: Springer, 2006), pp. 1–10.
4 Sarah Pessin, 'The Influence of Islamic Thought on Maimonides', in *The Stanford Encyclopedia of Philosophy* (2016), online at: https://plato.stanford.edu/cgi-bin/encyclopedia/archinfo.cgi?entry=maimonides-islamic
5 Moses Maimonides, *The Guide of the Perplexed*, Volume 1, translated by Shlomo Pines (Chicago: University of Chicago Press, 1965), p. 104.
6 Averroes, *The Incoherence of the Incoherence*, translated by Simon Van Den Bergh, pp. 250–1, available at: https://archive.org/details/the-incoherence-of-the-incoherence/page/3/mode/2up, accessed 01/07/2024.
7 Maimonides, pp. 85–6.
8 Janet Soskice, *Naming God: Addressing the Divine in Philosophy, Theology and Scripture* (Cambridge: Cambridge University Press, 2023), p. 32.
9 Janet Soskice, *Naming God: Addressing the Divine in Philosophy, Theology and Scripture* (Cambridge: Cambridge University Press, 2023), pp. 210 and 228.
10 Janet Soskice, *Naming God: Addressing the Divine in Philosophy, Theology and Scripture* (Cambridge: Cambridge University Press, 2023), p. 54.
11 Andrew Steane, *Liberating Science: The Early Universe, Evolution and the Public Voice of Science* (Oxford: Oxford University Press, 2023), pp. 139–42.
12 Soskice, p.179.
13 Pope Francis, *Fratelli Tutti*, 2020, para.209, available at: https://www.vatican.va/content/francesco/en/encyclicals/documents/papa-francesco_20201003_enciclica-fratelli-tutti.html
14 Raphael Zarum, *Questioning Belief: Torah and Tradition in an Age of Doubt* (London: London School of Jewish Studies, Maggid, 2023), pp. 59–63.
15 Raphael Zarum, *Questioning Belief: Torah and Tradition in an Age of Doubt* (London: London School of Jewish Studies, Maggid, 2023), p. 228.
16 James Hinton, *Mass Observers Making Meaning: Religion, Spirituality and Atheism in Late 20th Century Britain* (London: Bloomsbury, 2022), p. ix.
17 Zarum, p. 227.
18 Zarum, p. 308.
19 Jonathan Arnold, *The Everyday God: Encountering the Divine in the Works of Mercy* (Abingdon: Bible Reading Fellowship, 2024), p. 62.
20 Jonathan Arnold, *The Everyday God: Encountering the Divine in the Works of Mercy* (Abingdon: Bible Reading Fellowship, 2024), p. 140.
21 Jonathan Arnold, *The Everyday God: Encountering the Divine in the Works of Mercy* (Abingdon: Bible Reading Fellowship, 2024), p. 85.
22 Hartmut Rosa, *Resonance* (Cambridge: Polity, 2019).
23 Raymond Tallis, 'Human Transcendence: The Possibility of Spiritual Irredentism', in *Theology* 2019, 122.2.83–92.

7

POSTSCRIPT

Without Naming God

Brian Pearce

> The paper by Brian Pearce which introduced Part I of this book gave rise to a series of discussions, mostly in online conversations, some of which are reflected in the subsequent chapters here in Part I. In the light of those discussions, Pearce shared these further thoughts.

The paper which I circulated in 2020 included a substantial amount of material pointing to the possibility of a plausible concept of God. However, subsequent conversations made it abundantly clear that to find common ground between the religious and the non-religious, it would, unsurprisingly, be necessary to deploy more neutral language, setting to one side theistic terminology and instead 'unbundling' in the process the concept of 'God'. This would in no sense represent a religious 'surrender', but rather an attempt to establish how much genuine agreement might be found across the board.

In such engagement, it would seem particularly important to start from our shared human experience. My earlier paper concluded by identifying a series of aspects of human experience, starting with very general experiences which are not distinctively religious and moving towards more religious ones. In now seeking language which might be used to identify common ground, it would be appropriate to drop the latter, and I would also modify the wording of others which could be retained. What follows is an initial suggestion of terminology which it might be helpful to use in such an enterprise:

a A sense of 'oneness' in the universe of which we find ourselves a part – suggesting that everything is interconnected and, therefore, that we should

DOI: 10.4324/9781003536185-8

be cautious about binaries, even if, at a secondary level, distinctions can be important to identify and explain differences.

b A sense of awe and wonder at the magnitude and order of the universe.

c The recognition of an evolutionary process which started long before we humans came on the scene, displaying an extravagant abundance of novelty, which has led to a growth in the complexity of the universe and, in particular, in the life forms to which it has given rise.

d The sense of that which is 'more than' the mundane and the everyday, and which appears to be inexhaustible.

e A sense of gratitude for the opportunity to live the lives we do.

f The awareness of a universe which exhibits characteristics such as (in alphabetical order rather than an order of significance) beauty, creativity, empathy, enjoyment, fruitfulness, love and truth, as well as pain, suffering and tragedy – and many more – which can provide rich meaning for us.

These reflections and suggestions set the scene for the chapters which now follow in Part II of this book.

PART II

Opportunities for Convergence

8

THE KINDNESS OF STRANGERS

Empathy, Altruism and the Case for Convergence

John Saxbee

Introduction

When Blanche DuBois in Tennessee Williams' *A Streetcar Named Desire* signs off with "I have always depended on the kindness of strangers", the phrase took off as emblematic of what many felt to be a counter-intuitive notion – care and compassion shown to those beyond our circles of acquaintance and presumed responsibility. This links to one of the most challenging topics in the debate between theists and atheists/humanists – the relationship between religion and ethics, and specifically how care and concern for others relates to our respective moral leanings.

On the one hand, there has been appeal to human nature and how it has evolved, and needs to further evolve, to secure the well-being of humankind and the environment we share. On the other, there is appeal to a moral authority that transcends the human mind whilst inspiring and informing human attitudes and actions likewise conducive to the well-being of humankind and the environment we share. Whilst an atheist will most likely see the positive evolution of humanity as building on an instinctive concern for familial and local community networks, and onwards towards an ever more expansive concern for the flourishing of all people everywhere, a theist will embrace as fundamental a prior principle of moral theology that all of humanity is valued and loved – and cascade that love as expansively as their circumstances, resources and opportunities will allow. Local to global, or vice versa, the resulting beneficence can be of equal moral and practical worth, and if theists and atheists co-operate, there can be significant added value as their respective motivations converge.

DOI: 10.4324/9781003536185-10

58 Religion and Atheism in Dialogue

Countervailing considerations can also demonstrate convergence. For example, the humanist may gain meaning and significance for his or her life from familial and localised networks and, resting content, apply what may be described as a moral significance taper disincentivising practical, or even emotional concern for those less genetically, spatially or temporally proximate. But equally, the theists, whilst acknowledging the equal worth of all people and believing that, indeed, "God has no favourites", might well temper moral idealism with practical reasons when it comes to just how far his or her sense of moral responsibility might stretch. For them, as for many an atheist, charity begins, and resides, at home! This might be described as negative convergence and, if it is, then it may require to be countered by positive convergence centred on principles, virtues and values which transcend such quotidian considerations.

What follows is a summary of exchanges between myself and Richard Norman representing religious and humanist perspectives respectively. They focus on the extent to which our respective points of view differ to the point of being irreconcilable or, on the other hand, hold out the prospect of convergence with potential to promote further creative dialogue and practical co-operation. Neither of us claims to be an authorised spokesperson for our respective constituencies. But we have both felt the benefit of these exchanges which helped us to contribute constructively to a stimulating debate when the Religion and Atheism dialogue group dedicated one of its sessions to this topic. The to-and-fro format of these exchanges inevitably entailed a degree of reiteration which is to some extent evident in what follows. This edited version is included so as to capture both the substance of our exchanges, and the constructive and convivial spirit in which they were conducted.

1.

So what might humanists and theists bring to the table?

A humanist perspective typically:

1 poses a measured but effective challenge to any uncritical appeal to divine command and natural law ethics.
2 affirms positive quality of life *before* death, and *physical/psychological* well-being, as key moral objectives in countering the prioritisation of spiritual and post-mortem fulfilment.
3 emphasises networks of relationships and membership of an on-going human community as instrumental in giving meaning and significance to our lives, and illuminating why the lives and interests of others matter to us.
4 affirms the role of altruism as intrinsic to human nature, having evolved as essential to human growth and development.

The Kindness of Strangers **59**

Theists might challenge the instrumentalism implied in point 3 above, and be rather less sanguine about intrinsic altruism. But they are likely to acknowledge the critical force of points 1 and 2.

A theistic perspective typically:

1 prioritises the moral significance of all people, and their environment, as a theological imperative from which commitments to familial, local and wider social responsibilities are derived.
2 challenges confidence in altruism as intrinsic to human nature, and so places a premium on an educated conscience as key to the internalisation, articulation and activation of virtues and values conducive to the common good.
3 counters reliance on *ad hominem* subjectivism and authoritarianism in determining moral standards and embraces a moral measure which transcends the human heart and mind, and to which all are accountable at all times.
4 promotes belief in, and commitment to, unconditional love (*agape*) that transcends legalism, conformism and self-serving instrumentalism.

With regard to such a theistic perspective, humanists might well appreciate the moral integrity of point 1, whilst disputing its theological provenance. From their point of view, human nature, as it has evolved, is the sole source of an altruistic disposition, so they are reluctant to acknowledge the need for any extrinsic educative influence in moral formation and any accountability to a moral measure transcending the human mind. They are more inclined to credit human nature with an inbuilt capacity for altruistic love, notwithstanding a solipsistic instinct for survival towards which evolution has typically been seen as orientated.

So, by way of summary, atheistic humanists tend to advocate for a bottom-up, freed up and down to earth moral economy which can function as an effective antidote to the worst excesses of theological dogmatism, spiritual detachment and supernatural or eschatological escapism. Theists tend to advocate for a universal, self-sacrificial, unconditional and accountable moral economy predicated on agapeistic love as both mysteriously transcendental and immanently expressible. It can function as an effective antidote to the worst excesses of human arrogance, self-regard, moral nihilism and socioeconomic elitism.

2.

Whilst reason and tradition may well impact on how these respective positions arise and are articulated, and for theists revelation may feature as well, it is primarily on lived experience that the moral significance of who or what is other than ourselves is based. Apparently opposed interpretations of experience can appear to be irreconcilable, but if belief in human nature as intrinsically altruistic and belief in an intrinsic moral measure to which all are accountable are both acts of faith based on lived experience, then a degree of convergence can be acknowledged and explored further. Furthermore, the common good can be progressed by the sharing of perspectives, the pooling of moral sensibilities and joint enterprise in confronting the evils of injustice, oppression, exploitation and indifference – and so promote and normalise kindness of strangers.

Any theistic appeal to "a moral authority that transcends the human mind" has to acknowledge how simplistic appeals to, for example, scriptural authority, on the part of all the 'religions of the book', have contributed to inhumane treatment of some sectors of society. Humanists insist that care and concern for others is just that – human care for human beings. Theists, of course, may share such concerns when it comes to obscurantist fundamentalism, and atheists may acknowledge risks involved in reliance on human nature which we all know to be all too flawed. The apparent reliance on such flawed human nature, all too capable of leading humans to do terrible things, may render humanist ethics most vulnerable to challenge. If we are not accountable to anything outside our own humanity, do we lack a sufficient moral bulwark against what Robert Burns called 'man's inhumanity to man'?

Atheists may hold that it is not so much altruism as empathy which is a deep-seated feature of what it means to be human – and, it might be asserted, is not confined to responses to those nearest and dearest. Feelings are infectious and, as David Hume put it, "none are...entirely indifferent to the interests of their fellow creatures". Human beings are moved by the joys and sorrows of others. This is not to be seen as a mere incidental and occasional aspect of human behaviour but sufficiently deep-seated to be described as part of human nature. That said, empathy is not altruism, and if it does lead to altruistic action it is more likely to be towards those closest to us. But by application of our capacity for rational reflection, imagination, understanding and fellow feeling, we might, again to quote Hume, "render our sentiments more public and social". The consequent scope for convergence across any religious/non-religious divide is, at this concrete level, obvious. We – all of us – have a shared moral vocabulary, a shared language of values – of kindness, fairness, honesty and integrity – and though it does not guarantee agreement on moral conclusions, it makes reasoned debate possible.

Empathy, then, as a deep feature of our humanity, can be extended in these ways and is not a totally fragile basis for an ethical concern for others. At the same time, it is not a guarantee of altruism. Our sympathetic concern for others can all too easily be overridden by our indifference, our selfishness, by malign ideologies and belief systems and by the manifold ways in which we may dehumanise the other. This is as much a problem for religious people

The Kindness of Strangers **61**

as for humanists. Maybe the sense of a transcendent moral authority can strengthen people's care for others, but it too may fail. Maybe this is where common ground is to be found in the need for faith based on lived experience. Of course, atheists are likely to be wary of references to faith, conscious as they are of how appeal to faith can function as a substitute for reasoned belief. But as people of faith sometimes point out, the word does not have to be used in that way. In everyday speech, we talk quite uncontroversially of having faith in a person: "I know he's let us down in the past", we might say, "but I believe he's good at heart and I have faith in him". It's not a confident prediction that he will do what we rely on, it's a commitment to give him the benefit of the doubt, but it is not blind faith. It is grounded in experience.

We can, and do, extend this way of talking beyond faith in particular individuals and talk of faith in humanity. People do describe acts of kindness shown by strangers as having restored their faith in humanity. Nelson Mandela, who knew as much as anyone about acts of inhumanity, wrote in his autobiography:

There were many dark moments when my faith in humanity was sorely tested, but I would not, and could not, give myself up to despair.[1]

Our faith in humanity is strengthened by our knowledge of exemplars, by our experience of what human beings are capable of – people we know personally as well as public figures. Perhaps such a faith in humanity, based on lived experience, is common ground on which humanists and theists can converge.

3.

At this point, it is important to test the limits of reliance on deep-seated capacities for empathy as more or less evident in human nature but sufficiently evident to require no further accountability criteria, and no further basis upon which to value the moral worth of human behaviours, attitudes and judgements. If shared values are "a brute fact about what it means to be human",[2] it may not be clear how this differs from claims that, for example, empathy is intrinsic to human nature or a part of human nature – a notion on the face of it incompatible with how human beings actually behave, apart, that is, from those we admire as exemplars of empathy expressed as altruism. It might just be that they are exceptions that prove the rule, hence their Mandela-esque iconic status.

Also, appeal is made to something else deep-seated in human nature, that is, capacity for rational reflection to support confidence in the extension of altruism towards 'persons remote from us' (Hume). But is there sufficient evidence to support such an appeal? Again, the stories we tell about heroic

62 Religion and Atheism in Dialogue

exemplars of selfless altruism would suggest that kindness of strangers as testimony to such capacity for rational reflection is honoured more in the breach than in the observance. Might it just be that theists who promote accountability to a moral authority that transcends the human mind have a point when it comes to not resting content with empathy, however deep-seated in human nature, as a sufficient explanation of, and stimulus towards, the very best virtues and values? The point has been typically well made by John Cottingham:

> ....human nature has to mean more than just a collection of contingent facts about the sort of creatures we have evolved to be. Instead, it has to embody a normative ideal of what is noblest and best within us.[3]

This 'normative ideal' cannot be something we have created for ourselves if it is to be other than what we subjectively say it is – it must have a source outside ourselves. Except that non-theists might pursue a different path out of the dilemma by declaring one of the parties to be non- or sub-human on account of their deficient moral sensibilities. But that then consigns them to bestial status and so subject to the same moral neutrality as we afford animals. This could be a challenge to all moral philosophies exclusively predicated on human nature possessed of moral capacities, be they defined as 'intrinsic' or 'deep-seated'.

The scope for convergence on the strength of a shared moral vocabulary, a shared language of values – of kindness, fairness, honesty and integrity – is very real. A shared appeal to reason, imagination and experience will also provide crucial stimulus towards making common cause together. Faith in humanity as a commitment to give human beings the benefit of the doubt is certainly a commitment all right thinking theists should share – and if atheists likewise acknowledge that affirmation of moral accountability to a reality which transcends the human mind is based on lived experience, and not blind faith, then they can profitably probe together common denominators at the heart of moral philosophy and theology.

4.

As Christians and humanists, the same questions have to be faced. How far, and in what ways, can our aspirations to live a good life be built on our human nature and our human capacities, and how can we strengthen those capacities when in danger of failing? To some extent, undeniably, the answers will point in different directions. From a theistic ethical perspective, humans are accountable to something outside themselves. However, there is also a sense in which this can be said from a humanist perspective. They may be cautious about saying that we have created for ourselves our moral values, our normative ideal. But they would say that our values are *human* values which cannot just be invented out of nothing. They are a response to the world in which we find ourselves, a response to the human condition as we experience it, and above all a response to the Other, to our encounters with other human beings. Our values take shape with our growing awareness of the lives and aspirations of others, and our growing commitment to the life we share in common.

Most humanists would say that we are not just accountable to our fellow human beings but to other living things with whom we share the natural world. What humanists would not embrace is talk of moral accountability to the authority of a personal being transcending the human mind. That is likely to be the core difference between religious and non-religious perspectives. But common to both is the shared experience of being accountable, of values which make demands on us, and which also inspire us so that we can be caught up in and devoted to ideals which strengthen us and carry us along. Meanwhile, deployment of various forms of idealism across the atheism/agnosticism/theism spectrum suggests scope for convergence when it comes to affirming ethical norms and values short of belief in a personalised supreme being, but more than reliance on an exclusively human provenance.

The humanist account of ethical decision-making derives from reason and empathy. These might look like somewhat elusive qualities, but what is being referenced here are, quite simply, *thinking and feeling*. Human beings are, at least sometimes, responsive to other people's feelings. We share the feelings of others, *we feel with them*. That is what words like 'empathy' and 'sympathy' mean. This responsiveness can, of course, be all too limited, fickle and inconsistent, but it is a fact, a brute feature of human nature. It is the starting point, humanists would say, for any account of moral values and ethical decision-making, which would be impossible without it.

It means the ability to think about what others are feeling and experiencing, and the need to respond to that. Capacities for thinking and feeling are features of human beings quite generally, and any account of our ethical life, religious or humanist, must see them as an essential part of the story. To say that they are 'deep' features of human nature is not to say that they are steady and reliable, but that they are fundamental to our nature as a species. They are not just a collection of contingent facts about the sort of creatures we have evolved to be. Our ability to share our feelings, and our possession of a shared language which enables us to find a shared significance in our experience, are what make us, as a species, social beings.

But, of course, they may fail us, and this is a part of our shared human predicament. It is a shared challenge for all of us, religious and non-religious, and the recognition of that challenge is another important area of common ground, even if ways of responding to it may differ. Theists are likely to talk of sinfulness and identify a role for divine influence in dealing with it. Christians

64 Religion and Atheism in Dialogue

can draw on their membership of a religious community, they can be inspired by the life and teachings of Jesus, and they can be strengthened by prayer. But they recognise that these too may fail. Those who profess to live by the law of love all too often fail to live by it. Humanists draw on fellow human beings, appealing to the example of countless people who have worked in big ways and small, through large-scale social movements and small day-to-day acts of kindness to relieve human suffering and improve the lives of others. But legion examples exist of 'man's inhumanity to man' perpetrated by people whose sole moral horizon is at a human level. But notwithstanding these challenges, both religious and non-religious people do have their own specific resources of moral motivation, we can all of us draw strength from one another. We can do so because we are, at the most basic level, brought together by shared values. These are not an adventitious collection of values which just happen to coincide. They are values which we share because we are all part of the same interdependent human community. Dialogue, therefore, can and should help to deepen awareness of those shared values and so facilitate working together in pursuit of them.

Conclusions

Following a further discussion in the wider dialogue group focussing on morality, with particular reference to empathy and altruism, the following conclusions were reached, thereby developing the case for convergence between theist and atheist points of view.

At the heart of these exchanges has been a contrast between two perspectives. On the one hand, a theistic appeal to a normative ideal predicated on the moral authority of a personal being transcending the human mind, and to which we are all accountable at all times. On the other, an atheistic reliance on the capacity for empathy as a deep-seated feature of human nature, expressed especially in inter-personal and communal relationships and capable of being widened into a general altruistic concern. In light of these two perspectives, the following possible points of convergence might be discerned.

Shared challenges

We have noted the prevalence of failure to act on our altruistic imperatives. Recognition of this failure leads to a tension between optimism and pessimism both about belief in human beings as made in the image of God, and about belief in a human capacity for altruistic action. All fall short: what Christians would describe as the fact of human sinfulness is our shared predicament. Then there is the tendency to prioritise the well-being of those closest to us spatially, socially and temporally. The capacity for empathetic concern which humanists point to in our relationships with those near at hand is liable to taper off in our responses to more remote claims on our concern, whilst theists who assent to a transcendent imperative advocating universal care and compassion may routinely apply limits to the reach of their altruism. Also, the existence of those whose moral sensibilities are deficient to the point of being psychopathic challenges humanist reliance on human nature, and the status of those for whom a transcendent normative ideal has no significance raises issues for theists. By no means least, the prevalence of simplistic versions of both religious and atheistic ethical perspectives, taking the form of a fundamentalist use of, for example, biblical texts on the one hand or, on the other, an over-simplified view of evolutionary theory, is also a shared challenge, as are tendencies towards attenuated versions of human flourishing which fail to give due weight to spiritual well-being on the one hand or to physical well-being on the other.

These shared challenges render all the more significant the positive points of convergence which have characterised our exchanges.

Accountability

Both theists and atheists see themselves as being morally accountable to something. For theists, it is a transcendent reality beyond the human mind: as Rowan Williams has put it, "in what sense can ethics fail to be about the contest of power, if there is nothing towards which we are all accountable all of the time?"[4] Humanists would say that they are accountable to their fellow humans and other living things with which we share the natural world, and that our values must be responsive to the world in which we find ourselves, the human condition as we experience it. Common to both perspectives is the shared experience of values which make demands on us.

Shared values

These values, whether grounded in human nature or a moral authority beyond the human mind, encapsulate the shared recognition of a responsibility to aim at the well-being of humankind and the environment we share. We can all of us draw strength from one another because we are, at the most basic level, brought together by shared values – kindness, fairness, honesty and integrity – and dialogue between the religious and non-religious can and should help us to pursue them together.

Faith

The language of faith comes readily to those with a religious commitment. Humanists tend to be wary of the word, but at the everyday level, they can recognise the need for faith in our fellow human beings and, by extension,

66 Religion and Atheism in Dialogue

faith in humanity which can draw strength from those around us who remind us of the best of which we are capable. Faith of whichever kind, based on lived experience, can be a key contributor to our joint endeavours and reflections upon them.

Notes

1 Nelson Mandela, *The Long Walk to Freedom* (Philadelphia: Little, Brown, 1994).
2 Anthony Carroll and Richard Norman (eds), *Religion and Atheism: Beyond the Divide* (London: Routledge, 2017), p. 109.
3 John Cottingham, *On the Meaning of Life* (London: Routledge, 2003), p. 71.
4 Unpublished response to an article by Bishop John Spong.

9

CAN HUMANISTS BE SPIRITUAL?

Jeremy Rodell

Eighty or so humanists, all active in their local communities, were asked whether they agreed or disagreed that "Humanism and spirituality are incompatible."[1] The result was a complete spectrum. Some saw 'spirituality' as an irredeemably religious term, with no resonance for them as humanists. Others disagreed about its underlying meaning. Others felt there were things there with which they could identify, or at least recognise.

When a word is so contentious, there are two approaches. The safest is simply not to use it. But that means you either need a good alternative or must steer clear of the subject matter entirely, leaving others to take ownership. The alternative is to be willing to use it sparingly and carefully, making clear what you mean. When it comes to the S-word, many humanists choose the first option. As Peter Connelly, formerly of Chichester University, put it: "when people attempt to secularise the idea of spirituality, supernaturalism gets a toehold in humanist discourse."[2] Instead, he proposed 'trance experience.' But 'trance' carries its own baggage. Others have suggested that 'transcendence,' 'awe' or 'contemplation' can do the job. Often they can, but not always.

A strong case for willingness to use the S-word when appropriate was illustrated in a discussion on BBC Radio 4's 'Today' programme featuring Christina Rees, at the time a spokesperson for the Church of England's General Synod. She was arguing that humanists and other atheists should continue to be excluded from the programme's 'Thought for the Day' slot (as they still are) as they are "...coming from a position that denies the spiritual dimension... a partial and diminished perspective...There is more to life than you can see, touch and measure." The implication was that humanists and other atheists somehow have the essence of their humanity missing. Like Mr. Spock, we are all Vulcans.

DOI: 10.4324/9781003536185-11

68 Religion and Atheism in Dialogue

On the other hand, here is the former President of Humanists UK, Professor Alice Roberts, on Twitter/X in 2019: "I consider myself a spiritual person. But it's a natural sort of spirituality, not the sort that's tied up with supernatural beliefs." No taboo there.

But what might 'a natural sort of spirituality' mean? In answering that question, perhaps we can get beyond the long-running debate about the word and consider what are, I think, important elements of our humanity but without denying the real differences between humanist and religious perspectives.

What we don't mean

In digging beneath the hard crust of this contested term, we rapidly hit material which can be thrown on the 'not for humanists' spoil heap. Firstly, there are things to do with the Church as the 'spiritual' estate of the realm, dating back to a medieval worldview in which the supernatural was considered a very real presence, mediated by the clergy. The vestiges of that worldview remain with us today in the form of Church Establishment, and Lords Spiritual sitting in Parliament. This use of 'spiritual' is sometimes extended to refer to religions in general.

Secondly, there are varieties of 'spiritual' practice associated with what most humanists would consider supernatural ideas or beliefs, such as prayers seeking benefit in an afterlife, Catholic Communion, with its underpinning doctrine of transubstantiation, 'personal conversations' with God or 'speaking in tongues' (as practised daily by former Archbishop Justin Welby[3]).

New Age spirituality also falls into this category. David Webster, from the University of Gloucestershire, subtitled his book *Dispirited: "How contemporary spirituality makes us stupid, selfish and unhappy."*[4] His ire is directed not towards traditional religion, but towards 'spiritual-but-not-religious' worldviews, which he refers to as 'faith lite,' a pick-and-mix approach which he criticises as offering no challenge and propagating a belief that underlying all religions is a deeper spiritual truth visible only to those who have 'thought different' – a classic feature of conspiracy theories.[5] He is particularly critical of the Mind, Body and Spirit (MBS) variety of spirituality. This type of magical thinking can be found almost everywhere in the United Kingdom. Treatments offered by my local shop include chakra reading, crystal healing, past life regression and several types of tarot reading.

The use of 'spiritual' in a schools context suffers from a different problem: loose thinking. Schools in England are inspected for 'Spiritual, Moral, Social and Cultural (SMSC) development,' where "The spiritual development of pupils is shown by their: ability to be reflective about their own beliefs (religious or otherwise) and perspective on life; knowledge of, and respect for, different people's faiths, feelings and values; sense of enjoyment and fascination in learning about themselves, others and the world around them; use of imagination and creativity in their learning; willingness to reflect on their experiences."[6]

In criticising an earlier, equally muddled, version of this definition, Marilyn Mason – then Education Officer at the British Humanist Association (later Humanists UK) – suggested that they should have consulted the Dalai Lama, who provided this helpful distinction between religion and spirituality.[7]

> I believe there is an important distinction to be made between religion and spirituality. Religion I take to be concerned with faith in the claims to salvation of one faith tradition or another, an aspect of which is acceptance of some form of metaphysical or supernatural reality, including perhaps an idea of heaven or nirvana. Connected with this are religious teachings or dogma, rituals, prayer and so on. Spirituality I take to be concerned with those qualities of the human spirit – such as love and compassion, patience, tolerance, forgiveness, contentment, a sense of responsibility, a sense of harmony – which bring happiness to both self and others... This is why I sometimes say that religion is something we can perhaps do without. What we cannot do without are these basic spiritual qualities.

Two key types of spirituality

Dig a bit further, and we can identify two broad categories of 'spirituality' where there is a high degree of universality:

- Inner spirituality: Relating to our profound inner life.
- Experiential spirituality: A wide spectrum of experiences featuring a sense of transcendence or connectedness with something larger.

Inner spirituality

The Seamus Heaney HomePlace in County Derry, Northern Ireland, is a museum in the area where he grew up. It features written poems and recordings of him reading them. I rarely read poetry, and knew little about Seamus Heaney. Yet my response was an unexpected plunge into the deeper layers of my inner life, of thoughts about what I had – or had not – done with it, of important relationships, of gratitude for what I had.

These thoughts would no doubt be familiar to those working in hospital chaplaincy/pastoral support, supporting people facing illness, sadness and, often, the end of their lives. Many of those patients now are non-religious, and there is greater diversity among the religious. The result has been a reappraisal of 'spiritual care' in healthcare, which is now defined by NHS Scotland as "...care which recognises and responds to the needs of the human spirit when faced with trauma, ill health or sadness and can include the need

70 Religion and Atheism in Dialogue

for meaning, for self-worth, to express oneself, for faith support, perhaps for rites or prayer or sacrament, or simply for a sensitive listener."[8]

Religious or not, we can probably all recognise the universal humanity underlying this definition (which is the approach used by the Non-Religious Pastoral Support Network). Elsewhere, the NHS identifies 'religious care' as a subset of 'spiritual care.'[9]

As wider acceptance of the S-word is inhibited by its religious connotations, it is interesting that two other words with the same problem – chaplaincy and chaplain – have been consciously re-defined in the healthcare context. NHS guidelines now state: "The term 'chaplaincy' [refers] to the pastoral, spiritual and/or religious care and support that the NHS is expected to offer to all its users... [We] intend it to encompass care and support available to individuals of all religions and beliefs...[which] encompasses non-religious beliefs and the absence of a religion or belief."[10] There are now humanist, Muslim, Hindu, Jewish, as well as Christian, chaplains providing spiritual care alongside each other in the NHS.

Whether or not people choose to use the S-word, there is a universality at the heart of what the NHS refers to as 'spiritual care,' or what the Dalai Lama calls 'basic spiritual qualities' distinct from religion. This is about profound aspects of our inner life.

Both the NHS and the Dalai Lama refer to the 'human spirit' in this context. If that means 'soul' in the sense that a traditional Christian, or even a Mind Body Spirit practitioner, might use it, meaning something immortal and immaterial, then we have veered off the common ground. It would be hard to find a humanist who thinks such souls exist. But the problem disappears if human spirit simply refers to human consciousness. That is one thing we can all be sure of. While consciousness is not itself material, almost all humanists would recognise it as a natural phenomenon, which emerges from material human brains (and non-human brains too). When we die, that activity stops, and the light of consciousness goes out. Precisely how the matter of our brain gives rise to consciousness remains the so-called 'hard problem of consciousness.' But, unlike soul, there is no debate about its existence. That then takes us towards the other major aspect of spirituality.

Experiential spirituality

Here is André Comte-Sponville, former Professor of Philosophy at the Sorbonne, from his *Book of Atheist Spirituality*.[11]

The first time it happened I was in the forest in the north of France. I must have been twenty five or twenty six... That particular evening, some friends and I had gone for a walk in the forest we liked so much.... Gradually our laughter faded, and the conversation died down. My mind empty of thought, I was simply registering the world around me... And then, all of a sudden...What? Nothing: everything! No words, no meanings, no questions, only – a surprise. Only – this. A seemingly infinite happiness. A seemingly eternal sense of peace. Above me, the starry sky was immense, luminous and unfathomable, and within me there was nothing but the sky, of which I was a part, and the silence, and the light, like a warm hum, and a sense of joy with neither subject nor object...Yes, in the darkness of that night, I contained only the dazzling presence of the All.... 'This is what Spinoza meant by eternity', I said to myself – and naturally, that put an end to it.

Sam Harris, the American philosopher and neuroscientist, who became well known in the early 2000s as one of the 'four horsemen' of New Atheism, recounts a similar – albeit daytime – experience in his book *Waking Up*.[12] These are intense human experiences. And anyone who has had one will recognise what they are talking about. For me, the most powerful was when I was still at school, probably age fifteen or sixteen. For a reason I cannot remember, I was walking home alone in the middle of the day. It was a bright morning, and the sun was coming through the trees overhanging the lane outside the school gate. Then, exactly as André Comte-Sponville says, "all of a sudden...." Something wonderful. Paradise. It did not last very long. But I will never forget it.

Both André Comte-Sponville and Sam Harris refer to these as spiritual experiences. Sam Harris goes on to say:

> If I were a Christian, I would undoubtedly have interpreted this experience in Christian terms. I might have believed I had glimpsed the oneness of God, or been touched by the Holy Spirit. If I were a Hindu, I might think in terms of Brahman, the eternal Self, of which the world and all individual minds are thought to be a mere modification.

In other words, intense spiritual experiences become religious experiences when a religious person views them through the lens of their religion or, as Sam Harris puts it, draws 'metaphysical conclusions.'

They appear to have some common characteristics:

- They are non-intellectual. Sadly, for those of us who tend to over-intellectualise, they are short-lived, as André Comte-Sponville found when he thought about Spinoza.
- The core of the experience is a sense of transcendence or connectedness. That may mean with other people, wider humanity, the rest of the universe or simply 'something greater.' The experience carries with it a diminishment of the ego, sometimes to the point where there is no self-awareness,

or separation between subject and object. Rather than 'you' looking at 'it,' there is simply 'the looking.'

- They are individual. As far as we know, the others in André Comte-Sponville's party just carried on as normal.
- They are more common when we are young.
- Finally, they are powerful and positive, accompanied by feelings of elation, joy and compassion towards the world. They seem important. And memorable.

The psychologist, Abraham Maslow – of 'Maslow's Hierarchy' fame – studied these 'peak experiences' extensively. His work confirmed that they are quite common across the population. According to his biographer, "Maslow found it incredible that some of his undergraduates at Brandeis University unknowingly described their peak-experiences in language of rapture similar to those of famous spiritual teachers, East and West."[13]

It seems such spontaneous spiritual experiences are responses to combinations of the many inputs our consciousness receives at every moment: sound, sight, smell, touch or taste from our external environment (including other people), internal bodily sensations and what has been described as 'conceptive' thoughts,[14] the sort that well up from our subconscious: mind-wandering, daydreaming or random flashes of memory. It is almost impossible to say what the specific set of triggers were in a particular case. But the considerable body of credible research now accumulated on spiritual experiences and the brain has included the use of drugs to induce them. For example, a 2006 double-blind study with volunteers who had not previously had experience of hallucinogenic drugs concluded: "When administered under supportive conditions, psilocybin occasioned experiences similar to spontaneously occurring mystical experiences."[15] That may explain why plants containing psychedelic ingredients, such as magic mushrooms (the source of psilocybin), peyote and ayahuasca have been used to create or enhance mystical experiences for centuries. It seems that electrical stimulation of the relevant part of the brain, the anterior insula, can produce similar effects.[16]

Albert Einstein (a humanist and agnostic) understood such experiences in a cosmological context:

A human being is part of a whole, called by us the Universe – a part limited in time and space. He experiences himself, his thoughts and feelings, as separate from the rest – a kind of optical delusion of his consciousness. This delusion is a kind of prison for us, restricting us to our personal desires and to the affection for those nearest us.[17]

In other words, *not* experiencing a sense of transcendence is the delusion.

Maslow confirmed that peak experiences are more common and intense for young people. With age, they give way to a 'gentler, more sustained state of serenity' he called plateau experience, which he believed was more amenable to cultivation. The Buddhists and other meditation practitioners – and more recently medical science – teach us that this sort of contemplative experience is something we can consciously choose, develop and, to a degree, control.

Other experiences to which the 'spiritual' label is attached may not be as powerful but exhibit similar characteristics: the shiver down the spine from a Beethoven slow movement, the human connectedness staring at a Rembrandt self-portrait (or is it vice versa?), the wonder at the immensity of a starry sky. They all involve a non-intellectualised sense of joy, transcendence and connection, often communicated though the arts. We actively seek out circumstances which we hope will take us in the direction of this sense of transcendence, whether it is by buying a ticket to a concert, contemplating a beautiful view, stepping outside on a clear night or – for those so inclined – attending a religious service.

There is another category of experience to be considered here. In 1969, the Oxford marine biologist Sir Alister Hardy founded the Religious Experience Research Centre. He began by placing advertisements asking: "Have you ever been aware of or influenced by a presence or a power, whether you call it God or not, that is different from your everyday self?" The records of The Alister Hardy Trust,[18] now held at the University of Wales Trinity Saint David in Lampeter and Bishop Grosseteste University in Lincoln, include the thousands of replies he received, some of them peak experiences. As his question was clearly leading in a religious or supernatural direction, it is not surprising that a more recent analysis of the responses, supported by a BBC poll, illustrates the danger of confusing reports of subjective experiences with the interpretations the subjects put on them.[19] It came up with categories such as: meaningful coincidences that seemed 'meant to happen'; 'the presence of God'; 'prayer being answered'; 'a sacred presence in nature'; and 'the presence of the dead.' There has been so much subsequent research into the many varieties of such allegedly supernatural events that we can say with some confidence that there was nothing supernatural actually occurring. Some of them seem to be peak experiences.

There is one class of experience, well documented in the Alister Hardy archives and elsewhere, which has attracted particular attention: the Near-death experience (NDE). These have been reported by an estimated 10–20 per cent of people who have survived a close encounter with clinical death.[20] They vary, but common features include vivid imagery, such as a bright light, movement through a tunnel or visions of past life events. Some include 'out-of-body experiences' or visions of heaven. Most are accompanied by feelings of great serenity. Some are terrifying. Like peak experiences, they often have a positive long-term impact on the subject. NDEs have been reported for centuries, and there is no question that, like peak experiences, they are subjectively real, and powerful. They continue to be widely studied.

74 Religion and Atheism in Dialogue

According to Susan Blackmore, who has spent a lifetime researching in this and related areas, some explanations for NDEs can be dismissed. Religious expectations may have a role in the reported detail: "Christians tend to see Jesus in the light, and Hindus see the messengers of Yamraj [the god of death]."[21] But they happen to the non-religious and the religious alike, and the essential features are independent of religious belief or unbelief. And they happen regardless of whether people have been given medication or not. On the other hand, lack of oxygen reaching the brain (anoxia) does seem likely to play an important role in many cases. Given the unknowns surrounding human consciousness and the brain, there is clearly more to be found.

It is easy to see why such profound spiritual experiences are often given religious interpretations. Many of those experiencing them believe that they have had an insight into an afterlife, despite the fact that the one thing they all have in common is that in the end, they did not actually die. The fact that these and other spiritual experiences are clearly physiological does not reduce their power.

That takes us back to the issue of consciousness. Sam Harris's book *Waking Up* is sub-titled *Searching for spirituality without religion*, drawing particularly on his years of contemplative experience with a range of Buddhist and Hindu teachers. It encourages the use of meditation to develop a range of healthy mental skills. However, the core message is more profound. It is the realisation that what we feel as the 'self' is an illusion that arises because we confuse our consciousness with the thoughts and other experiences it contains. In this view, the 'I' is simply a feeling in a psychological continuity of consciousness that begins during foetal development and ends at death. Consciousness is all there is. His conclusion has been underlined by subsequent research, such as Thomas Metzinger's study of people experiencing 'pure consciousness' through meditation, which quotes an old Tibetan saying: "it is simply too close for us to see, too profound for us to fathom, too simple for us to believe, or even too good for us to accept."[22] They make a convincing case, and this does indeed seem an important insight, albeit one that is hard to hang on to in everyday life.

Whether or not this is right, it strongly suggests that we should consider spiritual experiences as differing states of consciousness.

What does it matter?

In a paper titled "Integrating spirituality into the public realm," Jonathan Rowson, former Director of the Social Brain Centre at the Royal Society of Arts, argued that spirituality is nothing if it is not 'transformative,' and that meaningful transformation is not in the realm of inner contemplation but should instead be a driver for political action to improve life for others.[23] Climate change was top of his priority list.

There is no doubt that many people are driven to do good works by their religious or non-religious principles, but why should subjective spiritual experience be politically *transformative*? Urging an undefined spirituality (in this case he was talking in a religious context) to legitimise political action might have a direct line to action on climate change, but it also has a direct line to White Christian Nationalism in America, or Boko Haram murders in Nigeria. We surely do not need to invoke spirituality or religion to do the right thing politically.

But the sort of universal spiritual experiences described here are usually beneficial in a different sense. Apart from the generally positive effects on the person involved, they do seem to have a wider benefit through that person's interactions with others. A study of reports in the Alister Hardy Trust archive concluded that "some of the most profound, life-changing experiences that people have, lead them to become more loving and altruistic."[24] Even without reaching the peaks, this is something we can all recognise. As Michael McGhee – a Christian turned Buddhist – says in his *Spirituality for the Godless*, "the sublime in nature and poetry have the effect of awakening a moral consciousness."[25]

This may not be the sort of political action Jonathan Rowson had in mind. But more love, altruism, heightened moral consciousness and the Dalai Lama's "love and compassion, patience, tolerance [and] forgiveness" must be a good thing.

Unfortunately, modern life is pulling in the opposite direction. As Thomas Metzinger says: "...social media and tech firms aim to maximize user engagement by creating ever better attention sinks and developing pathological, addictive forms of media consumption." Some of the most powerful and intelligent computer systems available are competing to monetise our time and attention, squeezing out the space for other activities, including those associated with spiritual experience and its positive results. This is surely something we should resist.

Defending that space is not to deny the divide between humanist and religious – or spiritual-but-not-religious – worldviews. In a 2013 discussion on spirituality,[26] Elizabeth Oldfield, then head of the 'Theos' Christian think tank, referred to Christianity as being about a relationship with, and response to, an 'objective transcendent' – God. The dividing line is between worldviews that incorporate an element of that objective transcendent – the supernatural – and those that do not. The former cover the range from unsophisticated superstition and magical thinking, through the various conceptions of a deity, to the sophisticated 'panentheist' concept of a universal spirit that is present everywhere, including within us, while also transcending everything.

If a typical humanist uses the word spirituality, they mean none of those things. While accepting that it will remain a contentious term, humanists

76 Religion and Atheism in Dialogue

should surely feel free to use it where they feel it is the best word to communicate what they do mean.

The inner spirituality described in universal terms by the Dalai Lama, and in the NHS approach to spiritual care, is something we can all recognise, whether or not we see a role for an 'objective transcendent.' Most of us can also recognise the non-supernatural sort of spirituality referred to by Alice Roberts, whether the silent drama of a peak experience, the calm and compassionate state generated by meditative practice, or the softer transcendence produced by nature, art or music. These are positive states of human consciousness which we can value and celebrate. They are part of our shared humanity.

Notes

1 Humanists in Action Day, Humanists UK Convention, Cardiff (2024).
2 Connelly, Peter, 'Humanist Spirituality: An Oxymoron', 2022, unpublished.
3 BBC News (21 Jan 2019), 'Archbishop Justin Welby prays in tongues every day' at www.bbc.co.uk/news/uk-46945022
4 Webster, David, *Dispirited: How Contemporary Spirituality Makes Us Stupid, Selfish and Unhappy* (Winchester: Zero Books, 2012).
5 Webster, David, *Dispirited: How Contemporary Spirituality Makes Us Stupid, Selfish and Unhappy* (Winchester: Zero Books, 2012), p. 23.
6 Ofsted School inspection handbook, 2019, quoted at https://www.smscquality-mark.org.uk/what-is-smsc/ (accessed July 2024).
7 Mason, Marilyn, '"Spirituality" – What on Earth Is It?', *International Conference of Children's Spirituality, Roehampton Institute*, 2000, quoting Dalai Lama, *Ancient Wisdom, Modern World* (London: Abacus, 1999), pp. 22–23.
8 NHS Education for Scotland (2009), *Spiritual Care Matters*, p. 6.
9 NHS Scotland (2009), *Spiritual Care and Chaplaincy*, Annex A.
10 NHS Chaplaincy (2023), *Guidelines for NHS Managers on Pastoral, Spiritual and Religious Care*.
11 Comte-Sponville, André, *The Book of Atheist Spirituality* (London: Bantam Press, 2008).
12 Harris, Sam, *Waking Up* (London: Transworld, 2014), p. 81.
13 Hoffman, Edward, 'What Was Maslow's View of Peak-Experiences?', *Psychology Today blogpost*, 2011. Maslow discussing peak experiences: https://youtu.be/TkqQX896WiA
14 Douglas, Kate, 'What is thought and how does thinking manifest in the brain?', *New Scientist 20 May 2024*.
15 Griffiths, Roland; Richards, William; Mccann, Una; Jesse, Robert, 'Psilocybin Can Occasion Mystical-Type Experiences Having Substantial and Sustained Personal Meaning and Spiritual Significance', *Psychopharmacology* 2006;187:268–283. doi: 10.1007/s00213-006-0457-5
16 Nencha, Umberto; Spinelli, Laurent; Vulliemoz, Serge; Seeck, Margitta; Picard, Fabienne, 'Insular Stimulation Produces Mental Clarity and Bliss', *Ann Neurol* 2022 Feb;91(2):289–292. doi: 10.1002/ana.26282. Epub 2021 Dec 20. PMID: 34877703; PMCID: PMC9300149.
17 Einstein, Albert, 'Letter to console a grieving father, Robert S. Marcus', 1950.
18 The Alister Hardy Trust at www.studyspiritualexperiences.org (accessed July 2024).

19 Culiford, Larry (2014), 'Spiritual Experiences: Eight Major Types – Spiritual experiences reported by over three-quarters of a large British sample', *Psychology Today blogpost*, at https://www.psychologytoday.com/intl/blog/spiritual-wisdom-secular-times/201401/spiritual-experiences-eight-major-types (accessed July 2024).
20 'Near-Death Experiences' (undated), *Psychology Today* at www.psychologytoday.com/us/basics/near-death-experiences (accessed July 2024).
21 Blackmore, Susan, 'Near-Death Experiences', *The Skeptic Encyclopedia of Pseudoscience*, Ed. M. Shermer (Santa Barbara, CA: ABC-Clio, 2002), pp. 152–157. Reproduced at www.susanblackmore.uk/chapters/near-death-experiences (accessed July 2024).
22 Metzinger, Thomas, *The Elephant and the Blind: The Experience of Pure Consciousness: Philosophy, Science, and 500+ Experiential Reports* (Cambridge, MA and London: MIT Press, 2024). Quoted in *New Scientist* 24 April 2024, p. 28.
23 Jonathan Rowson. 'Integrating spirituality into the public realm', World Congress of Faiths Conference, Salisbury, 2016.
24 *Journal for the Study of Religious Experience,* Vol. 9, No. 1 (2023), pp. 5–18.
25 McGhee, Michael, *Spirituality for the Godless* (Cambridge: Cambridge University Press, 2021), p. 34.
26 Royal Society of Arts (2013), 'Beyond Belief: Taking Spirituality Seriously', *RSA Replay*. www.youtube.com/watch?v=iyQILTtDUos&ab_channel=RSA at 39:08.

10

UNDERSTANDING SPIRITUAL EXPERIENCE

Two Approaches or One?

David Scott

Many would agree that, at a deep level, atheistic and theistic humanists share a common goal: to understand spiritual experience. For though they are divided, they take spiritual experience as a common starting point. In what follows I work with a kind of empty, placeholder definition of this term: I take "spiritual experience" to refer to whatever kind of special experience it is that brings us, *qua* atheistic and theistic humanists, to the same table. The expression stands as a kind of broad indicator of the idea that there is *something*—some matter of real value or import—which brings atheists and theists together. It is surely safe to insist that, despite enormous divergence in our views, no one is inclined to deny the existence of some "spiritual" interest animating us, some shared valuative enterprise in which we all have a stake.

Of course, because the expression "spiritual experience" carries so much interpretive baggage, it is natural that we should seek out concrete examples, in order more closely to define our subject's special nature. In our deliberations, with the help of a discussion paper by John Cottingham, we identified two paradigmatic examples of spiritual experience: the majesty and preciousness of the moral law we feel operate within us, and our responses to the wonders of the heavens.[1] These paradigm cases were ranged, respectively, under two general headings supplied by Jeremy Rodell—"inner spirituality" and "experiential spirituality". The latter heading encompasses a wide spectrum of experiences including (especially) "a sense of transcendence or connectedness with something larger"[2]; and it is this type of spiritual experience that will be the focus of this paper. More narrowly—and notwithstanding my stated non-committal stance on spiritual experience—in what follows I concentrate on the "wonders-of-the-heavens" example, not

DOI: 10.4324/9781003536185-12

least because of its immense popularity in discussions on our subject. In particular, I explore a tradition that approaches this example in such a way as to *discount* any instructional value it might be thought to have on the question of spiritual experience. If this tradition which holds the paradigm case of heavenly wonders to achieve nothing in the elucidation of spiritual experience is right, it goes a long way toward undermining the category of "experiential spirituality" as a tool for investigation into our shared reality of "spirit". Our options look thereby to be shrunk to one category alone— Rodell's "inner spirituality". By a process of elimination, then, we who seek to better our understanding of spiritual experience seem to be brought into closer quarters.

I.

The version of the wonders-of-the-heavens example considered here is the one set forth in Rodell's paper, the source of which is André Comte-Sponville's *The Little Book of Atheist Spirituality*:

The first time it happened I was in the forest in the north of France....That particular evening, some friends and I had gone for a walk in the forest we liked so much. Night had fallen. We were walking. Gradually our laughter faded, and the conversation died down. Nothing remained but our friendship, our mutual trust and shared presence, the mildness of the night air and of everything around us...My mind empty of thought, I was simply registering the world around me—the darkness of the undergrowth, the incredible luminosity of the sky, the faint sounds of the forest...only making the silence more palpable. And then, all of a sudden...What? Nothing: everything! No words, no meanings, no questions, only—a surprise. Only—this. A seemingly infinite happiness. A seemingly eternal sense of peace. Above me, the starry sky was immense, luminous and unfathomable, and within me there was nothing but the sky, of which I was a part, and the silence, and the light, like a warm hum, and a sense of joy with neither subject nor object...Yes, in the darkness of that night, I contained only the dazzling presence of the All.[3]

One of the compelling aspects of this passage—one of the reasons the example is regarded as paradigmatic—is that many of us, atheists and theists alike, have had experience(s) roughly similar to Comte-Sponville's. We do not find it too difficult to acknowledge some special quality of this experience. It is only when we endeavor to *interpret* such experiences further— beyond "special" or "spiritual"—that differences begin to emerge. Some regard such experiences as possible or meaningful only under the condition of an existing God. Others take a more naturalistic route, grounded in the

80 Religion and Atheism in Dialogue

empirical sciences, to explain spirituality's sources or conditions of meaning. To the former group, we might count theists like Cottingham, who has sympathy for panentheism though he grants there to be no strictly logical or even probabilistic compulsion to describe the mystery of spiritual experience in theistic terms. To the naturalist-leaning group belong atheists like Rodell, for whom the transcendent or extra-personal feel that attaches to spiritual experience is best interpreted not in terms of an external presence of the divine, but rather as something in reality generated endogenously—that is, from within a person's brain. To Rodell's physicalist, ultimately impersonalist account of spiritual experience, Cottingham opposes that experience's phenomenology which, he points out, does not involve endogeneity. Rather, phenomenologically speaking spiritual experiences point in the other, exogenous direction; they have the character of *responses*—specifically, of incomings from without rather than out-goings from within.[4]

For our purposes, we need not decide on the reconcilability of Rodell's endogenous account and Cottingham's focus on the responsive (exogenous) character of spiritual experience. For in their respective ways, Rodell and Cottingham both take Comte-Sponville's starry sky experience as a secure foundation on which to base deliberation on spiritual experience, and this is precisely what is rejected by the tradition I explore below. As noted, that tradition is distinguished by its *disavowal* of the capacity of the starry heavens example to illuminate our spirituality. Let us turn now to some representatives of this view.

II.

First in order of appearance is the Christian apologist Boethius (480–524). From a remark penned in prison, he makes it clear that when it comes to seeking out the true wonders of existence—i.e., when it comes to what is special about "spiritual experience"—looking to the heavens is looking in the wrong direction:

> Perhaps, again, you find pleasure in the beauty of the countryside. Creation is indeed very beautiful, and the countryside a very beautiful part of creation. In the same way we are sometimes delighted [when you] look up with wonder at the sky, the stars, the moon and the sun. However, not one of these has anything to do with you, and you daren't take credit for the splendor of any of them...You are in fact enraptured with empty joys, embracing—as if they were your own—blessings that are alien to you... [I]t is obvious that not one of those things which you count among your blessings is in fact any blessing of yours at all...It seems as if you feel a lack of any blessing of your own inside you, which is driving you to seek your blessings in things separate and external.[5]

Understanding Spiritual Experience **81**

There can be little doubt about just how uncompromising Boethius is in his repudiation of the "Big Nature" experience—the countryside, the sea and the starry heavens—as a genuine source of human spirituality, i.e., as itself an efficacious cause of human uplift. When it comes to our experiences of (e.g.) the beauty of a countryside (in which we justifiably take pleasure) or "the sky, the stars, the moon and the sun" (in which we legitimately take delight), there is nothing special or "spiritual" to be gleaned: there is just our pleasure and delight. To be clear, for Boethius, the countryside *is* beautiful, the starry heavens *have* their splendor; and in this sense, he fully accepts Comte-Sponville's objectivist-sounding attribution of beauty and splendor to those things. However, what for Boethius is missing from anything we might experience of the heavens is any connection or link they have to *us*. He sees them as "things separate and external", things which please (or even "enrapture") but do not normatively define us; they are grand, alright, but they are grand "out there". Absent from the stars is any sense in which, by beholding them, we come truly into our own or, as he puts it, come to be "blessed". For all the pleasures we might derive from it, Boethius holds the extended cosmos to lack the wherewithal—the spirit—to spiritualize us or to be "our blessing".

The second representative of the tradition which dispenses with the starry heavens as an instructive object of spiritual experience is Blaise Pascal (1623–1662), who famously writes:

> Man is but a reed, the weakest in nature, but he is a thinking reed. There is no need for the whole universe to take up arms to crush him: a vapour, a drop of water, is enough to kill him; but even if the universe were to crush him, man would still be nobler than his slayer, because he knows that he is dying and [he knows] the advantage the universe has over him. The universe knows none of this. All our dignity consists, then, in thought. By it we must elevate ourselves, and not by space and time which we cannot fill.[6]

Much in the way Boethius objectifies beauty and splendor in allowing such properties really to belong to nature, Pascal cedes to "the universe" its own sphere of "nobility". Its nobility resides in its unimaginable power, an infinitesimally small portion of which—e.g., a mere "vapour, a drop of water"—is sufficient to annihilate us. No question: relative to us, such power is infinitely humbling. However, as much as it confers nobility on the universe, for Pascal an even greater nobility accrues to us by dint of our *knowledge* both of it and (more pertinently) of our vulnerability in the face even of the weakest of natural forces. For Pascal, the difference-maker is not our smallness or fragility in relation to the cosmos but our knowledge thereof. Such knowledge is transformative; it convert our putative weakness into strength. It confers a nobility on us that far outstrips any worth nature might have in virtue of its raw power.

82 Religion and Atheism in Dialogue

Our third and final representative of the tradition that is skeptical of the power of the Comte-Sponville example to put us in touch with our spirituality is Raymond Tallis, our friend and fellow inquirer. There is much in Tallis' writing that affiliates him to Boethius and Pascal's approach. Consider how he directly connects (on the one hand) the importance—the virtue—which Socrates attaches to our self-aware ignorance of who we are and what or how we value, and (on the other hand) Pascal's celebration of our worth in the face of a cosmos that would crush us in a thoughtless instant:

> My awareness of my lack of insight into either what I am, or what I am like for others, surely suggests another kind of, possibly higher-level, insight. To know what one does not know is the venerable Socratic wisdom, however ill-defined it must be. A desperate remedy, perhaps—analogous to the Pascalian claim that, since we are capable of recognizing that we are minute accidents in a vast universe, we must be *more* than minute accidents in a vast universe. Our unique sense of insignificance makes us special—even significant: the knowledge that makes us small is a testament to our greatness.[7]

The "higher-level insight" which Tallis says is shared by Socrates and Pascal—the insight, namely, that we are "*more* than minute accidents in a vast universe"—is what drives the tradition that eschews the physical heavens as the fitting and responsive terminus of spiritual seeking. As incisive and as in keeping as this is with the tradition of Boethius and Pascal, Tallis pushes Boethius' skepticism *vis-à-vis* the starry sky's relation to spiritual satisfaction even further. Pascalian defiance has the feel for Tallis of a "desperate remedy", a point on which he expands in *Seeing Ourselves*:

> While it may seem to the eyes of science that we are *located* in a vast, largely meaningless universe, we do not *live* in that universe; rather we inhabit a small parish within it, populated by those whom we love and hate, like and dislike, our friends and our adversaries, where we pursue our projects and are immersed in our preoccupations. The poet Paul Valéry acidly responded to Pascal's famous cry—'The eternal silence of these infinite spaces terrifies me' [*Pensées*, 206] with 'However, the hubbub in the corner distracts me'. Being the most important character in the room, the life and soul of the party, can cancel one's objective insignificance. In part this is because meaning, and meaninglessness, begins far nearer home than (for example) the rocks on distant galaxies. The most obvious reason for our unconcern with ultimate meanings is that we are often too closely examined—or at least tested—by life. The spaces which might house our search for cosmic meanings that we would choose, and embrace, are already occupied by unchosen meanings that embrace, indeed engulf, us.[8]

The contrast drawn here between where we are *located* (our vast universe) and where we *live* (our small parish) adds a kind of existential nuance to the alternative account of spiritual experience we have been examining. Boethius and Pascal are skeptical that any understanding of our experience of where are *located* can serve to spiritualize us where we *live*. Tallis' point is not so much to solve the problem as to sharpen or vivify its contours. No doubt, he is on psychologically sure footing in asserting that our "[b]eing the most important character in the room, the life and soul of the party, can cancel one's objective insignificance". But his point is also that "can" is not "must", and that it is the "must"—our *need* for ultimate meaning, our need to cancel our objective insignificance—that we seek to satisfy as atheists and theists alike. Though the distractions of the salon can dispel our sense of cosmic insignificance, the question of our objective *significance* has real staying power; it haunts the antechambers, patiently waiting out our moments of local glory. The fact is, even in the place we call home, there are always tinges of evidence that we are *not* "the most important character in the room", *not* "the life and soul of the party". The permanent fact of our condition is that we lead an unsettled and unsettling existence wherever we are, be it at home or abroad. For Tallis, then, we are caught—succeeding in understanding things that fail to matter, but equally failing to understand those closer-to-home affairs that actually count. These are really two sides of the same existential coin. What guarantees Tallis' place in the company of Boethius and Pascal is his insistence that, whatever (if anything) mattering itself ultimately is, it must always take place at home; and in this sense, we need not pay much heed to those starry heavens.

III.

Boethius, Pascal and Tallis all reject the adequacy of the vast night sky, despite its natural splendor, to serve as an object of spiritual experience. They are skeptical of Cottingham's view that in contemplating the starry heavens, our response indicates that we have been put in touch with something of objective and ultimate significance. Still, while it is true that for these thinkers, such speculation is mistaken because whatever our experience is *of*, it is not "something objective that has ultimate significance", at the same time, there are elements of Cottingham's developed position that echo something of what they have in mind. For as Cottingham sees it, if there is such a thing as ultimate significance at the heart of reality, the only way of understanding such meaning would be by positing a kind of primordial "I", which is to say, a conscious mind. Such placement of "conscious mind" at the heart of reality to meet the requirements of ultimate significance is described by Cottingham as putting the personal at a metaphysically deeper level than the impersonal, and in one very important respect, this is profoundly in keeping

84 Religion and Atheism in Dialogue

with Boethius' skepticism about Big-Nature-inspired spirituality. Simply put, for *both* Boethius' tradition and Cottingham, something's being of ultimate significance consists in its being somehow answerable to a conscious *mind*— which is to say, to something personal. Despite contradictory approaches to what they hold the starry heavens to be able to do for spiritual experiencers, in their own ways both Boethius and Cottingham posit *some* sort of mental, personal reality that goes deeper than impersonal matter.

Granting such degree of agreement, the obvious question arises: Wherein lies the difference between Boethius *et al.* and Cottingham? It resides, I submit, in the fact that the "conscious mind" revealed for Boethius is not any mind that somehow inhabits, encompasses, stands behind or infuses the space and infinite variety of the extended universe. He is not a so-called "panentheist", for which appellation Cottingham has sympathies. Rather, for Boethius, any mind that is intimated or revealed as we plumb the depths of the extended cosmos is really just the mind that peers into it—which is to say, *our* mind. If there is anything approaching an objective, cosmic or public mind, i.e., a mind that is somehow discernible "out there" in or of the stars, for Boethius *et al.*, such a mind can only be our own individual minds understood collectively as contributors to the scientific project in which Nature (i.e., that thing outside of us) becomes "nature" (i.e., our collective doing). We can reasonably be said to see ourselves in "nature", but not in Nature; and that is as far as Boethius *et al.* are willing to go. When it comes the sphere of resonance generally speaking, the most our empirical sciences can do for us is constantly throw us back upon ourselves, since if nothing resonates in us, nothing resonates anywhere.

Still, matters cannot be left simply at that. Boethius *et al.* might reject a metaphysics of a personal mind "out there" among the stars, but at least for the theists among them, that does not close the question of the ground of ultimate significance. Are our individual minds sufficient indices of the meanings we manage to make? The question echoes the predicament of Descartes in the third of his *Meditations*, where the concern is whether he can be the sole cause of *all* those ideas (meanings) which exist within himself, including his idea of God *qua* source of meaning *tout court*. For Boethius *et al.*, ascertaining the existence of Cottingham's primordial "I" or conscious mind other than our own requires *both* consideration of something that is at a "metaphysically deeper level than the impersonal" (or is, as Pascal puts it, something beyond that "space and time which we cannot fill") *and* consideration of something that is, simultaneously, either in or accessible only through us. Such is the theistic commitment of those who accept the reality of spiritual experience but who hear only silence from the heavens.

In effect, what Boethius' tradition expresses is a demand for an inward turn for metaphysics—if, that is, the question of our "true blessings" is to be fully addressed. The dividing line for atheists and theists within that tradition

Understanding Spiritual Experience **85**

is over the question whether that inward turn, which begins with the self, ends there too.

IV.

We have considered a tradition that repudiates the starry sky example's ability to put us in touch with something objective that has ultimate significance; but we have said nothing about the countless *other* ways in which experience might be thought to lead us in the direction of a foundation of human spirituality. Those other ways fall under Rodell's general heading of "inner spirituality", under which are subsumed those innumerable occasions, extensively noted by Cottingham, when (e.g.) we recognize the power and authority of the moral law or are exalted by great music or art or are taken out of ourselves by love for another. Having given up on the starry heavens, an endless array of cases of inner spirituality remains for consideration on Boethius' approach.

As to the general profile of this remaining option, if one grants—as atheistic and theistic humanists appear to grant—that spiritual experience is of extraordinary significance and power, whereas ordinary experience by definition is not—then it seems we must allow that it is by some existing principle or value *within experience itself* that spiritual experiences are special. Given this, it would seem that whether the atheist's (Rodell's) endogenetic account of spiritual experience can meet what the theist (Cottingham) highlights as the specifically responsive or exogenic character of the same experience is a question addressable only with reference to something that is *both* within experience (since that is where it is agreed we must look) *and* beyond it (since we agree it is a *kind* of experience that needs to be differentiated). Looking forward, what Boethius has to offer looks something like this. We seek something that is both within experience and beyond it, and it is only the *experiencer* that is both within and beyond experience. Simply put: I experience (and so I am within it), but I am not an experience (and so I am beyond it); I am an experiencer, but *what I am* is not itself an experience. For Boethius, then, our next move is to ask what this subject of experience is that is simultaneously within and beyond its experience. Both Rodell and Cottingham agree that there are such beings as spiritual experiencers; indeed, both believe themselves to *be* such beings. The further question is who or what *they* are, such that their shared belief can be true.

Notes

1 On Cottingham's recommendation, then, we followed Immanuel Kant, *Critique of Practical Reason*, trans. M.J. Gregor (Cambridge: Cambridge University Press, 1997), p. 133.

2 Cf. Rodell's chapter in this volume.
3 Trans. N. Huston (New York: Viking Books, 2008), p. 156.
4 Trans. N. Huston (New York: Viking Books, 2008), p. 156.
5 *The Consolation of Philosophy*, trans. V.E. Watts (Harmondsworth: Penguin Books, 1969), pp. 66–67 (modified).
6 *Pascal's Pensées* (§347), trans. W.F. Trotter (New York: E.P. Dutton & Co., Inc., 1958), p. 97.
7 *Logos: The Mystery of How We Make Sense of the World* (Newcastle upon Tyne: Agenda Publishing, 2018), p. 199 (emphasis added).
8 *Seeing Ourselves: Reclaiming Humanity from God and Science* (Newcastle upon Tyne: Agenda Publishing, 2020), p. 265 (emphases added). For Valéry's response, cited in this passage, cf. *Collected Works of Paul Valéry*, vol. 4, p. 124 (as cited in *Seeing Ourselves*, p. 423, n. 39).

11

THE SPIRITUAL AND THE RELIGIOUS

Interlinked or Separable?

John Cottingham

In the fractious and polemical climate of our times, exacerbated by the unrestrained intemperance of social media postings, attitudes to religion (and to much else besides) have become increasingly polarized. So it is refreshing and reassuring when adherents to such very different worldviews as classical theism and secular humanism are able to occupy a measure of common ground. The distinguished humanist Jeremy Rodell, in his thoughtful and carefully argued contribution to the present volume, stresses both the *value* of spiritual experience, and also its *pervasive nature*: spiritual experiences are 'positive states of human consciousness which we can value and celebrate', and they are 'part of our shared humanity'.[1] Coming from the very different standpoint of a card-carrying religious believer, I have in my own previous writings reached very similar conclusions. As regards their value, I have described spiritual experiences as 'indispensable elements of what it is to be a fully flourishing human being, and something without which our species would be immeasurably poorer'.[2] And as regards their being part of our shared humanity, I have underlined that 'they are not the prerogative of any cosy club of insiders or the "saved", but a natural part of our ordinary human birthright'.[3]

With respect to the *kinds* of experience we have in mind in using the label 'spiritual', there is also a considerable measure of agreement. In my work, I have instanced our powerful responses to the beauties of the natural world or to great works of art, as well as certain deeply felt moral responses of love and compassion towards those who are dear to us[4]; and Rodell, albeit with an important caveat, also regards these types of human experiences as ones that are appropriately classified under the label 'spiritual'. His caveat is that in so describing them, there should be no implication or suggestion that

DOI: 10.4324/9781003536185-13

88 Religion and Atheism in Dialogue

they are to be interpreted as manifestations of anything supernatural. We should not view such experiences through a religious 'lens', or be tempted to draw any 'metaphysical conclusions'.[5] And he approvingly cites a remark of the former President of Humanists UK, Professor Alice Roberts, who classifies herself a spiritual person, but with the proviso that what is meant is a 'natural sort of spirituality, not the sort that's tied up with supernatural beliefs'.[6]

In fact, however, separating out religious from secular spirituality by reference to the concept of the supernatural is by no means as straightforward a matter as might at first appear. There may, admittedly, be some types of spiritual experience, visions of angels perhaps, that are supposed by those who have them to be of supernatural origin. But what of the widespread types of spiritual experience mentioned in the previous paragraph, those described by Rodell as 'powerful and positive ... peak experiences', accompanied by 'feelings of elation, joy, and compassion towards the world'?[7] When such experiences figure, as they often do, in the writings of religious believers, it is noteworthy that they are not typically described in supernaturalist terms. Rather, they are characteristically seen as disclosing a depth of meaning that is *already present* in the natural world around us, but which often eludes us in the humdrum routines of our quotidian existence. This surely is what the poet Gerard Manley Hopkins meant when he declared that 'the world is charged with the grandeur of God',[8] or when, in the sonnet *Ribblesdale*, he recorded his response to the overwhelming beauty of one of the Yorkshire Dales – 'Earth, sweet Earth, sweet landscape, with leavès throng/And louchèd low grass ...'.[9] In such cases (and many more could be cited from a wide range of other religious writers), what is being celebrated, often in ecstatic terms, is not some separate supernatural domain, but the mystery and wonder and grandeur, the goodness and beauty, of the natural world that is our home. The theologian and philosopher Judith Wolfe puts the point very aptly when she describes the Christian faith as 'a mode of seeing the world which beholds in that world an unseen depth of goodness, significance and love'.[10]

The key word here is 'significance'. What, for the religious believer, gives these widespread experiences their status as 'spiritual' is that they seem to be laden with a special kind of *meaning* – that they are taken to disclose something of profound significance for understanding the true nature of the reality we inhabit, and for appreciating how our own human nature is attuned to that reality. In such experiences, we seem to glimpse 'the sacred depths of nature', to borrow a phrase from the biologist Ursula Goodenough, who aptly describes herself as a 'religious naturalist'.[11] The same kind of idea appears frequently in the nature poetry of William Wordsworth (often classified as a 'pantheist' – wrongly, in my view, since his writing is largely free of metaphysical theorizing of any kind). What we find in Wordsworth's reflections on the natural world is an inextricable fusion of the moral, the aesthetic and the religious: the poet's exaltation and joy at the beauty of the woods and fields is closely bound up with a deep sense of their goodness and of the 'blessings' that they bestow[12] – a sense that is in turn linked to the upwelling in him of love and sympathy for humankind. These kinds of 'transcendent' experience described by Wordsworth – experiences by which our minds are 'nourished and invisibly repaired'[13] – involve not so much a revelation of supernatural entities as a heightening, an intensification, that transforms the way in which we experience the world. The term 'transcendent' seems appropriate not in the sense that there is necessarily any invocation of metaphysical objects that transcend ordinary experience, but rather because the categories of our mundane life undergo a radical shift: there is a sudden irradiation that discloses a beauty and goodness, a meaning, that was before occluded.[14]

So what are the implications of all this for the relation between spirituality and religious belief? As far as Rodell's take on these matters is concerned, I think a crude but fair summary of the lesson he wishes us to draw in his chapter would be that there is nothing wrong with using the concept of spiritual experience, and indeed that spiritual experience can be a very good thing, provided we 'strip it of its religious meaning'.[15] But if what I have just been suggesting in the previous two paragraphs is on the right lines, then the kinds of experience we call 'spiritual' are so called precisely because they stand out from ordinary experience in virtue of their special significance for how we understand ourselves and the reality we inhabit. Yet if we now 'strip off' the religious element, then it seems to me there may be a risk that this will erode the very aspect of such experiences that gives them their special significance. For it appears that for Rodell, and for those who share his secularist stance, such experiences are, when all is said and done, simply a loose assortment of endogenous subjective states of consciousness that happen to be 'triggered'[16] in various ways – for example, by 'buying a ticket to a concert', 'stepping outside on a clear night'[17] or indeed, in the words of the atheist philosopher Sam Harris, 'taking the right drug'.[18] But this now cries out for an answer to the question of why they should be accorded such special importance as bearers of significance for how we understand ourselves and our relation to the world.

For why should, for example, looking at the cosmos on a clear night have the profound and transformative moral significance that many atheist writers seem to want to accord it?[19] What precisely is it that allows them to describe their experiences in terms not dissimilar to those we find in the religiously resonant poetry of writers such as Wordsworth and Hopkins? The reason such a question poses itself here is that the secularist's list of the various heterogeneous 'triggers' of spiritual experience appears to lack any kind of principled linkage between the cosmological and the moral domains – the kind of integration that arguably only a religious outlook can provide.

90 Religion and Atheism in Dialogue

The 'integration thesis', as one may term it, has been persuasively presented in the work of Ursula Goodenough to which I alluded earlier. For Goodenough, what a religious outlook offers is a worldview that encompasses both *How Things Are* and *Which Things Matter*:

> The great religions address two fundamental human concerns: *How Things Are* and *Which Things Matter*. How Things Are becomes formulated as a Cosmology ... Which Things Matter becomes codified as a Morality or Ethos ... The role of religion is to integrate the Cosmology and the Morality, to render the cosmological narrative so rich and compelling that it elicits our allegiance and our commitment to its emergent moral understanding.[20]

It is this linking of the moral with the cosmological dimensions of reality that enables human life to be seen by the religious believer as more than a random by-product of the cosmic process, and as having a purpose and a destiny in the wider scheme of things. The cosmos, in short, is seen as having a teleology, a moral direction, goal or end; and as part of that process, we humans can, and indeed must, understand ourselves teleologically – as required (though we often fall short) to direct our lives towards that good.[21] The faith that striving for the good is not a futile endeavour, but accords with the way things ultimately are, is what allows the Judaeo-Christian worldview in particular to affirm the ultimate 'sovereignty of the good' (to borrow and adapt a phrase of Iris Murdoch).[22] For how else could all the widely described aspects of spiritual experience – the upwelling of joy and elation, the feeling of being 'nourished and invisibly repaired', and the calm sense that 'all which we behold is full of blessings' – how could such 'positive states of human consciousness'[23] be generated merely by our contemplation of a blank indifferent universe that is, in the immortal words of Bertrand Russell, 'just *there*'?[24] How could all this occur, were there not, deeply intertwined with what we call spiritual experience, some inchoate religious sense that we are somehow at one with creation, and that our aspirations towards the good are not mere futile subjective projections but longings that find an answering echo in the way things ultimately are? This is what the core religious faith in the sovereignty of the good amounts to,[25] and stripped of this religious element, the proposed secularist analogues of spiritual experience, so it seem to me, must lose their title to significance.

The upshot is that, while wholeheartedly approving Rodell's admirable project of mapping out those aspects of spirituality that are part of our shared human heritage, I find I cannot accept his conception of a viable spirituality whose religious core has been fileted out.

But before I move on, an objection needs to be addressed. In insisting on a religious core to authentic spiritual experience, if it is to make good its

The Spiritual and the Religious **91**

title to significance, have I not begged the question against Rodell by tacitly re-importing those very 'supernatural beliefs' that his secularist worldview rules out of order? I take it I have already partly pre-empted this objection by pointing out, as I did earlier, that when spiritual experiences figure in the writings of religious believers, they are not typically described in supernaturalist terms but are characteristically seen as disclosing a depth of meaning that is *already present* in the natural world around us. But to supplement that point, it may be helpful to refer to a very apposite distinction eloquently articulated by the philosopher and psychoanalyst Richard Gipps – a distinction between *theism* and *religious belief*:

> the *theist* thinks he understands what 'God' means independently of his disposition to pray and to experience and give voice to existential gratitude. It's precisely because he thinks he first knows what 'God' means that he then takes himself to be reasonable in suggesting God to be the proper object of his praise – and of his thankful and other prayers. The *believer*, by contrast, thinks that if you want to know what 'God' means, then understand that He is that to which one ... offers prayers and existential gratitude. The *believer* finds her way to belief in part in and through such attitudes; she doesn't take a living faith to involve a prior intellectual assent ... to the existence of 'a deity' followed by the direction toward that 'deity' of their prayers and gratitude. The *theist's* belief is, it might be said, a rather *philosophical* matter. *Theism is, if you like, a kind of theory ...* The *believer*, by contrast, is playing a different game. Nature is not explained by, but *seen as*, creation. And attitudes of awe and wonder and repentance, and existential gratitude and humility and openness to love, themselves help give meaning to religious belief. Where by 'give meaning to' isn't (or isn't only) meant: provide a point for, but rather: make for the very intelligibility of, the belief.[26]

Those who find this distinction persuasive, as I do, will probably also feel that Rodell's strictures against conceptions of spirituality that involve a 'metaphysical or supernatural reality'[27] do not really bear against the religious life as it is actually practised by religious adherents in their daily and weekly spiritual observances, any more than they bear against the modes of religiously infused spiritual experience of the Wordsworthian or Hopkinsian kind referred to earlier. In short, it may turn out that the secular humanist's austere distaste for the 'supernatural' domain, and in general for all things 'spooky', is better directed against the austere and abstractified tribe of philosophical cum theological *theorists* about God than against the much wider community of actual religious *believers*. And just to add one final twist to the argument: it may even turn out that a significant number even of theistic philosophers and theologians do not, in the way they speak of God, quite fit

92 Religion and Atheism in Dialogue

the humanist's target. They may admittedly sometimes use terms like 'supernatural' of God, but this is simply to emphasize God's absolute difference from any identifiable 'deity', or from any item to be found in the world. For it is a striking feature of what may be called classical theism, at least if the mainstream Catholic tradition derived from Aquinas is taken as representative, that human beings are pretty much in the dark as to the nature of God.[28] But to explore this further is a task for another day.

I turn now to David Scott's very interesting contribution to the present volume,[29] which turns out to be highly pertinent to the discussion so far, albeit he is mainly concerned with a somewhat different question from those we have been considering up till now, namely the question of the preferred *path* or *route* to spiritual experience. I have drawn attention to religious 'nature poets' such as Wordsworth and Hopkins, whose ecstatic responses to the beauties of the world around us seem paradigmatic indications of ways in which a certain kind of spiritual experience might arise. But Scott cites Boethius and Pascal, who echo Augustine's injunction *Noli foras ire, in teipsum redi; in interiore homine habitat veritas* ('Go not outside, but return within thyself; in the inward human being dwelleth the truth').[30]

But what is wrong with going outside? For Boethius, as Scott points out in his citation, the person who looks up in wonder to the starry heavens is 'enraptured with empty joys – blessings that are alien to you'.[31] And for Pascal, while we may be cowed by the vastness and power of the cosmos, it is we puny human beings, mere fragile reeds, who vastly surpass it in dignity; and this is because we are conscious – the human being is a *'thinking* reed'.[32] The lesson Scott derives from this, drawing on some reflections of Raymond Tallis,[33] is that 'we need not pay much heed to those starry heavens'. The universe, as Tallis puts it, may be where we are *located*, but it is not our home, not where we *live*. Our home is the human world where alone meaning and significance can reside. It may, for reasons of existential angst, be a precarious and unsettled home, but, so Scott concludes, 'whatever (if anything) mattering itself ultimately is, it must always take place at home'.[34]

The sharp distinction made by Tallis and Scott, between the physical universe in which we are located and the human world that is our home, is an interesting one because in a certain sense, it seems curiously pre-Darwinian. By this, I mean that it seems to take us back to the Cartesian view (shared in part by Pascal when he sets the 'thinking reed' against the inert, mindless universe) that consciousness is something radically distinct from the natural world. But since Darwin, we have surely come to realize that we are not these strange, alien, immaterial 'thinking things', separated out from the material world we inhabit. On the contrary, we are part of that world, ultimately formed of the self-same stuff as anything else on the planet, formed of the 'dust of the earth', as the Genesis story, has it[35] (and which we can now retrospectively see as containing a germ of truth). What is more, coming down beyond Darwin to more recent scientific developments, modern cosmology has now discovered that we are intimately related not just to other terrestrial items but to the wider cosmos, since the very materials from which we are made, the physical components that form the building blocks of life, come ultimately from stellar matter – from the heavier elements produced billions of years ago by the cosmic explosions of supernovae. We are quite literally made of stardust.

So the Cartesian separatist picture is no longer compelling because we now understand that, in one sense at least, Spinoza was nearer the mark – there is a sense in which we are but 'modes'[36] of that stupendous whole which comprises the starry heavens and the planets, and whose dwelling (to switch from Spinoza to Wordsworth) '… is the light of setting suns,/And the round ocean, and the living air,/And the blue sky, and in the mind of man'.[37] In a way, the scientific, the philosophical and the religious perspectives come together here: 'all things are in God … the infinite being we call God or Nature' (Spinoza)[38]; 'God is in all things' (Aquinas)[39]; and 'in God we live and move and have our being' (Paul).[40] I am of course aware that I am glossing over many important differences in linking these texts together, but they are intended to reinforce the central point (on which these different perspectives coincide) that we humans are not set over against the rest of reality but belong to it.

I hope it may begin to be clear from this why I cannot accept David Scott's central claim that the 'outward looking' part of spiritual experience, that which relates to the starry heavens and other non-human parts of reality, should be 'discounted'.[41] In affirming with wonder the integrated totality of the vast natural process from which we came, and of which we are a part, we can begin to see that we are not autonomous creators of our destiny, as the Nietzschean fantasy proposed,[42] but *creatures* – '*dependent* rational animals', as Alistair MacIntyre put it.[43] And what the framework of religious spirituality does is to acknowledge this, but not with fear or resentment, but with gratitude and joy.[44] So when the psalmist affirms that 'the heavens declare the glory of God',[45] yes, there is awe and fear, but not the 'terror' which Pascal felt for the 'silence of those infinite spaces',[46] but an upwelling of joy at the essential goodness and beauty of the reality from which we come, and to which we belong.

Here is the material for a true spirituality, one that does not overweeningly suppose that we can create our own meaning and value, but which acknowledges that we can only *respond* to meaning and value – respond to an awesomely wonderful reality that we did not create and cannot compass or fully comprehend. None of this is to deny David Scott's important point that what *processes* all this is the conscious human subject of experience, the 'spiritual experiencer', as he puts it, who is simultaneously both 'within and beyond' experience.[47] But that experiencer is not self-creating, nor the author of value, nor can its randomly generated or endogenously spawned conscious

94 Religion and Atheism in Dialogue

states somehow transform themselves into experiences of profound moral and spiritual significance. So with all due credit to the eloquence of his arguments, in the end, I find myself at odds with Scott's proposal for an 'inward turn' in metaphysics, at least if this is construed, not as Augustine meant it, as a route to acknowledging something infinitely greater than ourselves, but instead as an assertion of our human self-sufficiency as authors of meaning and value. For I fear that the inward turn construed in this latter way may isolate the human spirit within a prison of its own construction, a prison we can only break out of by turning, in joy and thankfulness, towards the mystery of a reality we did not create, the mystery that is the source of the completion and fulfilment for which, as Augustine himself famously put it, the restless human heart longs.[48]

Notes

1 Jeremy Rodell, 'Can Humanists be Spiritual?', pp. 76, above.
2 John Cottingham, 'Philosophy, the Good Life, and Spirituality' [2013], in John Cottingham, *The Humane Perspective* (Oxford: Oxford University Press, 2024), ch. 5, p. 83.
3 John Cottingham, 'Religion and the Mystery of Existence' [2012], in Cottingham, *The Humane Perspective*, ch. 11, p. 185.
4 See note 2, above.
5 Rodell, 'Can Humanists be Spiritual?', p. 71, citing Sam Harris, *Waking Up* (London: Transworld, 2014).
6 Rodell, 'Can Humanists be Spiritual?', p. 68.
7 Rodell, 'Can Humanists be Spiritual?', p. 72, citing Abraham Maslow; https://youtu.be/TkqQX896WiA
8 Gerard Manley Hopkins, 'The world is charged with the grandeur of God' [1877], from *Poems (1876–1889)*, in W. H. Gardner (ed.), *The Poems and Prose of Gerard Manley Hopkins* (Harmondsworth: Penguin, 1953). Compare the following: 'All things therefore are charged with love, are charged with God, and, if we know how to touch them, give off sparks and take fire, yield drops and flow, ring and tell of him'. G. M. Hopkins, *Note-books and Papers*, ed. H. House (Oxford: Oxford University Press, 1937), p. 342; cited in *Poems and Prose*, ed. Gardner, p. 231.
9 Hopkins, 'Ribblesdale' [1882], in *Poems and Prose*, p. 51, emphasis added.
10 Judith Wolfe, *The Theological Imagination: Perception and Interpretation in Life, Art, and Faith* (Cambridge: Cambridge University Press, 2024), ch. 1, p. 19.
11 Ursula Goodenough, *The Sacred Depths of Nature* (New York: Oxford University Press, 1998).
12 '... our cheerful faith that all which we behold/is full of blessings'; William Wordsworth, *Lines Written a Few Miles above Tintern Abbey* [1798], lines 135–136, in S. Gill (ed.), *William Wordsworth: A Critical Edition of the Major Works* (Oxford: Oxford University Press, 1984).
13 Wordsworth, *The Prelude* [1805 version], Book 11, line 265, in Gill (ed.), *Major Works*.
14 These observations draw on my paper 'Confronting the Cosmos: Scientific Rationality and Human Understanding' [2011], in Cottingham, *The Humane Perspective*, ch. 7.
15 The phrase is Maslow's, referred to approvingly by Rodell (see note 7, above).
16 The term, again, is Maslow's; see note 7, above.

The Spiritual and the Religious **95**

17 Rodell, 'Can Humanists be Spiritual?', p. 73.
18 Harris, *Waking Up*, pp. 43–4.
19 Rodell quotes Michael McGhee's claim that 'the sublime in nature and poetry [has] the effect of awakening a moral consciousness'. Magee, *Spirituality for the Godless* (Cambridge: Cambridge University Press, 2021), p. 34. A more specific example, also quoted by Rodell, is André Compte-Sponville's account of a night-time walk under the starry sky in a forest in Northern France, in *The Book of Atheist Spirituality* [*L'esprit de l'athéisme*, 2006] (London: Bantam, 2008), ch. 3, p. 156.
20 Goodenough, *The Sacred Depths of* Nature, p. xiv.
21 Compare Alasdair MacIntyre, defending this kind of Aristotelian-cum-Thomistic framework: human agents, 'as participants in the form of life that is distinctively human … can only be understood, they can only understand themselves, *teleologically*'. Alasdair MacIntyre, *Ethics in the Conflicts of Modernity* (Cambridge: Cambridge University Press, 2016), p. 237.
22 Iris Murdoch, *The Sovereignty of Good* (London: Routledge, 1970). Murdoch's conception of the sovereignty of the good leads her, however, towards a Platonist rather than a theistic metaphysics ('the Good is the reality of which God is the dream', p. 496); for discussion of this, see John Cottingham, *In Search of the Soul* (Princeton, NJ: Princeton University Press, 2020), ch. 3.
23 Rodell, 'Can Humanists be Spiritual?', p. 76.
24 In a 1948 debate on BBC Radio with Frederick Copleston; reprinted in Bertrand Russell, *Why I am Not a Christian* (London: Allen & Unwin, 1957), ch. 13, p. 152.
25 It's important to add, as is abundantly clear from both the Hebrew Bible (for example, in the story of Job) and the Christian Gospels (for example, in the account of the Crucifixion), that this 'sovereignty of the good' is not affirmed in a magical or a crudely triumphalist way but in a manner that does not at all try to deny our human vulnerability or gloss over the tragic aspects of the human condition.
26 Richard Gipps, 'Gratitude, Prayer, and Godly Vision', posted 20 December 2024 at https://afaithexamined.blogspot.com/2024/12/gratitude-prayer-and-godly-vision.html (emphasis supplied).
27 Rodell, 'Can Humanists be Spiritual?', p. 69.
28 'The divine substance surpasses every form that our intellect reaches. Thus we are unable to apprehend it by knowing what it is' (Thomas Aquinas, *Summa contra gentiles* [1259–65], I, 14). 'God is greater than all we can say, greater than all we can know, and does not merely transcend our language and our knowledge, but he is beyond the comprehension of every mind whatsoever' (Aquinas, *De divinis nominibus* [*c.* 1261–68], I, iii, 77). Both texts are cited in Brian Davies, *Aquinas* (London: Continuum, 2002), ch. 7, p. 66. See also B. Davies, 'A Modern Defence of Divine Simplicity' [1988], in B. Davies (ed.), *Philosophy of Religion: A Guide and Anthology* (Oxford: Oxford University Press, 2000), ch. 52, pp. 549–64.
29 David Scott, 'Understanding Spiritual Experience: Two Approaches, or One?', pp. 78–86, above.
30 Augustine of Hippo, *De vera religione* [391 CE] XXXIX, 72. In an earlier and more extended version of his chapter, Scott referred to the well-known passage from the *Confessions*, where Augustine remarks that 'people wonder at the height of mountains, the huge waves of the sea, the broad sweep of rivers, the size of the ocean and the circling of the stars, yet omit to consider themselves' [*Confessiones, c.* 397–401], Bk X, ch. 8. There is good reason to think Boethius was influenced by Augustine; see Seamus O'Neill, 'Augustine and Boethius, Memory and Eternity', *Analecta Hermeneutica*, vol. 6 (2014), pp. 1–20. The influence of Augustine on Pascal and the Jansenists (who explicitly invoked his teachings) is well established.

96 Religion and Atheism in Dialogue

31 *Quid inanibus gaudiis raperis, quid externa bona pro tuis amplexaris? Numquam tua faciet esse fortuna quae a te natura rerum fecit aliena.* Boethius, *The Consolation of Philosophy* [*De consolatione philosophiae*, 593 CE], Bk II, ch. 5. See Scott, 'Understanding Spiritual Experience', p. 80.

32 *L'homme n'est qu'un roseau, le plus faible de la nature, mais c'est un roseau pensant.* Blaise Pascal, *Pensées* [1670], ed. L. Lafuma (Paris: Seuil, 1962), no 200 (§347 in the Brunschvicg numbering); see Scott, 'Understanding Spiritual Experience', p. 81.

33 Raymond Tallis, *Seeing Ourselves: Reclaiming Humanity from God and Science* (Newcastle upon Tyne: Agenda Publishing, 2020).

34 Scott, 'Understanding Spiritual Experience', p. 83.

35 Genesis 2: 7.

36 Benedict Spinoza, *Ethics* [*Ethica ordine geometrico demonstrata*, c. 1665], Part I, prop. 25, schol.

37 Wordsworth, *Tintern Abbey*, lines 97–100.

38 Spinoza, *Ethics*, Part I, prop. 15; Part IV, preface.

39 Thomas Aquinas, *Summa theologiae* [1266–73], Part I, qu. 8.

40 In the speech at the Areopagus in Athens reported in Acts 17: 28.

41 Scott, 'Understanding Spiritual Experience', p. 79.

42 For Friedrich Nietzsche's 'revaluation of values', see his *Beyond Good and Evil* [*Jenseits von Gut und Böse*, 1886], § 202.

43 Alasdair MacIntyre, *Dependent Rational Animals* (London: Duckworth, 1999).

44 See further J. Cottingham, 'Engagement, Immersion, and Enactment: The Role of Spiritual Practice in Religious Belief' [2023], in Cottingham, *The Humane Perspective*, ch. 14.

45 Psalm 19:1. For more on this text, see John Cottingham, 'Spiritual Experience: Its Scope, Its Phenomenology, and Its Source', *New Blackfriars*, vol. 104, issue 1112 (July 2023), pp. 414–27.

46 *Le silence éternel de ces espaces infinis m'effraie*, Pascal, *Pensées*, ed. Lafuma, no. 201 (Brunschvicg, §206).

47 Scott, 'Understanding Spiritual Experience', p. 85. It seems that Hopkins is in effect acknowledging something like Scott's point, in the sonnet 'Ribblesdale'(mentioned above, see note 9), when he declares 'And what is Earth's eye, tongue, or heart else, where/Else, but in dear and dogged man?'

48 Augustine *Confessions*, Bk I, ch. 1: *fecisti nos ad te, et inquietum est cor nostrum donec requiescat in te* ('You have made us for yourself, and our heart is restless until it finds repose in you').

12

MORAL FAILURE AND SPIRITUAL PRACTICE

Michael McGhee

1.

Humanists ask more or less rhetorically whether we can be 'moral', or live a moral life, 'without religion'. The thought is that you don't really need to ask—obviously you can. And plenty of people of faith would agree.[1] So what is the source of religious anxiety about secularism? That question takes us to the political heart of the so-called culture wars at least as these are fought in North America, particularly by traditionalist Christians, Catholic and Evangelical, who have a dystopian view of the moral and social disorder they take to be entailed by secularism. They believe that our moral standards derive their authority *as* moral standards from a transcendent source, the divine will, and if the very idea of deity is rejected, then all that is left is the wayward human will as a source of what is to count as a moral standard at all, and what prevails in that environment is a complex *malaise* of relativism, permissiveness, debauchery, personal advancement, arbitrary power, with no space to spare for the development of character and virtue.[2] Secular humanists may politely recall the good pagan who pursues virtue despite the temptations of ambition and the flesh. More to the point, they may complain ironically that secularism is being read as what used to be called 'worldliness'.[3]

But should there not be at least some misgivings on the part of secularists about the loss of religion, even if they dismiss the late C19th fear that with loss of religion came loss of social control? The German philosopher Jürgen Habermas[4] has talked of 'an awareness of what is missing' in what he calls our post-metaphysical age. *Is* something missing? Perhaps it is this unease that leads, even among secular humanists, to the now routine appeal of 'spirituality'. But let us retrace our steps.

DOI: 10.4324/9781003536185-14

98 Religion and Atheism in Dialogue

2.

When Jews, Christians and Muslims talk about 'religion' they often conflate it with 'religious belief', and so do secular humanists, who are variously cultural Jews, Christians and Muslims. But there is a distinctive ambiguity in that reference to 'religious belief' since in these traditions, 'believer' is a religious *role and identity*. 'Belief in God' can mean belief in the existence of God, but it also has the religious double meaning of *trust* and *faithfulness*, the salient features of our notion of 'believer'. Indeed the *form* of 'belief in the existence of God' is just this attitude of trust and fidelity, its vicissitudes under pressure *and*, significantly, its defiant rejection, as exemplified, perhaps, in the figure of Milton's Satan. Crudely, believers *believe God*, believe God's promises and abide by his Law, though clearly there are important, not to say stark, differences of theological understanding.

But being a believer in this sense is a particular cultural variant, and we should avoid the Procrustean move that makes all religious adherents 'believers'. When atheism was a cultural newcomer, it was hard not to see it as a form of defiant infidelity, and this perception seems to lurk still in the account of secularism presented by religious conservatives. If you reject belief, you must be rejecting *God*, his promises and his moral law.

But the rhetorical question was, can we be moral without religion? The obvious answer remains yes, but it needs qualification. I think you can indeed be 'moral' without religious *belief*, understood in Abrahamic terms. But whether you can be so without *religion* ... I'm not so sure, mostly because the theistic traditions have handed down to us dramatic representations of the crises of moral and political life. In the Hebrew Bible, for example, 'fidelity' is constantly recalled in passionate denunciations of collective injustice and moral failure.

Some secularists will cautiously invoke the notion of 'spirituality' here and some *believers* will question its seriousness if it is not associated with the falterings of our relationship to God and receptivity to the grace which is necessary if we are to learn from sin (*pecca fortiter sed crede fortius*). But the problem and experience of 'sin', even if we no longer apply the term, can anchor 'spirituality' in the moral phenomena that caused believers to look for the help of the 'Spirit'. It is here, I think, that believers, non-theists and secular humanists come more closely together than might be expected, their main point of difference being how they make sense of what we might all call moral failure.

What we have in common, whether we are theists, atheists or non-theists, is that we are unreliable moral agents. Most of us recoil from our moral failure, and look for diagnosis and remedy, and this search is the *rationale* for what has come to be called 'spiritual practice', an endeavour both individual and collective, as we reflect on our conduct and the conditions that give rise to it. In other words, it is a *moral* endeavour, trying to find our way back onto the path, to echo a Hebrew notion of 'sin'. King Lear's daughter, Regan, said of her father: 'he hath ever but slenderly known himself'. That assessment could be applied to institutions as much as to individuals (including Regan). The search for diagnosis and remedy has led to the formation of concepts of interiority or inwardness, self-examination, self-awareness, and to a culture of forensic self-inquiry aspiring to an elusive self-knowledge, the opening and closing of horizons. The *language* is diagnostic and therapeutic, but it is also expressive, there is a *poetics* of the inner life and its relation to demeanour and conduct, it is agonised, despairing, hopeful, struggling to overcome cowardice, delusion, double-mindedness and self-deception, hypocrisy and collusion. Much of this inherited language is religiously inflected in a way that prescinds from 'belief'.[5]

3.

Students of moral philosophy are introduced early to the notion of *akrasia*, which is variously translated as 'incontinence', 'weakness of will' or 'lack of control', and this is contrasted with *enkrateia* (continence, (self-)control). They will hear references to the Latin poet Ovid's famous line '*video meliora proboque, deteriora sequor*'[6] and St Paul's 'For the good that I would I do not; but the evil which I would not, that I do'. This is presented as the pivotal dynamic of moral struggle—whether or not we can contain our contrary inclinations and do the right thing. But on either side of this dynamic, there are *akolasia* (excess, licentiousness, lack of chastisement) and *sōphrosunē* or 'temperance' or 'self-possession', a condition in which the capacity for ethical action is no longer threatened or undermined by resistance or reluctance or lack of attention. This seems an unassuming parallel to the more agonised 'It is no longer I who live, but Christ who lives in me'.[7] A believer would want at least to talk of the necessity for grace here, and the question arises, does this Pauline confession express in terms of a worldview we don't all share a human insight that a secularist could endorse, a revelatory experience made sense of in other language? A Christian believer might talk of a revelatory visitation, a secularist of a revelation, a shift of consciousness.

Akolasia and *akrasia* are signs and symptoms of a sickness in the soul,[8] whose treatment and cure, if there is one, inform our very notion of human harm and well-being. Students also encounter the Aristotelian notion of *eudaimonia*, variously interpreted as 'human flourishing', 'happiness' and 'well-being'; and they learn that a main criterion for the moral worth of an action is how it affects 'well-being', individually, collectively and ecologically. (We are less inclined to think in terms of, or refer in our teaching to, the interior conditions of such conduct.) The problem that they are then confronted with is how we are to understand 'well-being'. But crucially (and

100 Religion and Atheism in Dialogue

crudely), we are not talking of those for whom their well-being is *at risk*, but of those for whom it is already compromised, and a personal, even poetic register becomes appropriate. Our *plight* as unreliable moral agents not only impairs our capacity to *act* for the sake of well-being but also our capacity to *conceive* it, as T. S. Eliot soberingly puts it:

> the shame
> Of things ill done and done to others' harm
> Which once you took for exercise of virtue.

The trajectory from *akolasia* or licentiousness, which I shall read here as moral indifference, towards *sōphrosunē* is a trajectory towards the well-being of moral agents who are, on this criterion, only rarely well. The medical metaphor is in Plato, and it is there in the Buddhist doctrine of the 'three poisons' (of craving, aversion and ignorance) that infect and impair our moral and political life.

A condition of our moral impairment is brought out in this passage from Spinoza:

> For the ordinary surroundings of life which are esteemed by men ... to be the highest good, may be classed under the three heads—Riches, Fame, and the Pleasures of Sense; with these three the mind is so absorbed[9] that it has little power to reflect on any different good (*On the Improvement of the Understanding*).[10]

Notice that we are already involved in an aspect of moral psychology that is probably shared ground: we are talking of virtues and vices, the idea of incontinence or *akrasia* implies moral criticism of tendencies of character and conduct; and the *tone* of Spinoza's comment is one of moral regret, an *attitude* that is shown, not stated. And the question is, *whence* the regret? The 'little power to reflect on any different good' has always been politically convenient: unscrupulous politicians exploit ignorance and credulity, distort judgement by diversion, pacification, false narrative and so forth; they nurture with care the conditions for the failure of moral agency.

4.

Eliot's frequently quoted line,

> .... human kind
> Cannot bear very much reality

is often cited to clinch some reflection on the heavy burdens of human life. But it might be better to see it as part of a diagnosis of moral failure, in which 'reality' is construed simply as what we can't bear to acknowledge because it would force us to re-evaluate or change our lives. 'How can you live with yourself?' is a question that directs itself to this moral 'shadow'—we cannot bear very much of the reality of self-revelation or the human misery that surrounds us. It echoes the remarks of Spinoza about limitations on the 'power to reflect'. The line comes in *Burnt Norton*, the first of the *Four Quartets*, part of a poetic diagnosis of the strategy of avoidance. But the avoidance, and what is avoided, is encapsulated here:

> The world moves in appetency on its metalled ways
> Of time past and time future.

These lines return us to that notion of 'worldliness' that I mentioned at the beginning. 'The world' is familiar and traditional as a term of moral criticism, and it can be existentially deep or dogmatically shallow and repressive. Another aspect is that 'the world', conceived as such reality as we are able to appropriate, can be broken into. There can be an *irruption* of reality into 'the world'; there are circumstances in which it can force itself upon our attention, one of the conditions, perhaps, of moral conversion, a shift in sensibility which refocuses the will. 'World' appears to do a double service as an ethico-epistemological category. Firstly, it names a restricted set of interests, an orientation that determines the scope of attention and deflects us from the reality 'we cannot bear'. This is reflected in the uneasy self-distancing, the evanescent *mauvaise foi*, inscribed in this concept; but, secondly, it also names a population, as it were, the orientation's collective embodiment in a way of being or culture, a consensus, which restricts itself to the reality we *can* bear, and it resists criticism. To use a phrase from the literary critic F. R. Leavis, what focuses our attention as individuals is a kind of 'egocentric self-enclosure'—'the world' is the collectivity of such, pursuing, balancing and negotiating these interests. But now there is a use of 'self' which corresponds to that of 'the world'. It is the interior formation or mentality that inhabits 'the world'. The world is transcended to the extent that 'self' is in abeyance (in abeyance, one should say, rather than *repressed*, not the self-image of the 'selfless'). There are many conditions under which this 'self' is in abeyance—in which the negative passions are quiet or in retreat—including aesthetic experience, reflective attention to the arts, silent prayer, meditation—and moral possibilities present themselves that are not otherwise fully available, and the question arises whether the cultivation of these spiritual practices might itself start to lessen the impact of this 'self' as energy is transferred to a perspective that transcends 'the world'. But our projects can also be paused or suspended by moral shock, either at the conduct of others or of our own, one form of the irruption I mentioned earlier. But to *dwell* in the perspectival shift as a main focus of attention is a matter of spiritual practice which, without this end, can become merely narcissistic.

The existential question arises, then, whether and in what sense we can overcome 'the world'—whether and in what sense, to use a fraught term, we can 'transcend' it. But that we can distance ourselves from this orientation already reveals a critical moral purchase, an unwilling awareness of what we should be paying attention to. Ascribing the term to our own and others' interests in this way reflects the intimation of a *perspective* beyond it, a critical purchase on a dominant but not yet engulfing orientation. The *interest* that determines the scope of attention that belongs to 'the world' is partisan and self-serving or self-regarding and it generates only a precarious ethic for the ground rules of competition.[11] By contrast, and to use a much abused word, to be *dis-interested* is to be not thus limited either in awareness or conduct—more positively, we have the eighteenth-century Francis Hutcheson's reflection that benevolence is native or instinct within us and is a *disinterested* feeling, in the sense that it doesn't arise in dependence on self-love and, though it might give us pleasure, it is not done for the sake of pleasure. On the other hand, it is also true that this benevolence and its energy and scope are crucially limited, stifled and suffocated. Hutcheson's 'benevolence' is important, but the language is a little nerveless—it is hard to see 'benevolence' as passionate; it seems to me that when we represent moral failure, moral struggle, spiritual crisis, to ourselves in music, theatre and literature, we still draw on a religious lexicon, without thereby subscribing to belief. The language of 'crucifixion', say, or 'resurrection', reflect real and visceral human experiences. Eliot talks of 'darkness' and 'deprivation' ... of what one is reluctant to let go of, bearings, habits, strategies by which one keeps 'reality' at bay. Some secular humanists may be wary of using language that derives from such origins, as though in using it we were committed to the worldview within which it developed, the genetic fallacy patrolling our language, confusing origins with use. If Eliot writes about purgatorial fires, we don't think he must be committed to the doctrine of Purgatory (even if he is), though the question remains, what are the phenomena to which we apply the image? If we read 'I said to my soul, be still', do we have to believe in souls to accept the injunction? The injunction, however one expresses it, takes us back to the idea of the self in abeyance, as a condition of seeing what is there to be seen. Eliot talks of this stillness ('and let the dark come upon you') as a kind of 'waiting' (wait without hope, for hope would be hope for the wrong thing, etc.), as a condition of re-orientation in the direction of a perspective glimpsed rather than inhabited. Whatever form of expression we embrace, the language and landscape is that of *ascesis* and *therapeia*, self-overcoming, moral struggle, including the struggle to keep in view what we have seen but don't want to acknowledge. The 'metalled ways', by contrast, '(a)llow but a little consciousness'. 'Allow' is a good word here, ambiguous between 'permits' and 'makes possible'. It is worth comparing this with Rilke's talk in his *Duino Elegies* of our active avoidance of *das Offene*, of what lies *open* before us, though we determinedly look the other way. In a different idiom, Buddhists talk of the mental poisons of greed, hatred and delusion and project the possibility no longer of an evanescent but of a continuous dwelling in a form of consciousness that is free of them. Similarly, *metanoia* is a shift in consciousness in which 'the self' which was dominant is now in abeyance and we see and can keep in view what was previously obscured.

5.

Let us come back to the moral anxiety about secularism, that *unless* our 'moral values' are underwritten by a transcendent source or authority, we descend into relativism, conventionalism and sexual permissiveness; and this because under the condition of atheism, morality *can be no more than* a matter of the wayward human will, individual or collective. This position is stated, for example, by the conservative Catholic, William Barr,[12] who was Attorney General during the 2016 Trump presidency. Like Vance, he paints a profoundly negative picture of the consequences of secularism, with a particular focus on sexual ethics, and remarks that '... to control wilful human beings, with an infinite capacity to rationalize, ... moral values must rest on authority independent of men's will – they must flow from a transcendent Supreme Being'.

I think this is a false opposition. There is a third possibility, that 'moral values' derive *neither* from the transcendent authority of the divine will *nor* from the human will. But there is a sense of transcendence that might work here. Our 'values' are not the product of the human will but determine its possible directions and the 'authority', if that is the right word, is that of the *perspective* that transcends the 'metalled ways' of the world's 'appetency'. The possibility of such a perspective survives the loss of belief but is at the same time possible common ground in the dialogue between religion and atheism. In other words, there is another way of looking at this. A believer might say that our moral values rest on *this* authority, that we are made in God's image, and this is reflected in our native capacity for justice and compassion, impaired though it is by the Fall. It is our *nature* that bears the stamp of God's authority and this nature is reflected in our values, which should not be reduced to specific prohibitions and requirements, a set of singular prescriptions. This naturalism would be close to Hutcheson's position, that benevolence is instinct within us though compromised by self-love. I am drawing here on the tradition of the 'moral sentiments'—such as sympathy, benevolence, etc.—though I think this tradition needs to be modified, not only by the term 'perspective', which I have already used, but also by 'attitude'. The moral sentiments form our dispositions, and are expressed in *attitudes* towards others and their well-being; where this well-being is threatened by human agency, these attitudes fuse in the form of indignation in the face of what we call 'injustice'.

104 Religion and Atheism in Dialogue

However, and crucially, the range and scope of these attitudes is governed by the perspectives available to us. I have already named a particular and dominant perspective—the things we notice and respond to—that of 'the world' and talked also of a perspective that transcends it. But the moral sentiments straddle this distinction in terms of their energy, range and scope; and to talk about 'transcending the world' as I have presented it is to refer to a perspective disclosed when 'self-love' recedes. It's a matter of what we can see and respond to when perception is not thus circumscribed.

How does this relate to the criticism that we cannot rely on the 'authority' of the human will? I should say that 'the natural sentiments of humanity' *determine* the directions of the will, they are not, as I said, its product. We do not choose our values, our values choose us. The error is to abstract the human will from the sensibility that informs it, treating it as an independent and arbitrary agent. If we think of 'justice' as a 'moral value', we should nevertheless construe it as a *perspective* that calls forth or demands a response, an inner necessity rather than an imposed requirement. But it is also revelatory. For example, someone may resent being pushed around by more powerful others, but this resentment is compatible with a hoped for and revengeful reversal of roles. There is a perspectival shift when I come to see my personal plight as a *human* plight, reflecting a human struggle against oppression, a transition from immersion in immediacy to a reflective disinterestedness. There is the possibility, in other words, of a revelatory shift in consciousness, as when the smelly kid up the street is seen for the first time simply as a vulnerable child in need of help. Perhaps it is best to see this as a form of 'seeing as'—seeing them in the light of what we recognise as a shared human condition is an achieved but unstable perspective which determines attitude and demeanour: we behave differently towards them. If we are to talk of 'authority' here at all, it is not that of the human will but of a perspective that alters its possible directions and silences other interests. In other words, this 'recognition' of their humanity is essentially informed by a perspective that determines what we are *calling* 'recognition'. William Blake's *London*, the 'marks of weakness, marks of woe', 'the mind-forg'd manacles', the lines carry the pity and indignation but the feeling is directed towards a condition of humanity, and the perspective is precarious precisely because of the 'little power to reflect on any other good'. The point of the 'spiritual practices' I mentioned earlier is to increase this power to reflect—and thence act. This shift in perspective, its new hierarchy of needs, gives content to 'justice' as a moral concept. We see this particular person, but they exemplify something universal, the disclosure of an *idea* of what it is to be human fused with an attitude, perhaps of pity or compassion in the face of affliction. The crucial thing, though, is the *instability* both of the power to attend and the power to act. You *are* the perspective, but by the same token, you *are* the flickering oscillations and instability. Indeed, this is easily corrupted into a sentimental aestheticism, loving humanity but disliking people. Nevertheless, the poetry is a reflective site of revelation that awaits embodiment.

As for meditation and silent prayer as conditions under which the 'self' is in abeyance or even eclipsed, maybe humanists and believers are closer than they think. A believer may find in this silence the overshadowing presence of God, and emerge with a sense of wonder and a compassion for the world which shows what it means to be made in God's image. A humanist may share the silence and emerge with a sense of wonder and a compassion for the world. They may both in their affliction and moral failure feel included.

Notes

1 Aquinas' natural law theory claims that we can know what is right and wrong by the light of reason.
2 See, for example, J. D. Vance's comments on his conversion to Catholicism: https:// thelampmagazine.com/blog/how-i-joined-the-resistance
3 The notion of 'the world' will be discussed later in this essay.
4 Jürgen Habermas et al., *An Awareness of What Is Missing: Faith and Reason in a Post-Secular Age* (Cambridge, UK: Polity Press, 2010).
5 See elsewhere in this volume George Guiver's decentring of 'belief' in favour of practice.
6 I see the better and approve, but pursue the worse.
7 *Galatians* 2:20.
8 Cf. Plato's *Republic*.
9 'distrahitur'.
10 Compare Plato's account of the oligarchic personality.
11 Cf. Rousseau's notion of the 'will of all' in his *Social Contract*.
12 https://www.justice.gov/opa/speech/attorney-general-william-p-barr-delivers-remarks-law-school-and-de-nicola-center-ethics#:~:text=In%20the%20words%20of%20Madison,select%20a%20representative%20legislative%20body

13

PERSONS AND COMMUNITIES TRANSFORMED BY PRACTICES

George Guiver

For people in western society, discussions about religion usually assume 'beliefs' to be the topic to discuss. It may come as a surprise to hear that religion is not in the first place about beliefs – the higher religions normally, of course, present systems of belief, but the reality of the matter doesn't normally start there. A fairly wide consensus among anthropologists suggests that religion starts with practices, pure and simple. The second stage is when the affections and a sense of engagement come into play. There then follows a third stage when all of this is reflected on, and an attempt is made to describe and formulate what is being experienced – in other words to identify beliefs. First you have the experience, then you reflect upon it. One thing I hope to outline is the gradual gaining of religious perceptions and apperceptions through sustained engagement in practices. If these stages are the normal trajectory, then any exploration of religion through discussion of beliefs will be inadequate if it does not take account of religious practices. The discussion will be imbalanced because the fundamental insights of the religious participants aren't primarily indebted to discussing or weighing beliefs, but rather to what is largely physical experience. Some obvious examples are corporate worship, personal prayer, festivals, keeping Lent, decorating special spaces and all the rest of a large repertoire. The list also includes practices in daily life: love and service of our neighbour, for instance. If a discussion group made up of religious and non-religious people is not to remain limited to the world of ideas, how could participants jointly engage with this realm of practices? While it is not easy to see how this could be possible, there are some areas worth exploring. For instance, in the practice of service of others – engagement in it has an effect on you and can change you. This is a practice open to anybody to engage in and then reflect on. Another example would be religious practices regarding

DOI: 10.4324/9781003536185-15

engagement with one another. For instance, St Benedict wrote in the sixth century that when meetings are to be held to decide something, we should be slow to speak and quick to listen; we should expect to learn from the views of others, aware that our own views can be driven more than we recognise by passions and cherished positions rather than objective reflection. He also said that the meeting should take particular care to listen to the youngest in the group – this in a society where age gave status: status should not count for much in decision-making. It is not surprising that the monastic Rule of St Benedict is often used nowadays in management training. Making the effort to practise these principles can have an effect both on us, and on the way meetings work. Such a way of engaging in meetings is in large part a physical practice. As it happens, I think our atheist-religionist discussion group works well along these lines, and in that sense, we are already going beyond our reasoned discourse by practising something together to do with the way we conduct our meetings. You might however say, 'try this approach with Donald Trump, and see where you get – probably not very far'. This helps make clear that particular ways of participating in discussions are not simply for isolated individuals to seek to practise, as they can be quickly frustrated: the reference is more to a culture within a group that needs to be built up.

Other practices prove a little more tricky – prayer, for instance. It is not easy to see how this or its equivalents could be a part of shared experience between atheists and religious people. However, the notion of prayer is widely misconceived. Of course, it can involve addressing God and asking for things, but that on its own is another example of what I call head-stuff. Prayer includes physical actions of many kinds. For Christians, baptising with water, blessing bread and wine and sharing them, anointing the sick with oil, bodily postures (Eastern Orthodox bowings and prostrations are a good example, and, to the modern mind, good physical exercise as well), lighting candles, making the sign of the cross, using and looking after church buildings, processions, pilgrimages, festivals through the year, to give a few examples. The life of the Monastery where I live is sprinkled with practices of all sorts through the day and the year, which in their way are all prayer – that is, building up relationships horizontally and vertically. And there is a strong sense that such practices for any religious believer train you up in skills through your lifetime, schooling you in self-knowledge, in appreciation of others and in communicating with the deeper mysteries of life. All of this comes under the heading of prayer, and some of it is translatable into an atheist dimension, I should think. One obvious area where this is true is meditation, which has a very important place in Christian history and practice and that of other religions, but is also today part of the secular repertoire. These things depend on iteration: meditation, if it is to open us to change, needs to be practised regularly over a long enough period rather than simply tried once or twice.

108 Religion and Atheism in Dialogue

Much research has been done in recent decades on how symbols and ritual work. 'Ritual' (however it is defined, and that is not easy) is to be found everywhere in our lives and has its effects, which don't necessarily depend on any 'beliefs'. A recent article in the Economist said as much.

> Rituals aren't just about God, but about people's relations with each other. Everyday life depends on ritual performances such as being polite, dressing appropriately, following proper procedure and observing the law. The particulars vary, often mightily, across time, space and societies. But they are the foundation of all formal and informal institutions, making co-ordination between people feel effortless. They seem invisible only because we take them so much for granted. Organisations couldn't work without rituals. When you write a reference letter for a former colleague or give or get a tchotchke on Employee Appreciation Day, you are enacting a ceremony, reinforcing the foundations of a world in which everyone knows the rules and expects them to be observed—even if you sometimes secretly roll your eyes.[1]

'Religion', if we accept that word as a rough label, can be characterised as something that involves the whole person: mind, body, the physical world, surroundings and engagement with others. The mind, and our exercise of reason, have an essential place, but the question here regards not relative importance but the order in which things come into play. The order in which religion is best explored, as suggested above, is (1) practice, (2) engagement and (3) formulation of belief. Religion does not usually start with head-stuff – it gets you there through body-stuff. This is true not only about religion but about life as a whole. Here is something on which atheists and religious people could cooperate. Our society is ritually depleted, and this has costs in many ways. Think of the loss of rituals associated with death: holding a wake, viewing the body, drawing the curtains, wearing a black armband, talking together frankly, using stylised phrases according to convention rather than practising avoidance, and being free to weep. Psychological problems often result from having failed to grieve adequately over a death. The practices don't necessarily need to be religious. In fact, there is a need for both religious and secular rituals. Before modern times, significant events like death were marked in both secular and religious ways.

I think of a Romanian village wedding, where a great party is held in a central space, all the inhabitants engaging in a dance. I and some travelling companions once walked accidentally into such a wedding, and found ourselves taking part in a dance where a circle of young women was surrounded by a circle of young chaps. A battered brass band played, chickens scuttled among our feet, while the men revolved in one direction and the girls in the other. As they went round, a girl would drop a hanky in front of a boy, and they would kiss. Then the circling continued. At a certain point, everyone (or at any event a good number of people) decamped to the church for the Orthodox service where, among other things, bride and groom were crowned as kings and queens of creation. The service was taken very seriously, as you can find in Romania. After the service, all went back to the dance in the village square. This is as old as the hills: significant moments in life such as weddings, births, funerals, coming of age, moving house, have had secular traditions and church traditions living happily side-by-side. It occurs to me that humanists are attempting something important in evolving secular ceremonies for these occasions, and there is no reason why they should be in competition with faith practices. Our society needs to rediscover the dimension of secular rituals. The challenge is to evolve practices that will not only suit nice, tidy, polite educated people but also rise up from the vulgar and earthy, and usually the best way is for them to evolve from the grass roots. How can we help people in our society rediscover this dimension in our lives – corporate secular traditions and practices? The people who think about the question, like me, aren't so likely to be the ones who have the vulgarity to get stuff going that hits the spot. Liz Slade in her chapter provides good examples of two kinds of rituals identified by Ronald Grimes in his writings – rather than use his strange terminology, I'll refer to them as spontaneous and received rituals. Examples of the former are the spontaneously devised pilgrimages Slade describes. Any such ritual by the time of its second iteration, as with the meetings of the Sunday Assembly described in the same chapter, becomes more of a received ritual, something that you get the hang of and slot into, and through that slotting-in, find new vistas opening up.

One reason popular secular traditions are healthy and necessary is their capacity to involve the whole human person, mind and body, and above that, our unreflecting apperceptions, in a total, all-embracing expression. Like the pianist who forgets the written page and gives no thought to which finger goes where in any particular moment, in a whole-person 'swooping', where without attention to them, the fingers are left to get on with it. I was intrigued recently by a comment in our discussion group by two members who serve on ethical committees in the medical profession. One is a committed Christian and the other is a non-theist: in their experience, members of such committees can differ widely on moral principles, as they range from utilitarians to committed believers and everything in between, but when it comes to making decisions on particular cases, they usually reach the same conclusions on what action ought to be taken. In such situations, it seems that head-stuff is complemented and enlarged by whole-person-stuff. Our society needs to do some rediscovering of living as a whole person. We could say that our society has lost two primal elements: one is universal belief in God, on which we can differ, and another is the ability to live ritually, something on which we have the potential to agree.

110 Religion and Atheism in Dialogue

I should make clear that I am not wanting to downplay the vital role of human reason, without which we are surely lost. The question is of enabling it to find its proper place in the sequence. We have an inclination to take a particular aspect of our humanity and enthrone it rather than allowing it to find its proper place on the ladder. The Enlightenment was an epochal breakthrough, an immense gift, changing us for ever, but we can diminish it by giving it an imperial throne. Or perhaps we need to think of a throne with several seats on it. Reason for its own good has to work within that constellation which is the human being fully alive in every pore. Nor am I downplaying the role of belief, of doctrine, in religion. Its contribution is essential, but the question is rather of the point in the exploration at which it comes in, to play its role as guide and focus.

I am brought here to my second theme: the individual and the corporate. Inevitably, group discussions about beliefs unconsciously posit an individual doing the questing. It is an individual who asks, 'How can I as an individual make sense of the world and of the claims of atheism and religion?' 'How can I relate to the spiritual?' The individualistic presuppositions of our society are so strong that we may not realise how odd this is. Human beings are by nature corporate. Many people have gone into the making of me, and many of my characteristics, habits, and ways of acting and speaking I have picked up from others. We form each other, and all the people I know wander somewhere among the corridors of my mind. Most people do not find extended solitude easy, and in prison, solitary confinement is regarded as a particularly tough punishment. Our society, however, hypes to the skies the autonomy of the individual, and their capacity to make themselves – in a recent article in *The Guardian*, the writer gave the advice: 'you make you'. Here we see a reaction to ways in which society has cramped or manipulated people's individuality, and imposed restrictions that were needless, or to the advantage of others. We have made huge advances regarding our individual uniqueness and the rights that belong to the dignity of every human being. However, this progress has tended to occlude a fact that is unavoidable: we are irrevocably bound up together, and our society is riddled with avoidance of this fact. There are some areas, however, where our avoidance cannot be sustained. It is striking, for instance, how even the most individualistic of people can surrender to a common endeavour when they are admitted to that very corporate place, a hospital. Where is all this much-vaunted individuality when we have to submit to others in trust? Or in a society dominated, if not obsessed, by law, you can quickly discover how your individuality is circumscribed if you step beyond the law's limits. The courtroom is another corporate place in which our individuality is subjected to the community. There is furthermore something contradictory (or perhaps defiant) about laying ever more claim to the priority of individuality, while being limited on all sides by the exponential growth of regulation. A good deal could be said about the way our society resorts disproportionately to the law to solve its problems. Over-reliance on legal procedures edges out all that corresponds to the pianist's 'swooping'. There is something topsy-turvy about that: an individualism that relies on the law, with the result that individuality is diminished. Finally, beyond the bonds forged by the state, there are other areas of our deeper selves which cannot prioritise the individual. An obvious example is language – for most readers of this text, the English language is part of our grain, in the foundations of who we are. You would however have to stop using language if 'You make you' is taken absolutely. Concerts, art galleries, public transport, tax, neighbourhood, clubs and so on all reflect in similar ways this corporate reality of our nature. And so, in discussions about religion or 'spirituality' or 'meaning', it is perhaps somewhat odd to presume the explorer to be an individual, full stop. The point can come home if we imagine President Zelensky speaking to the world's leaders about the life of the Ukrainian individual, positing an individual faced with the war.

Religions evolved corporately and are corporately practised. The individual dimension derives from that. This suggests a need to find some way of engaging with a different question: not, 'how can the individual makes sense of the world the individual inhabits?', but something more like 'how can we join in a corporate quest to make sense of the world we inhabit?' Humanists UK and the churches are both examples of such a corporate approach, but they are hampered by two difficulties: firstly, neither of them at the moment engages enough people in our society to have sufficient corporate weight, and secondly, they are both hampered by our society's default position that the individual is the subject of the exploration. Indeed, most humanists and many Christians (if not most) assume that the individual is the principal actor and the starting point for the whole enterprise. Christianity in the West has been deeply influenced by the individualism which sprang from it but then took on a life of its own. So Christians will tend to posit the individual when talking about faith, even though they are deeply indebted to corporate practices in a way largely unrecognised. In any mutual exploration between atheists and people of religion, the participants need somehow to do justice to the corporate aspect of the exploration. In our theist-non-theist discussion group, the corporate is indeed at work, in our shared language, shared culture, and the awareness of work done together, and in friendships forged. But the subject under discussion needs somehow to engage with that corporate reality within which every individual is embedded.

This now leads me to a third consideration. The rather dead word 'corporate' does not say enough. 'Community' gets us a little further but is still abstract until filled out with further particularities. Those particularities lead us to the subject of culture. Human beings are not simply corporate – they generate and live within cultures. A culture could be called a whole-life language, if we are clear that the word 'language' is being used symbolically

112 Religion and Atheism in Dialogue

to embrace an entire way of living, physical, mental and intuitional. Like a language, a culture permeates and shapes a group; and like language, it provides structures and vocabulary within which we can come alive. The writer W. Somerset Maugham somewhere said we can only begin to understand our own country if we have lived in two other countries. Having lived in two other countries myself, and now in a somewhat offbeat third one if it can be called that (a monastery), I can see something of what he means. Living in Italy and, later, Germany has affected my mental filters so that I now perceive many things in British culture either as less universal than we think they are, or controlled by peculiar habits (like trying to eat peas perched on the curved back of a fork), or as gifts that need to be shared more widely, or as lovable characteristics that we should be careful not to lose. We need to grow in awareness of the relativity of our culture. Of course, the situation is not simple: in societies, there have always been subcultures and sub-sub-cultures, sometimes at variance with the overall culture. In our own world, it seems that there is a great umbrella represented by the mainstream media, politics, general public discourse, ideals and sense of the plausible. But it presides rather uneasily over a mosaic of cultural layers and pockets.

The umbrella, however, is formidably powerful and determining, and, crucially, incomplete. It has great power to become a procrustean bed, where vital limbs are chopped off to fit the frame. Religion is only one of such limbs. I have noticed how planning proposals in Italy treat 'beauty' as an important category in assessing plans for buildings or public works, to a degree unheard of in the United Kingdom. Beauty is key to human flourishing, and our British categories of the plausible have lopped it off or emasculated it, and we flourish all the less. Again, we have to be grateful for the fruits of the careful regulation and target setting that hold sway now in many professions and indeed in daily life, but the loss is irreplaceable: how do we deal with the restriction or loss of the freedom to take wing, in teaching, for instance, with a freedom of the spirit that cannot survive being policed? Another 'limb' is moral awareness. Michael McGhee in his chapter in this book raises questions about the sense of moral obligations in the minds of most people who live under the culture-umbrella, and our inability to face much reality; this in turn reinforces and shapes the umbrella: 'an orientation that determines the scope of attention and deflects us from the reality "we cannot bear" … a consensus, which restricts itself to the reality we *can* bear, and it resists criticism'.

This world, with all its gains and losses, has made us, and we each need to recognise the degree in which it is part of our own grain. And so, although I am an enthusiastically practising Christian, the society which presumes that God is not important is inside me. Its voice tugs at my sleeve. Its plausibility-structures subvert my ability to practise faith with conviction. When I pray, a little voice says, 'is God there?' Why is it that it gets nowhere with me?

Here I come back to the community (in my case, the Christian church) and its practices as I have called them. When practices are part of the mix, we find the sovereign liberty of the whole-person 'swooping' which takes off, and leaves the 'is God there?' question behind as head-stuff – important to ask and wrestle with, but incapable of lifting our feet from the ground and letting us swim. Correspondingly, in a person sustained and formed by a practice-rich culture that presumes God is *not* there, they ought to be able in the same way to say it launches their own swimming, 'swooping'. The same can be said of the arts and their corresponding rational questions (what is beauty?), or sport (what is competing?), or human love (what is human attraction?). 'Swooping' in the end trumps concepts. Am I saying, then, that the umbrella-culture of our society is 'wrong' in the way it sidelines rituals, and sidelines God? On the contrary, it is something from which we can and need to learn. Perhaps I can put it like this. Religions are cultures – not sub-cultures in fact, so much as meta-cultures. It is important for religion that it has challengers. This is partly because Christian practitioners have a long and tiresome history of subverting the very values they claim to represent. Just as I see some of our modern individualism to be an overblown fantasy supported by avoidance, so you don't need me to tell you that overblown fantasies supported by avoidance are always around somewhere in the world of religion. If we think, for instance, of Christian missions in the nineteenth century, there was often a tendency to presume missionaries had all the answers. We should not overlook the sacrifice and sensitivity to local culture often shown nor the great work of improving education and medical care which they usually brought, often at great cost to themselves. But this could in places lead to the absurdity of choirboys in surplices and ruffs singing Victorian hymns with harmoniums in the steaming jungle, and, worse, in some places, indigenous communities who lived exemplary family and community lives being forced to change these irreplaceable gifts by people whose own families were dysfunctional and their values narrow or limited – unaware, in fact, of the degree to which the true culture of the church they proclaimed had been colonised by the narrow culture of Victorian society. Religions are meta-cultures in the sense that they cannot tell us how to run a society. Religion is not in a position to tell a farmer how to farm or a mother how to mother. It needs to engage with these things and where necessary provide an alternative voice (e.g. on damage to the environment from over-use of fertilisers), but it can't oversee or determine the whole project of farming or mothering, and in this way, needs to have the humility to learn from those outside itself. The Christian gospel always engages with individual societies whose way of life has evolved from the ground up. You could say that when religion engages with a society, it needs to recognise that it has things to give but can only give those things well if it is prepared to receive and to learn. Furthermore, it needs to be prepared to come under judgement. This is why it is never a good idea to aim for a theocracy, or a society where the roles of religion and politics become too aligned. Even were the whole of British society to become practising Christians, their Christianity needs to know its proper place. This is why the default religionlessness of our society is something that needs to be listened to.

Au contraire, living as I do, as a monk in a monastery (and the reader shouldn't presume too easily to know what that involves!), I find myself in a Somerset-Maughamian 'other country', very conscious of the particularity and in some ways distinct oddness of the surrounding culture of our society. I wonder whether religions, as well as those corporate bodies which support atheism, need to work harder at trying to see our society from a slightly displaced vantage point, if we are to be of help to it. Our contemporary culture is in significant ways inadequate to the task of its own fulfilment, and we need to be able to see that and to identify where its weaknesses are. One contributory factor in the contemporary weakness of the churches is, in fact, that they have allowed themselves to hand over too much of the steering to the mindset of contemporary society.

Beliefs are the tip of an iceberg. This iceberg is greater and profounder than can ever be captured in words, and the individual is the tip of another, profounder, corporate iceberg. Societal culture, like earth's climate, perhaps needs closer examination and probing, if our icebergs are not to start breaking up. And I am left with the question I started with, without being clear at the moment how to take it forward: how can questions of faith, life's significance and the deeper questions we find in life about our humanity be responded to with the whole human person in the plural, and not with the head alone?

Note

1 'Large language models will upend human rituals – the results could be disturbing', Marion Fourcade and Henry Farrell, *The Economist*, 24 September 2024.

14

RITUAL FOR THE NON-RELIGIOUS

Elizabeth Slade

In leading a national church organisation, it's easy for me to forget that for most people in Britain today, religion and ritual are far from their minds and their lives. The 2021 census showed that fewer people than ever identify as religious, and church attendance is a rare activity.

As a child, going to the village church with my family, I don't remember any rituals being particularly important to me. I went up to the altar for communion, receiving a hand on the head, marking me (in my experience) as 'less than' by being a child, while the adults had a sip of wine from the golden cup. I remember feeling indignant not to have the wafer, and my mum explaining to me that it wasn't a snack. At Easter, they handed the children a Cadbury's Creme Egg as we walked out the church – a much more satisfactory ritual. My mum prayed with me and my brothers as she tucked us up in bed each night. At a certain age, I was expected to say them on my own, and asked if I'd done it in the same tone as checking whether I'd cleaned my teeth.

As a teenager, the Christian context dropped away as other more compelling ideas filled my mind. The local vicar asked me a few times whether I'd like to get confirmed, but it seemed so far away from the cultural concepts that drew me. Christianity seemed parochial, boring, and about conforming, whereas the bands I listened to and read about in magazines were exciting, rebellious, and spoke to the ideas that were on my mind. Aged around 15, in the mid-90s, some of us at school were invited to join a 'self-hypnosis' group to help us with examination stress. Nowadays, I think it would be billed as mindfulness meditation. It wasn't framed in any wider cultural, religious, or philosophical context than coping with examinations.

Travelling around European cities as a University student, I visited churches. One of my travel mates would always sit down quietly in a pew in

DOI: 10.4324/9781003536185-16

116 Religion and Atheism in Dialogue

each one we visited, and the others just looked at the stained glass windows and peculiar relics. I wasn't sure which was the right option for me. Those were the first times I had stepped into a church by choice rather than dragged by parents, or for a school event. On the cusp of adulthood, I realised that I had a choice about how I engaged with this. I tried sitting quietly in some of the churches, in a way that felt like I was expecting something to happen, and it never did. Was I doing it wrong? Or did religion just not work on me?

During my 20s, living in London, I nearly went to meditation groups plenty of times. I never did. Part of what was in the way was the sense that I would be making a choice that to my knowledge none of my friends or peers was making, and I wasn't sure what I would be saying about myself if I went. I never considered going to a church; the idea of believing in God made me laugh or snort. I had studied neuroscience, and the curriculum did not include God. How could He have any bearing on my consciousness?

I was working among other scientists, and there wasn't any hint of religion anywhere, at least among my British peers. I remember on the 7th July 2005, the day of the terrorist bombings in London, and being in the office when none of us really knew what was happening, how bad it was, or what we should do. The managing director had gathered us together to tell us what they knew, and to tell us we should leave and go home. Someone, not a British person, asked if they could say a prayer. The managing director paused for a telling beat before saying yes, knowing that for most people in the room, a prayer was the last thing on their minds. That evening, everyone I know went to the pub, and drank together in secular sacrament.

It was in my early 30s that I first stepped through the doors of a church by choice not as a tourist, but as a tentative congregant. I knew that something was missing in my life, and knew it couldn't be religion, but somehow wished that it could. I discovered that the Unitarian church ten minutes from my flat had a minister who was a scientist by background, and was also an atheist. I knew that the framework of his thinking would be compatible with mine, although I found it hard to trust that there wouldn't be some sort of trick, that there would be some God or Christianity in the service as a final reveal. But although we sat in pews, sang hymns and listened to a sermon, and candles were lit, God was not mentioned, the Bible was not read, and there weren't any ideas that required me to make a leap of faith that I didn't have in me. As I slowly got more involved in the congregation, I talked to the minister about the things that I found difficult – the word 'church', and the ideas it brought with it, the idea of 'membership' of the congregation, and the design and imagery used to promote the church. Mostly, I found it all terribly awkward and embarrassing – totally at odds with anything, I was choosing to turn my attention to in my young professional lifestyle in an exciting metropolis.

But once I'd found this new door in my life that led to a spiritual life, all sorts of things began to change for me. It prompted me to learn more about

Buddhism, which benefited me enormously – the closest to an instruction manual for having a human mind that I've found. It also led me to meet other people who were on similar paths of exploration, and these new spiritual friends became an incredibly important part of my life, and my uncovering of what living a good life might look like. I also grew to see how societally important this experience of meaningful community was. I was working in health system improvement at the time, and it seemed so glaringly obvious that the nation's health would be so much better if more people had a community like mine in which to belong and thrive.

* * *

This telling of my personal story is in part because I am in a minority in the group of contributors to this book in that I am not an academic, and I am not clergy. I am writing from my practical experience of serving the spiritual spaces outside of religion – often places that do not conform to the institutional structures of academia and church.

* * *

In 2013, a year or so after I'd started attending the Unitarian church, a gathering called Sunday Assembly started half a mile down the road in a deconsecrated church. Two stand-up comedians, Pippa Evans and Sanderson Jones, imagined a congregation that anyone could go to, where you didn't need to be religious. The congregation sang pop songs, backed by a live band formed by volunteers. There was a secular sermon about living well, or on a topic of awe and wonder, often from a marine biologist or astrophysicist. There was poetry, and a member of the community gave their testimony, telling a story of overcoming personal adversity. Two hundred people went to the first meeting, and three hundred went to the second. At its peak, the central London Sunday Assembly filled Conway Hall to its four-hundred-person capacity, and people were turned away at the door – and meanwhile 80 other Sunday Assembly chapters had opened up all around the world. They tapped into an unmet need. All the chapters had the shared values of 'Live Better, Help Often, Wonder More', and a set of principles around inclusivity, particularly that all beliefs were welcome. Although it was often known as 'the atheist church', it was important to its founders that it was welcoming to everyone, including religious people.

I met Sanderson Jones in 2015, not long after the courage given to me by my congregation led me to leap out of a job that had stopped being the right shape for me. He and I giddily compared notes on our experiences of non-religious congregation, and quickly realised that we would work together. In early 2016, I became chief operating officer for Sunday Assembly's

118 Religion and Atheism in Dialogue

global network of secular congregations. Our work supported the congregations around the world while developing a financial model that could sustain the infrastructure that had been put together in a whirlwind of growth and excitement. We met with leaders of housing associations and with public health directors, senior council executives, and with the Cabinet Office to seek funding and support. We made for an interesting meeting – the loud stand-up comedian who looked a bit like a bespectacled Jesus, and the quiet, sensible health system manager coming to talk about an atheist church – but the novelty factor alone wouldn't have been enough to get us in the room. These senior leaders knew that investing in communities of meaning and purpose made sense. They knew that the people they were trying to help lived atomised lives, and that the epidemics of loneliness and mental illness were connected to the lack of community and meaningful connection.

Meanwhile, the Sunday Assembly chapters came up against the limitations of being part of a spiritual community that didn't have much money, infrastructure, or theological underpinning. Conflicts arose around strategy, chapter autonomy, and the movement's priorities. There were the usual challenges with any start up around money, clarity of direction, and speed of progress. On top of that, everyone we worked with – volunteers and staff – were connected deeply to the work by the heart. Sunday Assembly meant so much to people. Some were there having grown up in a faith tradition but now no longer believing in God. But the majority had little experience of faith community in their background.

I noticed a strong difference between British and American chapters. In Britain, there was a background tone of being a little tongue in cheek, a sort of nod towards 'did you remember that church even exists?' as it was so far out of mind for most participants. In the United States, where the general culture is very much more religious, Sunday Assembly offered a place of belonging for atheists who were holding a lot of hurt or a sense of persecution about their lack of beliefs. Many leaders in Sunday Assembly in the United States had dropped out of seminary after losing their faith. When chapters from all over the world met for the annual international conference, someone from the Nashville chapter had written a 'hymn' about their pride in being an atheist. I remember it feeling a little bit like the moment when someone asked to pray in the office after the 7/7 bombs – a realisation that we were not all on the same page.

In the United Kingdom, given my experience as a white British older millennial moving in broadly middle class circles, it is generally assumed that people you meet are atheists; if people get married in church, it's because they wanted a nice building. If someone says they go to a meditation group, it is likely to be met with acceptance, whereas if someone says they go to church, there will be a faint sense of unease. As for the minister of my Unitarian congregation, he found his way there only after he became a father and people kept asking where they went to church. The Unitarian Universalist church offered the possibility of welcome to an atheist.

Another American in my home congregation observed that British people like to be a bit subversive, and don't like being too earnest. This is a fine line to tread – taking spiritual work seriously but not taking ourselves seriously. That Sunday Assembly was led by two comedians made it somehow non-threatening, but they were leaders who were really rooted firmly in the goodness and depth of spiritual community, and so there was no chance of them laughing *at* the idea of congregation. The ideas and values at the core were serious, and the ways of gathering and being in them were full of joy and lightness. There were balloons, bunting, uplifting songs, hugs, high fives, and laughter. That created the possibility of depth without frightening people off. I remember, one Sunday, the guest speaker was Shamash Alidina, the author of *Mindfulness for Dummies*, who led the congregation in a group loving-kindness meditation. It was introduced after a lot of laughter, finding that balance of light and serious, creating the conditions where a hall of Londoners felt comfortable shutting their eyes, and conjuring an inner sense of care for each other. The group meditation culminated in each person reaching out and touching another member of the community, so the three hundred or four hundred participants were all physically connected as well as being in the same attitude of loving kindness. It created a collective spiritual experience in a deeper, more direct way than the spoken words of an inspiring sermon can achieve. Practice and ritual like this are important in creating the conditions of personal transformation, allowing people to feel something different to the day-to-day, not just to think something different. Hearing inspiring ideas or being reminded of one's values are valuable, but in my experience, it is rare that the purely rational and intellectual conveying of ideas will shift our perspective enough to carry with us very long. Felt experience lasts. What I saw Shamash do so effectively was create a shared ritual experience that didn't require a shared religious context in order to be meaningful to participants; nobody needed to know anything about Buddhism or even that it was an adaptation of a Buddhist practice in order to benefit from taking part.

* * *

I dug deeply into spiritual exploration around that time, feeling aggrieved on getting some first tastes of wisdom that I had not been taught any of this before. It was 2016, and the political events of that year, the Brexit referendum, the first election of Donald Trump, brought a sense of urgency into the work. Among those of us exploring spirituality outside of religion, there was a recognition that there was a link between our secular, atomised cultures and the disenchantment many people held with the mainstream political systems.

120 Religion and Atheism in Dialogue

The need for more community felt clear, as did the need to find wisdom that the individualistic consumerist culture didn't seem to offer. This urgency grew with each new revelation about the climate crisis. The 2018 IPCC report announced we had twelve years in which to avoid unrecognisable disaster. Around that time, I was working with Vanessa Zoltan, a Jewish atheist alumna of Harvard Divinity School, to develop her vision of pilgrimages that centred around using sacred reading practices with beloved novels, and walking in the landscape of their settings and authors.

We had started with Virginia Woolf's *To The Lighthouse*, meeting a group of a dozen pilgrims on the steps of St Paul's Cathedral, leading them through Bloomsbury, then travelling to the South Downs, staying in a house across the lane from where Virginia Woolf's sister, Vanessa Bell, had lived, hosting the Sussex home of the Bloomsbury Group. Each day we used an adapted, secular, *lectio divina* practice to explore the book, and we made space for pilgrims to get to know each other and themselves. Zoltan had developed her approach first by treating *Jane Eyre* as a sacred text in the context of her divinity studies, and then during her podcast *Harry Potter and the Sacred Text*. Readers are guided to absorb a passage of text four times; first reading it at a narrative level – what's actually happening? Then, as allegory – what does it remind you of? Thirdly, the passage is read as contemplation – what does it make us think of in our own lives? And finally, the text is read through the lens of what it invites us to do or consider differently in our lives.

The pilgrims on this first trip ranged from those who loved Virginia Woolf deeply, to those who had read *To the Lighthouse* only for this trip, but were aficionados of *Harry Potter and the Sacred Text*. They were mostly women, and ranged from their 20s to their 60s, including a mother and daughter pair. Most of them would not describe themselves as people of faith, but of course signing up for a pilgrimage needs a certain amount of spiritual curiosity. After reading and reflecting each day, we walked in the South Downs, visiting sites that were important to Virginia Woolf, including her house, and we spent a couple of nights in a lighthouse. Over our few days together, deep connections were made.

In the planning of the pilgrimage, we knew we would need to address Virginia Woolf's death, her suicide by drowning, and with a group of strangers, together only for a few days, that would need care. We created a ritual by the banks of the river she died in, within a mile of her house. We had asked pilgrims to collect an object – a stone, a flower – on their way there, walking as we often did, in silence. It was a bright summer's day. As we approached the river, the pilgrims laid their objects into a central shrine, and then knew without instruction to stand in a circle around it. We said some words, which felt like a prayer, and we stood in silence. None of us had known Virginia Woolf personally, of course, but we all had stories to hold silently about the mental health struggles of people in our own lives – or ourselves. The ritual by the river spoke to all of those, and the space we created – a collective witnessing, with intention and beauty – allowed something important to happen. We closed the ritual with some words from Woolf's diary in 1924, when she had been reflecting on the anniversary of her mother's death – 'But enough of death; it's life that matters' – and continued our walk to Monk's House, where Virginia and her husband Leonard had lived, and its spectacularly abundant midsummer garden.

Later that year, we led a *Little Women* pilgrimage in Concord, Massachusetts, home of the author Louisa May Alcott, and the wider Transcendentalist community such as Henry David Thoreau and Ralph Waldo Emerson. Flying across the Atlantic having freshly read that IPCC report, knowing that pilgrims were flying from all over the United States, I wondered about the jet fuel our work relied on. So I designed our ritual dinner around the idea of loving nature, hoping to create inspiration for actions that could go some way to offset the carbon. As the pilgrims walked around Walden Pond, where the leaves were just starting to turn to their autumn colours, and we passed the site of Thoreau's hut, we invited them to bring back leaves and pinecones that we then arranged on our dining tables. Noting the exacting detail with which Thoreau's diary entries in *Walden* described those woods, over the first course of our dinner, we invited the pilgrims to talk with that level of precise detail about places that they loved. Over the main course, we reflected on the season, sharing some autumnal passages from *Little Women* and *Walden*, and talking with each other about what was ripe and ready to harvest in our own lives, and what was ending and ready to fall. Finally, with dessert, we reflected on a passage from Emerson's essay *Self Reliance*, tuning in to the genius and power of our own ideas. (We used versions of those 19th-century men's writings with the pronouns reversed, and reading them in the feminine seemed to unleash new energy.) As with the ritual by the river in the South Downs that summer, there was space for things in the pilgrims' lives to shift; the collective witnessing of each other's lives allowed for change. And although the ritual was underpinned with the sense of agency needed to prevent total climate breakdown, the space we designed spoke first to the personal in people's lives.

We went on to develop *Jane Eyre* and *Pride and Prejudice* pilgrimages, and they are going strong, covering novels from *Harry Potter* to *Frankenstein*, poets like Emily Dickinson, and even the lyrics of Taylor Swift. Each time, there will be pilgrims who have a transformational experience; they go home and quit their job, or choose to start a family, or commit to their creative practice. And deep relationships will be made – friendships of people who came together around the book they loved, in a new landscape, with just enough structure and practice to allow them to step outside of their day-to-day habits, and into something transformational. I have seen time and again the power of ritual in a secular setting. People seem to step towards it with only a gentle nudge, and even a simple structure can let the usual protective outer layer of cynicism be dropped in relief.

These experiences took place before the COVID pandemic, a collective experience that has created even more openness to ritual and spiritual community. Not just the collective acts such as clapping and cheering from front doors and balconies for the NHS workers but in the self-reflection that it forced all of us to do, against the backdrop of continued fraying of political norms, increasing division, and worsening climate breakdown – the polycrisis. Those in the West lucky enough to have enjoyed a lifetime of stability are feeling that the ground underfoot is no longer steady. Noticing the limits of the status quo opens more minds to spirituality. For some, that might look like joining the church or faith group of their family. For many more, it's looking beyond traditional religion to find meaning, purpose, and belonging.

In my early experiences of spiritual community, with the Unitarians, or working at Sunday Assembly, I felt the goal of helping people cope with the trials and tribulations of everyday life, and maybe even helping to make the world a little better. A decade of political and environmental upheaval later, that's no longer what feels most alive. Yes, we must meet people where they are in this secular, unhealthily individualised, consumerist culture, but we cannot leave them there. By inviting them into ritual in secular settings, we offer a glimpse of a different sort of world, one that's shaped to help all life flourish. Like the group loving-kindness meditation at Sunday Assembly that left four hundred people connected with a shared experience of compassion, ritual and spiritual practice can conjure the feelings in people that can lead them to act towards creating a world that is more loving.

Much in our mainstream culture creates feelings of lack, or anxiety, which can lead to individualistic actions, harmful to people and planet (even if we are far removed from the damage we cause). Ritual can help remind us of our values, and spiritual practice can create a sense of balance, away from anxious thinking, and into a sense of unity with humanity and nature. When we are in balance, connected with our care for the world, and having a sense of our own power, we naturally make decisions that benefit others, not just ourselves and people like us.

There is much to learn from traditional religion and its carefully stewarded wisdom and practices. And I can see there may be value in surrendering into a vast tradition carried by countless generations. But so many of those centuries of tradition are bound up in unhealthy power structures that cause systemic harm to life. Ritual and community can be vehicles to invite people to experience a taste of something different, and carry the inspiration to make a better world.

15

SCIENCE, HUMANISM, AND RELIGION

Raymond Tallis

There is a narrative in what we might call 'folk historiography' according to which religion and science are direct adversaries and that the truth or otherwise of what science has to say about the universe is one of the hinge issues that divides religious believers and secular humanists.

Did we not, after all, learn at school that Galileo, a key figure in the emergence of science in the early modern period, displeased the religious authorities by embracing the Copernican revolution that displaced the Earth from the centre of the universe? Was he not rewarded with persecution, threatened with physical maltreatment if he did not disavow heliocentrism, and kept under house arrest for the final years of his life? The claim that he muttered '*Eppur si muove*' after he had publicly abjured his claim that the earth moved round the sun has added to the resonance of the tale. What is more, it took until 1992 before the Catholic Church issued an apology for the way it had treated Galileo.

Equally iconic is the story of the debate in the Oxford University Museum a few months after the publication of *The Origin of Species*. It is particularly remembered for the exchange between religion, represented by Bishop Samuel Wilberforce, and science, represented by Thomas Huxley, 'Darwin's Bulldog'. Wilberforce, so the story goes, asked Huxley whether it was through his grandfather or his grandmother that he claimed descent from a monkey. Huxley's reply echoes down the ages: though he would not have been ashamed to have a monkey as an ancestor, he would have been ashamed to be connected with a man who used his intellect to hide the truth.

The accounts of these legendary clashes between science and the church have been questioned. Pope Urban's harsh treatment of Galileo may have been influenced by an uneasy sense that he had been lampooned in Galileo's

DOI: 10.4324/9781003536185-17

124 Religion and Atheism in Dialogue

Dialogue Concerning the Two Chief World Systems, and by political manoeuvring in the Vatican. And there is no first-hand verbatim account of the Huxley-Wilberforce exchange.[1] What is not in doubt, however, is the influence these stories have had in reinforcing the notion that science and religion have been historically, and indeed are of necessity, at odds because science has been at the forefront of an Enlightenment that has liberated humanity from the 'Endarkenment' of religion.

This account of a head-on collision between religion and science has been decisively challenged by Nick Spencer who also reminds us of the profound religious convictions of perhaps the greatest scientists of the last 500 years.[2] Isaac Newton's religious beliefs were at least as important to him as his science or 'natural philosophy'.[3] Michael Faraday, a Sandemanian Christian, saw his scientific work as a natural expression of his religious values: "he understood the physical universe as a divinely ordained natural economy...his science was directed to ascertaining the way God had created the universe".[4] As for James Clerk Maxwell, "His Christian faith gave him a vital framework for his research. He believed that because the universe had been created by God and that human beings had been made in God's image, it was perfectly reasonable that we could – and should – try to understand the universe".[5]

This may seem a surprising, even odd, place for a humanist such as myself to situate a discussion about religion and science. I do so in the dialogic spirit of this volume: to set aside the conventional, narrowly adversarial, and indeed superficial, account of the relationship between religion and science, in which religious belief and its institutions amount to a collective cognitive darkness from which scientific enlightenment, embraced by humanists, has awoken. Which is not to downplay the legitimate reasons many secular humanists have for regretting the influence of organised religions on the societies over which they have exercised power.

This regret remains valid irrespective of whether the net impact of religion on human history has been for good or ill. It is, after all, not possible to determine the contribution of religion to the making or amelioration of human suffering. We cannot run history twice – with or without religion. Besides, it makes little or no sense to pass a single, summarising judgement on numerous, profoundly different religions and sects.[6] They have competing visions of the world unpacked into profoundly different doctrines and moral codes; they mobilise vast and varied casts of deities, prophets, and spirits; and they have in some cases radically changed over the centuries.

That is anyway a story for another occasion.[7] The focus of the present chapter is on something that religious believers and secular humanists share – or should share: a rejection of the assumption that science, more precisely natural science, is the sole or ultimate source of truth about the fundamental nature of things, including ourselves. We have, that is to say, a common interest in rejecting *scientism*.

It is important to flag up the distinction between science and scientism at the outset because there are overwhelming reasons for being grateful to science, not the least for its practical applications. The astonishing transformations in life and health expectancy that have taken place since the 19th century – accelerating over the last few decades – are due in no small part to advances in theoretical and applied science. Infant mortality, malnutrition, and accidental death have fallen precipitously since the 1950s.[8] And this is in despite of the continuing propensity of humanity towards wickedness.

In my own profession of medicine, the journey from futile faith healing, and therapies based on pseudoscience, to evidence-based effective medical treatments has produced extraordinary advances not only making life longer but also less uncomfortable. And, beyond its direct application, the example of science and its methods in extending our empirical knowledge of how the natural world and our bodies work has influenced the way we conceive of, develop, and evaluate evidence-based approaches to social problems that have (for the most part) been beneficial.

Enough already. The point is, I hope, made that what follows is not an attack on science. The position I wish to put forward in this chapter is that religious believers and secular humanists have a common interest in resisting a scientism that elevates science to the status of the last word on what there is, what is reality, and (most importantly) what we human beings are.

Scientism has been a longstanding adversary of mine. My initial target was the appeal to biology to 'explain' our human nature. Biologism had two particularly striking manifestations which I baptised 'Neuromania' and 'Darwinitis'.[9] Neuromania identifies the mind and all its manifestations with neural activity. Its advocates envisage a future in which brain science will transform the humanities – hence, neuro-literary criticism, neuro-ethics, neuro-law, neuro-theology that identifies the 'God spot' in the brain, and so on. Darwinitis is a pathological variant of (entirely respectable, endlessly validated) Darwinism. It claims that evolutionary theory not only accounts for the origin and function of the organism *Homo sapiens* (which it seems to do) but also explains the lives, behaviour, aims, and ends of individual human persons and the societies to which they belong (which it most certainly does not).

There are many reasons for resisting biologism. The most obvious is that Neuromania has not been able to address, never mind solve, the fundamental problem of explaining how neural activity is somehow identical with, or causally generates, consciousness, in particular the phenomenal (in both senses of the word) consciousness of the human subject. The mental gymnastics of those who cannot let go of the idea that the mind – and the human person – are to be found in the brain are a wonder to behold.[10] What is more, Neuromania overlooks the distinctive nature of even the most ordinary human activity and, as a result, feels obliged to deny the possibility of genuine

126 Religion and Atheism in Dialogue

agency.[11] This is no place to defend free will – though it is central to the sense that our lives have meaning – but it is possible to do so if one does not uncritically accept scientism.[12]

Scientism goes beyond biologism. Another important source is the worship of physics and the elevation of fundamental physics to metaphysics. This is reflected in what we might call the 'science-cringe' of certain philosophers. Consider, for example, this passage from James Ladyman and Donald Ross:

> Any new metaphysical claim that is to be taken seriously should be motivated by, and only by, the service it would perform, if true, in showing how two or more specific scientific hypotheses jointly explain more than the sum of what is explained by the two hypotheses taken separately, where a 'scientific hypothesis' is understood as an hypothesis that is taken seriously by institutionally *bona fide* current science.[13]

Philosophy that does not take its orders from physics is dismissed as 'Neo-Scholasticism'. The philosopher's role is at best that of a Lockean humble under-gardener clearing away the litter from the path to truth – litter often dropped by other philosophers. Physicist Carlo Rovelli has allowed that philosophy may have something to say but he believes that "we need to adapt our philosophy to our science and not our science to our philosophy".[14]

Given the extraordinary predictive and explanatory power of physics, and its countless applications in the technology that has transformed our lives, deference to science might seem to have something going for it. What is more, conventional metaphysics, that does not seem to have progressed from unchanged questions to universally accepted answers in 2,500 years, hardly seems to be able to compete with contemporary science that has delivered so many answers to so many questions, some of which have been posed only recently.[15] The story is not, however, so straightforward.

Most obviously, there are unresolved conflicts as to the interpretation of what is observed at the cutting edge of science. (Understatement of the century.) As Richard Feynman, a leading 20th-century theorist, pointed out, quantum theory is unintelligible: anyone who thinks they understand it clearly doesn't understand it.[16] And there may be reasonable grounds to suspect that a science is in some sort of trouble if it has to invoke virtual particles bubbling in and out of a vacuum, fundamental entities that wobble between being particles, waves, and wave packets that deals in *negative* probabilities (I kid you not), invokes 'renormalisation' to head off impossible infinities, and permits fundamentally incompatible views about what happens when measurement 'decoheres' ranges of possible values of a parameter to a definite value.

As if the internal problems of quantum theory were not bad enough, there is the problem of its incompatibility with the other major theory in fundamental physics: general relativity. As for the latter, it is having to invoke dark energy and dark matter – mysterious stuffs of uncertain nature – to fiddle the books to account for certain observations on the macroscopic scale.

Nevertheless, presented with the practical and predictive success of quantum mechanics and general relativity, some might be tempted to say, "I could wish for such troubles". A theory that is responsible for technologies that by 2000 accounted for 30% of the GDP of the United States[17] and which have transformed every aspect of our lives must have got something – and something very big – right.

Any critique of the kind of scientism expressed in elevating physics to the status of metaphysics does not need to defend itself against the theoretical and applied success of theoretical physics. The case against scientism can be made by looking at the basic, ubiquitous features of science. It is to be found in the very life-blood – and rather bloodless lifeblood it is – of science: measurement.

If scientism has a founding doctrine, it is captured in this famous *profession de foi* of the great 19th-century scientist, William Thompson, a.k.a. Lord Kelvin:

> [W]hen you can measure what you are speaking about, you know something about it; but when you cannot measure it, when you cannot express it in numbers, your knowledge is of a meagre and unsatisfactory kind; it may be the beginning of knowledge, but you have scarcely, in your thoughts, advanced to the stage of science.[18]

Measurement is so familiar that it is difficult to see it for the distinctive, not to say strange, mode of perception that it is. It has two essential features: it is quantitative – resulting in numbers – and it is objective in the sense of marginalising the subject making the measurement. Because it is objective, it seems to be on the side of the object, or closer to the object in itself. It seems to correspond to a relatively unpeeled gaze. But is that really the case?

Consider a homely example: measuring the width of a table. The outcome of the encounter with the table is a peculiar kind of not-quite-experience: a *result* that refers to a parameter, which could not stand alone, extracted from the table. The result has two aspects: a number and a unit, for example, 'two metres' wide. I shall address numbers first and deal with units presently.

What is striking about the number is that it tells us nothing about the *qualities* of the table. We do not know whether the table is black or brown, shiny or dull, spanking new or old, beautiful or ugly. We have no idea what it looks or feels like, where it is, and how it relates to other things in the world. This is not a defect if all I want to learn from the measurement is (for example) whether the table can be carried through a door, also reduced to a quantity. The measurement has extracted one aspect of the size of the table.

The record of the size – still called an 'observation' though there is no longer an observer once it is written down and stored – can be transported to other places remote from the actual table and it will outlast the moment when the measurement was made.

Let us now look at the second aspect of the measurement: the unit. The width of the table is not translated into a naked number. It is a number of *units*: it is not '2' but '2 metres'. Units, which are universally applicable, have nothing specific to do with the table. They are ratios. To say of an entity that it is two metres wide is to say that it is two times the abstracted size of a standard of length.

It might be objected that, while it is remote from the table as it is experienced, the record of its size seems to capture something intrinsic about it. Measurement appears to cut through phenomenal appearances, that are in part dependent on the properties of the observer, to the table itself. Hence the tendency to think of measurement being 'objective' or on the side of the object. You and I may disagree about whether the table is 'big' or 'not very big' but we cannot legitimately disagree as to whether or not it is two metres wide. In such cases of disagreement, one of us is right and one of us is wrong.

So much for a homely measurement such as determining the width of a table. This is only the first step in humanity's cognitive pilgrimage to a purely quantitative, subject-free portrait of the world. Fundamental units become ever more distant and abstract. While this is not evident when we apply a tape measure to a table, metres are ultimately defined as the distance travelled by light in a specific fraction of a second. This is several orders of remoteness and sophistication away from the ordinary experience of objects as they are encountered in daily life. Measurement abstracts one aspect of an entity drained of all of its qualitative aspects and transforms it into a number by expressing it as units – the ratio of the abstracted extension to an absent, generalised, standardised entity or event.

I have focussed on individual observations but in its pursuit of general truths, science typically makes numerous measurements on samples of objects or events. These in turn stand for entire populations of such objects or events. Samples may be averaged or graphed. Observations, what is more, are increasingly mediated by ever more precise, sophisticated and complex instruments whose reliability is subject to quality control. They are themselves the progeny of other measurements. The parameters, variables, or features that are extracted from the measurement target are not naturally stand-alone. A gas does not have just a pressure or a volume or a temperature. It inevitably has all three, not to speak of other properties that are often treated as noise to be controlled lest the relationships between controlled and uncontrolled variables are obscured.

The most important product of the extraction and processing of a multitude of observations is the equation. It is worth pausing for a moment on the most famous of all equations, as it gives us a measure of the distance between the world in which we live and have our being and the scientific portrait of the fundamental material of that world: $E = mc^2$. In this equation, reality is simplified to energy (E) and mass (m). In accordance with the most fundamental scientific presumption of the underlying uniformity of nature, it is homogenised: even the differences between the kinds of energy – already reduced to a small handful – are lost in quantification. Likewise, the boundless variety of material objects is gathered up into the single kind of quantifiable stuff – mass – typically defined by resistance to acceleration. Further homogenisation results from seeing mass and energy as equivalent and consequently interchangeable. Light is present as that which determines their exchange rate, though its presence is in the form of its (not terribly luminous) velocity multiplied by itself.

Thus, we have one terminus of an approach in which the world is reduced to quantities. It does not provide any basis for the distinction between the reality in which we live and the billions of miles of a largely empty universe void of any sentient creatures. The entirely objective 'view from nowhere' sought in science looks perilously close to delivering a view of nothing in particular or, indeed, a view of nothing.

The success of the reduction of what-is to measurable quantities has led some physicists to embrace mathematical idealism – an industrial-strength Pythagoreanism according to which everything boils down to mathematics.[19] We may see this as the endpoint of a journey which began when Galileo famously asserted that:

> [Nature] is written in the language of mathematics and its characters are the triangle, the circle and other geometrical figures without which it is humanly impossible to understand a single word of it.[20]

It is interesting that Galileo chose geometry for the language of the book of nature. Many mathematical idealists do not specify the relevant branch of mathematics and, given that mathematics is a 'colourful medley' of disciplines[21] and given the failure of the endeavour to unify mathematics in set theory, this is a decisive objection to this claim.

But there are more serious objections. The most important becomes evident when we reflect on the nature of the quantitative, objective approach to the natural and human world and its reduction of the reality in which we live to numbers or structures created out of numbers. It is made possible only by progressively excluding the very thing that made science possible: the conscious subject or the community of conscious subjects who experience and observe the world, and make, or endeavour to make, scientific sense of it. The progressive reduction of the world as an object of measurement, to the kinds of relationships between numbers seen in equations, depends on marginalising, indeed deleting, the measurer or community of measurers. Notwithstanding the problematic role of the observer in the quantum collapse that reduces a range of possibilities to a single, definite value, fundamental physics overlooks that which makes physics possible: the physicist.

We can of course admire its extraordinary achievements and the benefits physics has conferred on humankind, without succumbing to an uncritical scientism. We need to remind ourselves that "Not everything that counts can be counted and not everything that can be counted counts".[22] Otherwise, we arrive at the much-quoted view of Nobel prize-winning physicist Steven Weinberg that "the more the universe seems comprehensible, the more it also seems pointless".[23] This is an entirely unsurprising conclusion if making the universe 'comprehensible' consists of reducing it to a mathematical portrait and consequently pushing meaning to one side – and if, as Weinberg claims,

> The explanatory arrow points downwards from societies to people, to organs, to cells, to biochemistry, and ultimately to physics. Societies are explained by people, people by organs, organs by cells, cells by biochemistry, biochemistry by chemistry, and chemistry by physics.[24]

Given the present situation of physics, the explanatory arrow seems to be pointing into the void.

What conclusion may we draw? Cringing before the cognitive tyranny of the quantitative approach to the world in which we live empties that world of meaning. Notwithstanding that we are the beneficiaries of the practical applications of science, secular humanists and religious believers have a common interest in rejecting a world picture built on the reduction of what is before us to mathematical abstractions. And, more broadly, in rejecting scientism which, as Tzvetan Todorov expressed it, "is not science but a worldview that grew fungus-like on the trunk of science".[25]

Unfortunately, that is probably where the consensus ends, and we part company. The possibility spaces opened up when we cut measurement down to size and identify the intrinsic limitations of natural sciences do not add up to accommodation for God or gods creating and shaping the universe and intervening in our lives, for an afterlife, or for other aspects of the apparatus of religion.

Nevertheless, secular humanists and religious believers have a common interest in rejecting scientism and the currently popular notion that science, and in particular physics, is the ultimate guide to metaphysics. The mysteries in which our existence is immersed, the question of our fundamental nature and of how we should live our lives, are not clarified by what fundamental science (that marginalises our humanity and the qualitative world in which we live our value-driven lives) has to tell us about the material world. Humanists looking to science to fill the spaces vacated by departure of religious belief will be disappointed.

Notes

1 J.R. Lucas, 'Wilberforce and Huxley: A Legendary Encounter', *The Historical Journal* 22; 2(1979):313–30.
2 Nick Spencer *Magisteria, The Entangled Histories of Science and Religion* (London: Oneworld Books, 2023).
3 Robert Iliffe, *The Priest of Nature. The Religious Worlds of Isaac Newton* (Oxford: Oxford University Press, 2018).
4 Geoffrey Cantor, 'Michael Faraday's Religion and Its Relation to His Science', *Endeavour* 22; 3(1998):121–4.
5 J. John, 'James Clerk Maxwell: The Physicist Who Had Deep Christian Faith', *Christian Today*, 9th July 2022.
6 According to one estimate, there are "roughly 4,200 religions, churches, denominations, religious bodies, faith groups, tribes, cultures, movements, or ultimate concerns". *World Religions. Religion Statistics.*
7 It is discussed at some length in Raymond Tallis, *Seeing Ourselves: Reclaiming Humanity from God and Science* (Newcastle: Agenda, 2020), especially pp. 3–29, 'Humanism and anti-humanism' and pp. 255–317, 'Flourishing without God'.
8 The statistics set out in Hans Rosling, *Factfulness: Ten Reasons We Are Wrong about World – And Why Things are Better than You Think* (London: Sceptre, 2019) are astonishing.
9 Discussed in Raymond Tallis, *Aping Mankind: Neuromania, Darwinitis and the Misrepresentation of Humanity* (Durham: Acumen, 2011, 2012).
10 Surveyed in Robert Lawrence Kuhn's masterly 'A landscape of consciousness. Towards a taxonomy of explanations and implications'. *Progress in Biophysics and Molecular Biology* 190; (2024): 28–169.
11 Robert Sapolsky, *Determined: Life Without Free Will* (London: Penguin, 2023) is the best account of biology-based determinism.
12 For a defence of free will, see Raymond Tallis, *Freedom: An Impossible Reality* (Newcastle: Agenda, 2021).
13 James Ladyman and Donald Ross, *Everything Must Go: Metaphysics Naturalized* (Oxford: Oxford University Press, 2007), p. 30.
14 Carlo Rovelli, *Helgoland: The Strange and Beautiful Story of Quantum Mechanics*, translated by Erica Segre and Simon Carnell (London: Penguin, 2021), p. 118.
15 This is, of course, a simplification. For a less naïve treatment of the question as to whether philosophy makes progress, see Raymond Tallis, 'The 'P' Word'. *Philosophy Now* April/May 2016, pp. 52–3.
16 He also (in)famously said "I think I can safely say that nobody really understands quantum mechanics". Richard Feynman, *The Character of Physical Laws* (London: BBC Publications, 1965), p. 129.
17 Max Tegmark and John Archibald Wheeler, '100 years of the quantum', 2001, arXiv:quant:ph/0101077v1.
18 William Thomson, 1889, 'Electrical Units of Measurement', *Popular Lectures and Addresses* (Volume 1) (London: Macmillan, pp. 73–136).
19 For a discussion of this idea, see 'Mathematics and the Book of Nature' in Raymond Tallis, *Of Time and Lamentation. Reflection on Transience'* (Newcastle: Agenda, 2017; 2019), pp. 99–213.
20 Galileo G., *The Assayer* in *Discoveries and Opinions of Galileo*, edited by Stilman Drake (trans.) (Garden City, NY: Doubleday, 1957), pp. 237–8.
21 Ludwig Wittgenstein, quoted in Karl Sigmund, *The Waltz of Reason: The Entanglement of Mathematics and Philosophy* (New York: Basic Books, 2023).
22 Often attributed to Einstein but it is due to William Bruce Cameron, *Informal Sociology. A Casual Introduction to Sociological Thinking* (New York: Random House, 1967). I owe this attribution to *Quote Investigator.*

132 Religion and Atheism in Dialogue

23 Steven Weinberg, *The First Three Minutes. A Modern View of the Origin of the Universe* (New York: Basic Books, 1977), p. 149.
24 Steven Weinberg quoted in Stuart Kauffman, 'Breaking the Galilean Spell' *Edge*. Excerpted from *Reinventing the Sacred. A New View of Science, Reason, and Religion* (New York: Basic Books, 2008). As Andrew Steane says in 'Physics, humanism, and openness' – page 151 of the present volume – 'the explanatory arrows are two-way'. Even if atomic theory explained society, we would still have to appeal to society to account for the fact that there is atomic theory.
25 Tzvetan Todorov, *Hope and Memory,* trans. David Bellos (London: Atlantic Books, 2004), p. 21.

16

MAKE UP A STORY

Joanna Kavenna

The editors of this volume seek to foster dialogue between those with differing views. In our febrile age of tribalism, seething binaries, algorithmic storms, this seems like a very good idea. A while back, I offered to write on 'the potential of the arts to convey ideas and insights which are common ground.' Now it's December and I'm quarrelling with my past self, an odd thing to find yourself doing when the sky is such a lovely shade of blue and it's briefly stopped raining. Can the arts really claim to offer lustrous ideas and insights? What about my discipline: the shabby old novel, which is always on the verge of obsolescence?[1] Besides, writers can be ferociously partisan: there are manifestos, hostile cliques, wild furies. Equally, representatives of other disciplines may be far more conciliatory and ecumenical than plaintive novelists. Nonetheless, I focus on literature because it's the discipline I love and work within. The writers I consider in this essay are opposed to fixed categories, adamantine certainties, 'shrieking voices' (as T. S. Eliot calls them).[2] Instead, as Toni Morrison writes, they perceive that reality is 'formlessness.' By writing, speaking, allocating concepts, we draw this formlessness into forms. The trouble arises when we mistake metaphorical forms for the formlessness, the map for the territory (to use another metaphor). I draw on these ideas about forms and formlessness throughout my essay.[3]

In terms of form and formlessness: as Morrison knows, any attempt to debate language within language is fraught with paradox. Words change their emphases and meanings over time; they are steeped in mystery and we can't even get back to the foundational language or languages beneath those we speak and write today. Language is both extrinsic – it comes from beyond each one of us, from long-gone ages, from the world around – and also intrinsic – we speak and think to ourselves in words. Consciousness co-evolves

DOI: 10.4324/9781003536185-18

134 Religion and Atheism in Dialogue

with language and each one of us is inducted into language without our prior consent. We cannot return to a pre-linguistic Ur-self. Language is also rife with judgements, value-laden terms, notions of good and bad. As Virginia Woolf explains, there is no absolute agreement on the meaning of such terms: '"this great book", "this worthless book", the same book is called by both names.'[4] As soon as you start writing a novel, you embark on a discussion about values. Who is a good character, who is a bad one? What are the values of the reality you have invented? This applies beyond novels, of course. We find examples of what Eve Sedgwick calls 'good dog/bad dog rhetoric' all over the place, with accompanying further arguments about whether these values are societal and mutable, or whether they are bolstered by eternal referents.[5] In *Thus Spake Zarathustra* (1883–1885), Nietzsche famously argues that 'everlasting good and evil do not exist!'[6] In *A Pluralist Universe* (1909), William James outlines a then-contemporary form of adamantine dualism:

> [T]he absolutists smashing the world of sense [...] the empiricists smashing the absolute—for the absolute, they say, is the quintessence of all logical contradictions. Neither side attains consistency.

For James, anti-absolutism has become as absolutist as absolutism. He diagnoses the problem as one of 'conceptual decomposition,' a taxonomical discrepancy between 'the essence of life in its continuously changing character' and our concepts which 'are all discontinuous and fixed':

> You can no more dip up the substance of reality with them than you can dip up water with a net, however finely meshed. [...] When you have broken the reality into concepts you never can reconstruct it in its wholeness.

James's metaphor of dipping up water with a net is a powerful one. We must use forms and concepts, he writes; there is nothing else to be done. The trouble arises, he adds, when we mistake such forms and concepts for the 'substance of reality,' forgetting that '[n]o philosophy can ever be anything but a summary sketch, a picture of the world in abridgement, a foreshortened bird's-eye view of the perspective of events.'[7]

Passing bells, bees, fragments, anarchy

World War I was fought with an array of new technologies: machine guns firing hundreds of rounds per minute, heavy artillery, motorised tanks, aeroplanes including aerial reconnaissance cameras, field radios and telephones. Some writers were thrilled by this and wrote worshipful paeans to mechanisation. The Vorticists, including the artists Wyndham Lewis and Henri

Gaudier-Brzeska, published their 'Manifesto' in June 1914: 'So much vast machinery to produce...BLESS these MACHINES.'[8] They despised antiquity, the past, the Edwardians and nature. Gaudier-Brzeska went to fight in France, writing back to the Vorticists in an article published in their magazine BLAST in June 1915. In this, Gaudier-Brzeska described the war as a 'great remedy': 'in the individual it kills arrogance, self-esteem, pride. It takes away from the masses numbers upon numbers of unimportant units...'[9] In the technophilic mode, humans are 'units' in a vast mechanised system.

Other soldiers adhered to a more venerable, romantic-chivalric tradition. Rupert Brooke's 1914 sonnet 'The Soldier' opens with the famous lines: 'If I should die, think only this of me/That there's some corner of a foreign field/That is for ever England.'[10] In 1915, Brooke heard he was being posted to the Dardanelles (formerly known as the Hellespont). He wrote a rapturous letter home to Violet Asquith, daughter of the then-Prime Minister Henry Asquith: 'Oh Violet it's too wonderful for belief... I'm filled with confident and glorious hopes ... Will Hero's tower crumble under the 15 in. guns?'[11] Brooke is alluding to the myth of Leander. The story had earlier inspired Byron – a literary hero of Brooke's – to swim the Hellespont. In April 1915, Brooke died on a hospital ship moored off the Greek island of Skyros, at the age of 27. Gaudier-Brzeska was killed by machine-gun fire in June 1915, at the age of 23. The Vorticist worship of machines, the Romantic worship of experience: both were smashed to pieces by the war.

In his 'Anthem for Doomed Youth,' written in September 2017, the English poet Wilfred Owen marks a drastic shift in tone:

What passing-bells for these who die as cattle?
— Only the monstrous anger of the guns.
Only the stuttering rifles' rapid rattle
Can patter out their hasty orisons.
No mockeries now for them; no prayers nor bells,
Nor any voice of mourning save the choirs,—
The shrill, demented choirs of wailing shells;
And bugles calling for them from sad shires.[12]

Owen brilliantly evokes the chaos of mechanised slaughter: the 'stuttering rifles' rapid rattle,' soldiers dying not as heroes but as 'cattle,' the 'shrill, demented choirs of wailing shells.' Owen was killed in the fighting in France on 4 November 1918, at the age of 25. The Armistice was signed just under a week later, on November 11, 1918 at 5 am in Compiègne, France.

Between 15 and 22 million people were killed during the war. Roughly 50 million died in an ensuing global influenza pandemic. In 'The Second Coming' (1919), Yeats writes: 'Things fall apart; the centre cannot hold/mere anarchy is loosed upon the world.' Amidst such carnage, he adds: 'The best

136 Religion and Atheism in Dialogue

lack all conviction, while the worst/Are full of passionate intensity.' At first glance, these lines seem counterintuitive. What's so terrible about passionate intensity? Isn't it good to be passionate about things? Why do the 'best lack all conviction'? But Yeats seems to mean that the febrile certainties of the 'worst' have embroiled the world in chaos. The 'best' are those who have dispensed with such adamantine precepts, but are weary and demoralised. It is a bleak view of society, to say the least.[13]

In 1922, D. H. Lawrence turns to this question of certainty in a teeming, eccentric essay called *Fantasia of the Unconscious*. He wants to thank Einstein for the theory of relativity, which has set everyone free:

> Now we know the universe isn't a spinning wheel. It is a cloud of bees flying and bearing around. Thank goodness for that, for we were getting drunk on the spinning wheel. And now we've escaped…we won't be pinned down. We have no one law that governs us.

Like Yeats, Lawrence calls for less, not more, conviction: 'One is one, but one is not all alone. There are other stars buzzing in the centre of their own isolation. And there is no straight path between them.' For this reason, Lawrence continues:

> [D]on't blame me if my words fly like dust into your eyes and grit between your teeth, instead of like music into your ears. I am I, but also you are you, and we are in sad need of a theory of human relativity. We need it much more than the universe does.

I love Lawrence's prose here, the way he wrangles old forms, old words, into novel and arresting combinations. There is no straight path, he explains, between the writer and the reader, the speaker and the audience. The only possible solution to these misunderstandings, the chaos of words, is a theory of 'human relativity.' Without this, he suggests, 'we are always falling foul of each other, and chewing each other's fur.' Another wild thing about Lawrence's prose here – his metaphors are all over the place. Words are dust, grit, rather than music. We are predatory lions or tigers, prowling around each other. Or, perhaps we are just small, angry cats. Instead, Lawrence suggests, we should think of ourselves as bees in a cloud: a group of discrete entities, each one of us buzzing in the centre of our own isolation.[14]

The literature of this period is fractured and fragmentary. The world is in ruins. The ostensibly teleological project of modernity now includes a mechanised war in which millions of souls have perished. In 1920, Hope Mirrlees's fragmentary epic, *Paris,* is published by the Woolfs' Hogarth Press. In this extraordinary poem, Mirrlees describes dreamlike, shattered crowds, moving across the Pont du Neuf, marked by death.[15] In 1922, perhaps influenced by Hope Mirrlees, T. S. Eliot publishes *The Wasteland*, another fragmentary epic in which – once more – dreamlike, shattered crowds process across London Bridge, with lines borrowed from Dante's *Inferno*: 'I had not thought death had undone so many.'[16] In 1929, Robert Graves publishes *Goodbye to all That*, describing his horrifying experiences as a soldier in World War I, the physical and psychological injuries he suffered, and his decision to leave England. Reminiscing about how strange England looked to soldiers returning from the front, Graves writes: 'We could not understand the war-madness that ran wild everywhere...the civilians talked a foreign language.'[17]

A raid on the inarticulate

Things have fallen apart and yet – as Yeats discerns – the 'worst' maintain their 'passionate intensity': extremists, zealots, ignoring desperate pleas for a theory of human relativity. In 1936, as German troops under Hitler reoccupy the Rhineland, among other indications that Europe is once again descending into war, T. S Eliot publishes 'Burnt Norton.' It is the first of his *Four Quartets*, and includes some oft-quoted lines about the trouble with language:

Words strain,
Crack and sometimes break, under the burden,
Under the tension, slip, slide, perish,
Decay with imprecision, will not stay in place,
Will not stay still. Shrieking voices
Scolding, mocking, or merely chattering,
Always assail them.[18]

Like Yeats, like Lawrence, Eliot discerns a tension between those who perceive this decay, this imprecision, and those 'shrieking voices' who busy themselves instead with scolding, mocking, assailing words.

A year later, in 1937, Woolf records an essay on 'Craftsmanship' for the BBC, part of a series called 'Words Fail Me.' For Woolf, 'a word is not a single and separate entity, but part of other words' and each word is 'full of echoes, of memories, of associations.' For example, the word 'incarnadine' is always – for Woolf – accompanied by a memory of 'multitudinous seas' and *Macbeth*. Words fail when they are pinned down, trapped in dictionaries, Woolf argues. Instead, words are alive and mutable, they are never fixed. They live 'on people's lips, in their houses, in the streets, in the fields [across] many centuries.' They cannot stay in place, cannot stay still.[19]

In the second of his *Four Quartets*, 'East Coker' (1940), Eliot returns to the question of words, describing each attempt at writing a poem as a 'raid

138 Religion and Atheism in Dialogue

on the inarticulate' with 'shabby equipment always deteriorating/In the general mess of imprecision of feeling.' He's wasted 20 years between the wars, he says, 'trying to learn to use words, and every attempt/Is a whole new start, and a different kind of failure.' Now it is 1940, and the world is embroiled in genocidal carnage, once again. The following year on March 28, 1941, Virginia Woolf drowns herself in the River Ouse. She leaves a note for her husband, Leonard:

> You see I can't even write this properly. I can't read. What I want to say is I owe all the happiness of my life to you. You have been entirely patient with me and incredibly good. I want to say that – everybody knows it. If anybody could have saved me it would have been you.

Woolf can't write properly, she says, can't read. Yet her final words are luminous with love and gratitude, agonisingly powerful even to strangers reading them almost a century later. Woolf thinks words have failed her; but they haven't at all.[20]

A celestial emporium

In 1942, Jorge Luis Borges writes an essay called 'The Analytical Language of John Wilkins' (or in Spanish 'El idioma analítico de John Wilkins'). Borges applies his vaulting, surrealist imagination to the real-life English 17th-century polymath John Wilkins. Among his many interests, Wilkins maintained a robust belief in the power of words to encapsulate reality, and aimed towards a universal language. In riposte, Borges invents a fictional encyclopaedia called the *Celestial Emporium of Benevolent Knowledge*. This great compendium, he writes, will catalogue every single sort of animal and must, in homage to Wilkins, be exhaustive. The categories of animals include:

> (a) those that belong to the Emperor, (b) embalmed ones, (c) those that are trained, (d) suckling pigs, (e) mermaids, (f) fabulous ones, (g) stray dogs, (h) those that are included in this classification, (i) those that tremble as if they were mad, (j) innumerable ones, (k) those drawn with a very fine camel's hair brush, (l) others, (m) those that have just broken a flower vase, (n) those that resemble flies from a distance.

The categories swiftly become parodic: 'those drawn with a very fine camel's hair brush' or 'those that have just broken a flower vase.' In this essay, Borges continues: 'there is no classification of the universe that is not arbitrary and conjectural. The reason is very simple: we do not know what the universe is.' We do not even know if the universe is created in a realistic or fantastical mode. If it is the latter, then the most careful and rational precepts will never fathom it. Of all the categories in Borges's fictional encyclopaedia, the most paradoxical is (l) others, for it seeks to categorise what cannot be categorised.[21]

Industrial strength Pythagoreanism

In his essay for this volume, Raymond Tallis argues that mathematical idealism exsanguinates our portrait of reality, excluding or ignoring elements that cannot be fathomed within numerical categories.[22] Tallis's excellent phrase for this is industrial strength Pythagoreanism 'according to which everything boils down to mathematics'; a 'quantitative, objective approach to the natural and human world and its reduction of the reality in which we live to numbers or structures created out of numbers.' As Tallis writes:

> [This] is made possible only by progressively excluding the very thing that made science possible: the conscious subject or the community of conscious subjects who experience and observe the world, and make, or endeavour to make, scientific sense of it. The progressive reduction of the world as an object of measurement, to the kinds of relationships between numbers seen in equations, depends on marginalising, indeed deleting, the measurer or community of measurers.

This introduces another paradox: 'fundamental physics overlooks that which makes physics possible: the physicist.' Furthermore, are the constituent elements of reality discrete or continuous? Is the universe effectively like an infinite game of Minecraft, pixellated into tiny bits and if we zoom in closer and closer we'll fathom everything? If we cite Heisenberg and zero-point energy, the tiniest particles are not like billiard balls but like coral atoms emerging from a formless field. This evokes the Vedanta, or the Ancient Greeks with their theory of reality emerging from a formless ocean, or Zeus born from chaos. All such theories beg the further question of what lies beyond the system of calibration – whether we call it the field, the primordial ocean, the category of (l) others, or formlessness.

Tallis also clarifies a vital distinction between science and scientism. Science, the rational method, is hugely important and allows us to intervene in the world, to put rovers on Mars, to cure diseases, to fly planes. Yet, the rational method has limits, including those eloquently attested by the Borges of the rational method – Gödel with his 1931 incompleteness theorems, along with Tarski's 1933 undefinability theorem. Tallis is rejecting not science but scientism, which 'elevates science to the status of the last word on what there is, what is reality, and (most importantly) what we human beings are.' This important distinction also applies to the arts, and the writers I've

140 Religion and Atheism in Dialogue

mentioned herein. Many forms of 'abridgement' or 'summary sketch' – to return to James's terms – are highly serviceable in many ways. Morrison, Eliot, Woolf, Borges, Mirrlees, Yeats are transfixed by their own attempts to raid the inarticulate, to create summary sketches. They are not against Form, only Form-ism, to echo Tallis's distinction between Science and Scientism. As Tallis writes, 'the entirely objective "view from nowhere" sought in science looks perilously close to delivering a view of nothing in particular or, indeed, a view of nothing.' This also applies to the arts: James's conceptual decomposition again.

Like the modernist authors I've cited, we are living through another era of accelerated change: the Digital Revolution. This is accompanied by new forms, new concepts. For example: each one of us deals every day with a cyber-architecture founded on algorithms and binary digits: 0 or 1. Cyber-reality is fraught with oppositional binaries, oddly redolent of the forms of Manichean dualism: Yes/No, Like/Dislike, Thumb up/Thumb down. Subjective emotions are correlated with ostensibly objective numerical referents. There is, for example, the protocol of star rating experiences; for example, 'my experience of this film was 3 stars,' 'my experience of this restaurant was 2 stars.' This advances a quite extraordinary proposition that inner experience can be captured and expressed in numbers. Yet more extraordinary is the further proposition that thousands or millions of these objective numerical correlates for inner experience can then be amassed into a single, universal numerical value for a given book, film, play, or other concept or entity. A global cyber-architecture deploys these mathematical precepts as if they have some certain attachment to the inner reality of billions of humans on earth.

Again, it seems otiose to mention that the internet is fantastically useful in many ways. Again, this is a question of the claims that are being made for the intrinsic systems of categorisation. Human experience does not align with industrial strength Pythagoreanism. Our desires, fears, hopes are complex, ambiguous, at times inchoate. We aren't exactly unitary in value. We sometimes do things for many reasons. We sometimes do things for no apparent reason at all. We're not much like binary digits, 0 or 1. If anything, we're more like qubits, existing in a state of indeterminacy, in danger all the time of succumbing to decoherence. An algorithmic heaven-on-earth converts humans into flawed anomalies in a perfect system. Yet, at times this mythical-mathematical reality fractures entirely: a Google map conveys me into a lake, while maintaining that this is the fastest route home. I find myself arriving at a hotel that no longer exists; the temporal flatness of the internet has scuppered my travel plans.

Yesterday, ChatGPT informed me that T. S. Eliot wrote a beautiful poem called 'The Weight of Words.' I asked ChatGPT if it was quite sure about this. Yes, it said. In that case, I replied, I'd love to read some of 'The Weight of Words,' if you know any of it? Of course, said ChatGPT and in a second, it had scrolled out a five-stanza poem 'by' T. S. Eliot. It begins:

The words, once bright, are brittle now,
Cracked beneath the pressure of the hours,
Shattered beneath the weight of want—
The whispered cry of empty tongues,
Sucked dry by time,
Fading in the dark.[23]

This is obviously not the work of T. S. Eliot, but neither is it the work of anyone. There is no animating consciousness behind these words, no finite mortal who feels or dreams or speaks. The forms have been untethered from human experience. Above, we have physics without the physicist as Tallis writes. Here, we have poetry without the poet. A view of nothing, from no-where, indeed.

Barfield's chess set and riding the blinds...

I've written about adamantine certainty, or 'passionate intensity' as Yeats defines it. I've written about fixed categories and algorithmic compression; industrial strength Pythagoreanism, as Tallis defines it. I've emphasised – along with Tallis, along with other writers I cite – that there's nothing fundamentally wrong with summary sketches, or with forms in response to formlessness. The trouble arises when partial, tenuous forms are mistaken for complete portraits of the formlessness itself. Or, to use Owen Barfield's phrase, when poetic metaphors are ossified, and adulterated with conceptual cement.

Owen Barfield was a philosopher and one of the lesser known Inklings. He loved to play chess. He had a beautiful red chess set which is now held at the Wade Center in Illinois. Barfield wrote about 'polarity' – an idea he derived from Coleridge and offered as an antidote to warring absolutes and two player games of mutual 'smashing.' For Barfield, a two-player game can be a good thing, so long as no one hurls the board across the room.[24] There are warring binaries, then there is polarity: a dynamic interplay of opposites, a debate perhaps between those with differing views, but one that proceeds quietly and even playfully. This summons William Blake's idea that 'without contraries is no progression' – and Blake's rebellion against imposed, tyrannical systems of thought in general. Contraries may illuminate, so long as we agree they are a summary sketch.[25]

Earlier, I mentioned Sedgwick's idea of 'good dog/bad dog rhetoric.' In fact, I found this phrase again recently in Maggie Nelson's *Freedom: Four Songs of Care and Constraint*. For Nelson, the idea that everything must

142 Religion and Atheism in Dialogue

have a single unitary value 'echoes capitalism's own fixation on quantifiable results.' While the tech companies simplify our desires, ostensibly to fulfil them, Nelson finds reality far more inchoate:

> Each of us has our own particular body, mind, history, and soul to get to know, with all our particular kinks, confusions, traumas, aporias, legacies, orientations, sensitivities, abilities, and drives.[26]

Nelson urges us to let go of any hopes for the 'big night' and instead ride 'the blinds,' not knowing precisely where we are going most of the time. In this respect, the arts have something to offer, she suggests:

> [W]e go to art [...] precisely to get away from the dead-end binaries of like/ don't like, denunciation/coronation—what Sedgwick called the "good dog/ bad dog rhetoric of puppy obedience school"—all too available elsewhere.[27]

This nods back to James, to Morrison, to Mirrlees, to Woolf, to Eliot. Art can perhaps offer a place away from, perhaps even beyond, 'dead-end binaries.' Lawrence called the novel 'the one bright book of life' – because it is about warm human complexity, rather than chilly absolutes.[28] This only works if the novel – if art in general – eschews 'dead-end binaries' however. Otherwise art, novels, become another version of 'puppy obedience school,' another kind of chilly utopianism, filled with lifeless abstractions. (And Chat-GPT can generate that sort of etiolated stuff in a second.) I began with Toni Morrison, so I end with her: in that way my form is circular. In her 1993 Nobel Prize acceptance speech, Morrison said: 'Don't tell us what to believe, what to fear.' Instead, 'make up a story...'[29]

Notes

1 On this subject: my footnotes for this article are somewhat in the Nabokovian tradition.
2 'Shrieking voices' is quoted from T. S. Eliot's *Burnt Norton,* first published by Faber in 1936.
3 David James, '"Seeing Beneath the Formlessness": James Baldwin, Toni Morrison, and Restorative Urbanism' in N. Waddell, & A. Reeve-Tucker (Eds.), *Utopianism, Modernism, and Literature in the Twentieth Century.* Palgrave Macmillan 2013.
4 Virginia Woolf, *A Room of One's Own.* Hogarth Press 1929.
5 Eve Kosofsky Sedgwick, 'Queer Performativity: Henry James's *The Art of the Novel*', in *GLQ* 1 (1). Gordon and Breach Science Publishers 1993.
6 Friedrich Nietzsche, *Also Sprach Zarathustra: Ein Buch für Alle und Keinen.* Ernst Schmeitzner 1883–1885. There's a new English translation by Michael Hulse published by Notting Hill Editions 2022.
7 William James, *A Pluralist Universe.* Longmans, Green, and Co. 1909. (James first delivered these remarks in the form of a series of lectures given in the United Kingdom and United States during 1908.)

Make Up a Story **143**

8 Wyndham Lewis (Ed.), *Blast No. 1*. John Lane, The Bodley Head 1914.
9 Henri Gaudier-Brzeska, 'Vortex (Written from the Trenches)' in W. Lewis (Ed.), *Blast*. John Lane, The Bodley Head 1915.
10 Brooke's poem 'The Soldier' was first published in *New Numbers*. Crypt House Press 1915.
11 Brooke's letter appears in *Royal Naval Division*. Produced, printed and published by Leonard Sellers 1997–2003.
12 Owen's poem appears in *Poems* – a collection of his verse published after his death, with an introduction by Siegfried Sassoon. Chatto and Windus 1920.
13 Yeats's poem was first published in *The Dial*. Thayer and Watson 1920.
14 D. H. Lawrence, *Fantasia of the Unconscious*. Thomas Seltzer 1922.
15 Hope Mirrlees, *Paris: A Poem*. Hogarth Press 1920.
16 T. S. Eliot, *The Wasteland*. Boni and Liveright, 1922.
17 Robert Graves, *Goodbye to All That*. Jonathan Cape 1929.
18 T. S. Eliot, *Burnt Norton*. Faber 1936.
19 Virginia Woolf, 'On Craftsmanship'. Recording for the BBC 1937.
20 Leonard Woolf reprinted this letter in his autobiography *The Journey Not the Arrival Matters*. Harcourt, Brace and World 1970.
21 Jorge Luis Borges, 'El idioma analítico de John Wilkins'. *La Nación* 1942.
22 All quotations from Raymond Tallis here and henceforth are taken from his essay in this book.
23 It feels odd citing ChatGPT when its output derives from untold quantities of previous poems and other words, etc. So let's say that ChatGPT 'emitted' this in December 2024.
24 Owen Barfield, *What Coleridge Thought*. Wesleyan Press 1971. Also: Owen Barfield, *Saving the Appearances*. Faber and Faber 1957.
25 William Blake, *The Marriage of Heaven and Hell*. Also printed and published by Blake 1790.
26 Maggie Nelson, *On Freedom: Four Songs of Care and Constraint*. Jonathan Cape 2021.
27 Maggie Nelson, *On Freedom: Four Songs of Care and Constraint*. Jonathan Cape 2021.
28 D. H. Lawrence, 'Why the Novel Matters' in *Phoenix* (published after Lawrence's death). William Heinemann 1936.
29 Toni Morrison, at the Nobel Prize Ceremony in Stockholm 1993.

17

PHYSICS, HUMANISM, AND OPENNESS

Andrew Steane

This chapter addresses various concerns around the intersection of science, especially physics (my own area of expertise), humanism, and certain kinds of religious commitment. Some of the points I shall make come from contemporary physics, and some concern assumptions in contemporary culture which are questionable and ought to be questioned, as well as values which can be held in common.

One questionable (and in fact, wrong) assumption is that modern science belongs to, or is more at home with, a non-religious outlook than it is with a religious outlook. This involves the assumption that science and religion are alternatives or at best awkward companions. There is a widespread prejudice which says that to embrace science fully, to really understand and welcome the insights of science, a person should first jettison the various religious traditions of human history and raise the flag of modern-day secular humanism. There are several reasons why this untruth has gained traction in the modern west. These include the increased role of secular government in public life, the inertia of any large and long-standing institution, and the tensions that have arisen. I mean the tensions that are commonly described as between 'science and religion', but if one looks into it more carefully they concern the interaction between the values which religious bodies treasure, the physical processes which science elucidates, and the unavoidable tension between freedoms of different kinds. The freedom to try out ideas such as Marxism or eugenics runs up against the freedoms associated with financial security and fair treatment, for example. Both Marxism and eugenics presented themselves as 'scientific' in their day. Both were resisted by religious bodies. This illustrates the fact that some of the tensions that have been said to be between science and religion were really symptoms of another tension:

DOI: 10.4324/9781003536185-19

the perennial difficulty of understanding what justice in human affairs looks like, and how it can be achieved.

Related to these concerns is the separation of church and state, and the importance of a secular governing apparatus. This notion, valued by many of us, is not (or should not be) a conception opposed to good religion, but rather it is the very approach which thoughtful religion advocates, at least from Jewish and Christian perspectives. (Islam, by contrast, is not well placed to recognise the importance and value of this separation.) We welcome this separation because the abuse of religious authority is so dangerous, and because it liberates the church and synagogue into their proper roles of prophet and teacher, not governor.

The term 'humanism' has a twofold meaning. In one meaning it affirms that we intend our outlook on life to be humane, treating human beings fairly and squarely as they are in their finite, ordinary, humble position in the scheme of things, and we want to affirm that human life is precious whether or not it is entirely curtailed by death. In this sense of the word, we (contributors to this book) are all humanist, I suggest. The second meaning of the word is as a label under which various further commitments and concerns can gather. This second meaning would exclude, typically, a positive assessment of the evidence for life beyond human death, and it would exclude any celebration of, or reaching towards, a reality which exceeds what the physical universe contains, or at least such a reality having personal characteristics or fittingly described by personal metaphors. I will regard this second meaning as a proper noun and signal it with a capital letter, as Humanism. By pointing out this double meaning I do not wish to curtail the right of modern-day Humanism to adopt the word as a title. But I have noticed a tendency in this kind of Humanism to be a little slow to see that humanism in the first sense is a wider phenomenon and they are not its only champions. This might be compared to the way some versions of modern-day Christianity think they are the only ones who understand grace and forgiveness.

Some modern-day Humanists may be open to the possibility that reality exceeds what the physical world can contain. They are resistant, perhaps, simply to naive use of personal language for matters which are, to such a large extent, beyond our ken. I mean the language of God as 'Father' or 'Mother' or 'Shepherd' or 'Judge' or 'Friend' or 'Teacher' or 'Captain'. The sense of hesitation about such words is not limited to Humanism. It is to be found in every religious tradition wherever deep thinking occurs. The difference between deep thinkers of different persuasions is that some find, in all honesty and humility, that these simple terms are better than nothing. Human parenthood is seen as a symbol of another and fuller parenthood.

A related concern is the intellectual and philosophical movement known as The Enlightenment (or Age of Enlightenment). This movement championed freedom of speech, the value of human happiness in the here and now,

146 Religion and Atheism in Dialogue

toleration, reason and evidence, and democratic representation and governance. It critiqued and resisted certain forms of religion, especially religious bodies exerting unchecked worldly power, or lacking tolerance, or paying scant attention to reason and evidence. For this reason, those who champion the Enlightenment nowadays tend to assume it was and is a broadly atheist movement. But this assumption is unhistorical, unfair, and unenlightened. The Enlightenment was itself in part Jewish and Christian, as well as atheist, and this is unsurprising because the critique of worldly religious power has a continuous history within Christianity and Judaism, going back to ancient Israel. Prophetic objection to the abuse of power is a central theme of the Hebrew Bible, especially kingly and priestly power. This is also central to the attitudes so bravely proclaimed and lived out by Jesus of Nazareth. The exploitative use of religious authority was conscientiously resisted by him, at great personal cost, sixteen hundred years before the Enlightenment thinkers were born.

If we are to treat history correctly, and allow it to teach us, then one should also note that modern-day democracy does not conform to the ancient Greek model. The ancient Greek model had some democratic features but remained essentially a form of aristocratic and dynastic rule supported by slavery. It was less egalitarian than Jewish society in that period, for example. Modern democracy grew out of a set of ideas developed and applied in Jewish and non-conformist Christian groups in the seventeenth century.

Along with its benefits the Enlightenment also, arguably, produced an overemphasis on the notion of the isolated individual and thus contributed to increased isolation in modern life, and it tended to be over-optimistic about the choices humans would make, which made it easier for totalitarian regimes to gain footholds in the twentieth century in Russia, Germany, and China.

I include these comments about the Enlightenment in order to make the point that, like humanism (small 'h'), its values do not imply atheism nor are they chiefly championed by atheism. We can regard them as common ground in the kind of meeting of minds which this book is about.

In the rest of my contribution I shall focus on matters scientific: to be precise, physics and the nature of the physical world. I would like to bring out two features: (1) the fact that physics does not present us with a clockwork universe and there is good reason to think the future is open (not fully determined by the past); (2) the structure of scientific descriptions and reasoning more generally.

The open future

There were two revolutions in physics in the early years of the twentieth century: Relativity and Quantum Mechanics. Both were remarkable; the second was the more profound. To these I would add a revolution in formal logic and mathematics associated with the work of Gödel, Church and Turing and connected to *undecidability* in formal logic and *computability* in computer science.

It is in common between these areas of physics that the nature of the physical world is much more subtle than the picture of billiard-like particles careening in space which was widely imagined in the nineteenth century, and which continues to be roughly the picture entertained in engineering and biology today. That simpler conceptual picture can still be used for many purposes because it gives a good first approximation to aspects of the behaviour of materials and of proteins and things like that. However, quantum physics declares that no molecule is really like the ball-and-stick model you see in biology textbooks. It is far from clear, and probably not true, that the simple picture is adequate for understanding how humans are embodied and enabled to be the people that they are.

A central insight of quantum theory is the property called *quantum entanglement*. This is widely exhibited in atoms and molecules, solids and liquids, and in human-made devices, especially quantum computers. A striking feature of quantum entanglement is that it represents a limit on the degree to which physical things can be decomposed into parts, as I next discuss.

All of science involves adopting what are called *models* of physical things. A scientific model is not the actual physical entity (a ball, a cell, a brain) nor does it capture the whole truth of any physical entity. A scientific model is a human-constructed set of ideas and relationships intended to capture some aspects of the entity or entities in question. In almost all of science the models assume that a large or complicated entity can be understood by dividing it into smaller, simpler parts and considering their individual behaviours and their interactions with one another. Quantum entanglement, by contrast, exhibits physical characteristics of a whole which cannot be understood as if they were carried by the parts one by one. When two entangled particles (say photons for example) have the same colour it may simply not be possible to assign colours to the photons one by one. The physical state expresses the correlation between the particles without expressing the presence of any single individual colour for each photon. Entanglement is involved in many natural phenomena and we are only now beginning to probe its role in materials science and biology. It will likely play a large role. And this means that the programme of understanding the natural world by breaking it down into simple parts does not always succeed.

Another pervasive aspect of modern physics is *indeterminacy*: what happens next, in some given physical scenario, is not completely determined by what happened before: more than one outcome is possible. The canonical example is the process called *quantum measurement*, which is a catch-all

148 Religion and Atheism in Dialogue

term for any process whereby a comparatively large and complicated physical thing (such as a retinal cell or a light-sensitive pixel in a camera) has its evolution steered by a smaller simpler physical thing such as a single photon. In such situations, there is openness in the development of the physical world over time. What is called 'classical' or Newtonian physics also admits an indeterministic formulation. In both classical and quantum physics the future has a degree of openness: it may come to be one thing or another, not entirely dictated by what went before.

Human freedom and divine action

Present-day quantum theory characterises the openness of the future purely in terms of randomness. The model, as it stands today, simply asserts that each outcome is arrived at randomly from amongst the possibilities, with a probability which the model specifies. The past fixes the probabilities and the physical process in the present converts one probability to a certainty. This is very likely all that can be said about vast numbers of measurement-like processes going on continuously in the world around us. However, this is just a model and it may be failing to capture the whole truth in some cases. The whole truth may involve considerations that are irrelevant for simple systems, but relevant in a highly complex signal-processing system such as a mammalian brain.

We are now entering unknown territory. Notwithstanding large amounts of marvellous progress in neuroscience and brain imaging in recent decades, we really do not know how decisions are arrived at by the physical apparatus (brain, body as a whole, other people, wider environment) which supports the expression of human personhood. There are two possibilities. Either the microscopic processes at work in each atom and molecule, and between adjacent molecules taken in pairs or small groups, give the whole story, or else there is also a component contributing at a larger scale and which cannot be entirely broken down in that way.

The view that the whole truth is expressed via simple, microscopic developments from moment to moment is termed either 'reductionism' or the 'algorithmic paradigm'. An algorithm is a kind of recipe: it consists of a sequence of steps, each of which is simple in itself, involving only modest resources and such that a simple machine could be constructed to perform it. By putting together large numbers of such steps, one arrives at complex behaviour overall, such as the behaviours exhibited by modern-day computers. This shows that algorithms are powerful and can achieve much. The mathematics developed to describe physics has, so far, been entirely of an algorithmic type. Given the success of this approach, many experts would be ready to assert with confidence that the algorithmic paradigm is indeed sufficient to capture correctly, and in full, the nature of the entire physical world. However, we do not know that, and to assert it as though we did would be a failure in logic. It is a failure which I have elsewhere dubbed the *Babel fallacy*:

Definition. The *Babel fallacy* is the fallacy of claiming that a given low-level grammar is capable of expressing a given high-level language when this has not been shown to be true.

Examples of the Babel fallacy abound in economics and political and military decision-making and in the history of science. In economics, investment decisions have repeatedly been taken on the basis of models which did not capture the behaviour of economic agents sufficiently well. Businesses, and sometimes entire economies, suffered as a result. In the history of science a prominent example of the Babel fallacy is the belief, expressed by many, that physics was coming to a completion at the end of the nineteenth century because (it was supposed) Newtonian mechanics and classical electromagnetism gave a complete and accurate model. Such assertions were wrong: not just slightly wrong but deeply misconceived. In view of this, we should be wary of making the same mistake again. We ought to keep an open mind about the possibilities when it comes to structures such as brains which exploit signal-processing in highly complex ways.

The possibility that human thought is not entirely algorithmic has been discussed by philosophers. In 1961 John Lucas, and in 1994 Roger Penrose, put forward arguments intended to show that a human mathematician could complete a certain piece of mathematical reasoning that is known to be inaccessible to algorithmic methods. If the argument of Lucas and Penrose holds good then we can infer that human brain processes are not entirely algorithmic in character. C. Wright commented that this offers 'as clear a demonstration as philosophy could reasonably hope for that our arithmetical capacities in particular, and hence the powers of the human intellect in general, cannot in principle be simulated by machine'.[1] However, as Wright goes on to point out, it is not clear that the Lucas-Penrose argument succeeds in fact. Counterarguments can be made. They in turn have received responses and as things stand the situation is inconclusive.

A legitimate reaction is as follows.

The openness of physical evolution, combined with the limits to reductionism entailed by quantum entanglement, combined in turn with the limits of algorithmic methods associated with Gödel's work, combined again with our experience of human life, together invite the conclusion that *the algorithmic paradigm does not convey the whole truth about the nature of the physical world*. Put more bluntly, the conclusion is: mammals and the like (and everything else, at some level) are not just complex machines; they are

150 Religion and Atheism in Dialogue

more subtle and more free. In our present state of scientific knowledge, this is a reasonable view to hold.

Note, I do not conclude that such an assertion about the physical world is *certainly* the case; I say merely that *it is reasonable to hold that* it is the case. A non-algorithmic model would not need to assert that brains have some special 'stuff' in them, but that there is *no mere stuff* at all, anywhere. Those who advocate an entirely algorithmic model will appeal to its success in wide areas of science. But the extrapolation to neuroscience is a guess, not a conclusion for which there is anything but small amounts of evidence. The place where the evidence has to be sought – the flow of events leading to human decision-making and consciousness – is far from understood. Contemporary supercomputers cannot simulate the brain of *Caenorhabditis elegans*. In other words, we do not know how even a worm arrives at its humble decisions.

This bears on human freedom; the freedom known as free will. If indeed humans are not entirely algorithmic creatures then aspects of their physical nature will require for their description types of scientific model which have not yet been formulated and which we do not know how to formulate. They will involve some kind of feedback process which allows the individual human (and to a lesser extent, presumably, other animals) to act as a centre of creative power in their own right. By creative power I mean the ability to introduce into the world a new avenue which is not merely the result of inexorable machinations like the cogs of a clockwork, nor the result of a random element, but the result of that person's contribution as the person that they are. Every new insight into mathematics, art, science, music or diplomacy may be of this kind, as may many of the decisions we all take in our everyday lives.

If humans have this freedom then the divine has this same freedom. The natural world is, of its own nature, a world in which new creative possibilities, and new acts of creation, can arise at any moment, without contradicting those patterns which we call 'laws of nature', and furthermore without running contrary to the artistic style of nature. Nature has a certain artistic style, and it is a style which both allows and invites our creativity. We are invited to join the project of creation and make the world embody the justice and beauty which it struggles to achieve.

I think the presence of ongoing divine action in the world is chiefly through inspiration, as people open themselves to degrees of insight, and capacities of the will, which they could not achieve unaided and which take the form of a partnership: a partnership with the larger reality which is the context of the whole natural order. The reasons why I think this go well beyond the remit of this chapter. My purpose here is to point out that such a position is in keeping with all that we know about the nature of the physical world.

The structure of science

Scientific study is loosely divided into the areas we call physics, chemistry, engineering, biology, social science, neuroscience and so on, and these areas are in turn divided up into sub-disciplines. All these divisions are somewhat artificial (the areas overlap and interact) but they are useful nonetheless. Faced with this set of scientific disciplines, the question arises, how best to see relationships between them? Is it the case, for example, that physics explains chemistry? After all, the physics of electrons and atomic nuclei gives a thorough description of all the elements of the periodic table, including a precise account of the way atoms form chemical bonds of all types. So, one might wonder, doesn't this amount to saying physics provides the 'real deal', the truth of chemical elements and their interactions, and the study of chemistry is 'merely' an offshoot, one engaged in finding simpler, approximate descriptions when solving Schrödinger's equation is too difficult for our computers?

The answer to this question is certainly 'no', but it takes a little thought to see why. I have written about this at length in *Science and Humanity*. Here I merely summarise. For this purpose the analogy of the arched stone bridge is useful. Consider an ordinary stone bridge in the form of an arch. Let it be made of limestone blocks and mortar and nothing else. If we first develop a thorough understanding of limestone blocks – their strength under compression, their stability over time etc. – and also a thorough understanding of mortar and the way it binds to stone, then we shall have discovered everything there is to know about what the bridge is made of. And since there is nothing else there but stones and mortar, someone might argue that our knowledge is then complete and there is nothing further to learn. Such a conclusion is certainly false. This is because arches can also be made of other materials – one can have arched bridges made of wood or iron, for example – and until one understands why the arched shape has itself certain relevant properties, irrespective of the component materials, one has not understood a bridge.

In a similar way, if we adopt the ordinary and useful division of science into its disciplines as they are ordinarily labelled, then the point is that no discipline within science offers a complete explanation of any part of the natural world. The 'explanatory arrows', as Steven Weinberg put it, are not all downward, as he thought. They are two-way. The processes at one level of description *support* or *make possible the operation of* those at another, and in turn the larger or higher-level description *enarches* or *elucidates what is possible* amongst those supported processes.

A classic example of a misleading statement in this area is the one offered by Steven Hawking at the end of his (otherwise wonderful) book *A Brief History of Time*. In a rhetorical flourish, Hawking asserted that once (if that day

152 Religion and Atheism in Dialogue

ever came) the human race had discovered a quantum theory of all the basic forces of the world, then we would 'know the mind of God'. Hawking was not, by this statement, asserting a commitment to theism as such. But he was asserting that, for him, the notion of the ultimate, or the notion of perfect knowledge or highest aspiration, has the form of a collection of mathematical ideas that cohere together in some profoundly elegant way, and that is all. There is no need, in this rhetorical statement, to assert any longing for justice and peace, or any aspiration to know what love is, or what is the quality of mercy. To 'know the mind of God' it is sufficient to know quantum field theory.

That is almost entirely false.

The life Professor Hawking led was distinguished by courage, great learning, humour, and humanity. I think what he really saw as our highest aspiration is some combination of the qualities and virtues by which he lived. His mistake (in the line from *A Brief History of Time*) was to invoke the notion of the divine in connection with mathematics, but not in connection with the humane and the just and the merciful.

Once we have grasped the network-like structure of science correctly, we shall be open to seeing that other disciplines, those we know as the humanities (literature, history, art, jurisprudence, philosophy, etc.), each also have their own valid discourse and contribution, and they cannot be replaced by science. Their relationship to science is comparable to that of the scientific disciplines to each other. The humanities are not a collection of vague or loose ways of speaking, waiting for some more 'sciencey' way of speaking to arise and replace them. They are already engaged in a discourse which science can only hope to learn, not replace. The comparative merit of the poetry of Keats and of Pound, for example, is already correctly described in insightful works of literary criticism. Chemistry and neuroscience will have nothing to add.

Learning

Contemporary society in the United Kingdom (where I write) is, in my opinion, in danger of undervaluing the role of the humanities in education. What we owe to the next generation of young people is not to make them more technically savvy at the expense of their own roundedness as human beings. What we must aim to do is transmit an entire civilisation, so that our young people can develop greater wisdom and greater capacity to enact the requirements of justice and of peace. From such a base they can acquire the more technical types of knowledge as and when they need them.

I began this chapter with a remark on values held in common, as well as points for dispute. Amongst the values held in common I singled out such 'Enlightenment values' as reason, tolerance, freedom of speech, ordinary

Physics, Humanism, and Openness **153**

happiness, democratic process. One can easily add such ancient values as courage, humility, truthfulness, and fairness. Nevertheless, atheism and theism disagree on some matters, and we think the disagreement is important enough to discuss, and the discussion is itself fruitful. As I heard a Roman Catholic bishop remark once, we all have in us a little atheist and a little theist arguing away. God has to remain silent, or at least extremely quiet, because once G speaks undeniably then all others voices cease. It would be as if justice itself had spoken. At that moment life changes forever or else ceases entirely. Atheism says there is no such G. Theists, in the present dialogue at least, have agreed that efforts to speak of such a G as just another voice amongst many, or as another thing alongside all other things – a 'god' like the ones you see in fantasy novels and movies, only much bigger and invisible – are futile. So we are all atheists in this important respect. What we might continue to discuss is whether the theist vision is liable to disrupt Enlightenment values, and whether the atheist one is liable to see the whole scheme of things, and people in particular, as other than they truly are.

Physical indeterminacy and limits to both reductionism and algorithms, along with philosophical reflection on our experience of reason, aesthetics, and moral value, together suggest that the physical world is not correctly construed as a vast machine. Rather it is a meeting place, one where centres of creativity, each having the risk and the dignity of responsibility, and able to know the joy and the pain of love, can come to meet one another. They share home and hospitality, and come to know and love, and thus go in to one another and look out with another's eyes, seeing themselves as they are seen. This is the best kind of mirror. And in all this they also experience the mystery of existence and they encounter, through it all, the sense that love and mathematics govern our existence, not mathematics alone.

Learning to see

I'll admit: I took to the poem
because I did not know what I wanted to say.
Or, nearer, because I knew that
what is to be said is unstateable.
It is the gaps in these lines that hide the treasure,
and all you can do is buy the poem,
—after selling all you have, of course.

But this much let me show, that rings
from what I heard to what I found:
it is something to do with being sought-after;
it is a way to discover,
a threshold which a little child could easily step across,

but it is not objectifiable.
It is the lesson itself, not what the school inspector sees.
It is what it is, not what science can say;
Cariad pure and daunting,
inexhaustibly and unconquerably bearing all things.

It is the space that my spirit expands into.
It is the iron that insists I get a better spirit.
And there is that Spirit, about whom we are rightly warned:
"You need not be afraid".

Note

1 C. Wright. Philosophia Mathematica, 3:86–102, 1995.

PART III

Religion and Diversity

18

RELIGION, NON-RELIGION AND VALUES

What Has Changed and What Stays the Same?

A conversation between Linda Woodhead and Andrew Copson

Andrew Copson (AC)

I think the most remarkable large-scale change that's happened in our lifetimes is the big shift in the 1980s, from a majority of people identifying as Christians to a majority identifying as non-religious. I sometimes think that, in the wider conversation about increasing diversity in society, that's not been given the sort of attention it should have. This big generational and ongoing trend that doesn't seem to show any signs of reversing, even if it is flattening out a bit.

Linda Woodhead (LW)

It is an enormous change in this country, given that Christianity has had a monopoly for so long and is so integral to our culture and society. It's interesting to ask why it hasn't had more press. I would guess it's because it's been happening for so long. What we're seeing is a change in what's habitual, what's socially acceptable, what's normal, and those changes never happen in a generation. It's been happening for a century or more, until it's got to the point where there's a majority of people for whom it's not normal to be a Christian. That is a really big change, but because it's been happening for so long, it doesn't seem like one. News only focuses on sudden changes.

AC

Maybe in a sense it's only the latest change. We've started the discussion by talking about identity, but that's not the only measure, of course, and the other measures, like practice or belief, were tailing off already.

DOI: 10.4324/9781003536185-21

158 Religion and Atheism in Dialogue

LW

Yes, I would always separate them out. 'Are you religious or not?' covers a whole set of things, as you say, from identity, through to practices, to ethics, and to actual spirituality. It's very hard to prove this, but I think that the level of lived, practical spirituality probably doesn't change much over time. A colleague of mine, Bobby Duffy, Director of the Policy Institute at King's College London, said to me the other day, 'There's this odd figure that we just keep getting the same. Since 1950, the number who are involved with fortune telling and the paranormal is 25%. It's completely static, it never changes. What's going on here?' And that really does never change. Each generation is just as likely to do these things. And in terms of actually having a spirituality, if we could measure it – which we can't very easily – it's probably always been about one in five. What changes is what we do as a family on a Sunday, what we read, what's socially acceptable, and what carries our ethics. That really has changed. Our ethics is a very good example. When I was young, a lot of people would still say they're Christian to signal that they were a decent person. Today, they are more likely to say in some circles that they're 'EDI' (Equality, Diversity, and Inclusion). I've just been through a whole batch of application forms for a job, and every one made a reference to EDI. I thought 'This is exactly like living with Christianity, this unquestioned way of saying "I'm a decent person"'. We've got a new ethical framework.

AC

I guess we will come on to values, but I think this idea is really interesting, that there is this permanent fixture, and that it's the social respectability that changes. I spend a lot of my professional time looking back, and looking around the world too, because there are other societies in different states from ours, and I think there's a solid core of people with a humanistic approach. I always pitched it at about a third, because that's what seems to recur and be pretty standard wherever I look – of people who have always been completely worldly in how they think of reality and their values and meaning and everything else.

LW

I think you've put it very well. That is the key difference. 'Are you worldly? Do you think this is really all there is? Or do you think there is something more that we can't quite explain, that's really important, that I spend time with?' That's the difference. And probably in most societies that doesn't really change over generations very much. But the social manifestations of all these approaches change hugely, and that's incredibly important.

AC

I think you're right about that. There's a worldly tribe and an otherworldly tribe in every society. Every culture we know of has produced these two ways of thinking, whether Classical China or ancient India or pre-modern Europe or modern Europe.

LW

That's true, absolutely. Look at ancient Indian philosophy.

AC

Yes. You've got the worldly ones, the Lokayata, the lay people, the materialists. And then you've got the Brahmin-enthused. Today, there's a lot of fierce discussion about what people are really up to. Are they perhaps belonging without believing? Are they practising? These arguments are important in the world that I work in, because government likes the social utility of bringing people together in community, for social good (or social control, depending on who's making the policy!). But I'm not so in touch with what the social facts on the ground are. How are people manifesting? I can think of big instances of non-religious social institutions, such as funerals, not just humanist funerals but all sorts of bespoke non-religious funerals. Weddings are the same. Other ways of celebrating other things. Christmas and other seasonal festivals have become quite secularised since the 19th century, maybe even longer. But what's it like amongst the religious? Is there a diversity amongst religious people, as to how important their religious manifestation is to them, and what they're doing with it?

LW

I recognise what you're saying about a concern for social cohesion amongst politicians. There's this nostalgic view that 'Christianity was wonderful at bringing people together', which I've never really been convinced of. Christianity was highly divisive – you're a Catholic or some version of Protestant. I don't think it ever had that nationally binding power that Labour politicians, and Tories sometimes too, have nostalgia for. Religion in this country doesn't have a binding power. Where it does – let's go back to India – it very often binds an in-group and an out-group. Politicians worry about what does bind us today when, strangely, Britain is quite a cohesive society. Compared with the United States, we're not polarised in that sort of way. It's not entirely clear what it is that holds us together. There are certain common values still perhaps, things that there's a common commitment to.

160 Religion and Atheism in Dialogue

AC

Back to Bobby Duffy's work. I think that research has shown us to be a cohesive society?

LW

Yes, he's done research on this and, interestingly, we're not much polarised over values in this country. The closest religious comparisons with England and Scotland are other northern European countries, Denmark, Finland, Sweden, and Norway, because they all had national churches at the Reformation in exactly the same way, which formed a container for their sense of ethnicity and unity. They're the same, these societies: not much polarised, quite strong national identities. Incidentally, the Scandinavian churches are doing rather better, there's more commitment to them still than there is to the Church of England or Scotland. We have an odd religious situation here in that is a national religion in England and Scotland, and to some extent, the chapel movement in Wales. And then Northern Ireland and the Republic of Ireland. So here religion was not one thing, but that national sense of unity is still there. It doesn't seem to be disappearing with the religion declining, does it?

AC

No.

LW

Another major change, of course, is that we're more religiously plural in the sense of having different world religions. We've always been religiously plural in the sense of having different kinds of Christianity. In 1851, when they asked a religious question tied to the Census, the Anglicans were terribly shocked to find that in England, there were as many nonconformists in church on a Sunday as members of the established church. We've always been religiously diverse. And of course, there have been Jews and Catholics, as lobby groups that achieved more toleration from the end of the 19th century. People overestimate what a big change it is to be religiously diverse. But now, because of migration, we have greater diversity – more than the United States, which thinks it's a plural nation and isn't as religiously plural as the UK. And the UK has actually integrated that religious diversity without much fuss.

AC

So far.

LW

Do you think it will change?

AC

I think it will *probably* carry on, but I'm very worried about certain things, like religious schools. I think the long-term trend towards religious separation in schools is a problem for integration. I always think of the example of Jews, an extremely well-integrated minority, whose children almost all went to non-Jewish schools, and now over a period of a couple of decades that has switched, so that most children of Jewish parents are going to Jewish schools. And I do start to worry whether or not that might have a disintegrating effect. I wouldn't say that any current division is a consequence of that, but I would hypothesise that in the education sector, if this goes on over time, we might see problems. I think the funny thing about this integration was that it just happened…

LW

It just happened. It is interesting to look at our RE curriculums over time, to see how diversity is institutionalised, because we are unusual in having religion in the curriculum by statute. It moved without much fuss from nondenominational Christian instruction, which was established in the 1944 Act, really just enshrining what was happening anyway, and then we get RE, particularly in late 70s, early 80s, and Ninian Smart and the Birmingham curriculum and the Shap working group saying, 'Christianity shouldn't be privileged and we should learn about all religions' and indeed humanism. The rationale for that was social cohesion: 'We need to learn, we need to be respectful and learn about our neighbours'. RE teachers don't get enough credit for being really quite radical in what they did. And they did help integrate. Now we've come to another phase, where RE professionals want to change it again, to 'Religion and Worldviews'. That's a recognition of a new approach to diversity, where it's not just 'We're all really nice, we must love each other'. It's 'We're all minorities. Now, there's no majority'. And each minority has got to have its say, including the non-religious.

AC

What are the implications for dialogue? Hyper-diversity surely has a lot of implications for dialogue. A lot of the old-fashioned ideas about dialogue – think about something like the Council for Christians and Jews in the early 20th century, or a lot of interfaith dialogue movements in the 20th century –

162 Religion and Atheism in Dialogue

assume that worldviews are impermeable blocs that can engage with each other on that basis, but each having a united front within themselves as they encounter each other and trade knowledge and understanding. What about a hyper-diverse context, where not only is everyone part of a minority, but everyone is in a sense in a minority of one? We recognise that everyone has a unique and distinctive worldview. Everyone who's a humanist has a different humanism from every other one. Once we start taking the concept of personal worldview seriously, it turns out everyone's a unique individual. Of course, many traditions have believed this for some time, but what are the consequences for dialogue?

LW

Well, it depends on your take on it. If you take Alexis de Tocqueville, he thought that this was mass society and was very dangerous, because we are just a set of atomised individuals with nothing to hold things together. And then you get mob movements, where it's just about who shouts the loudest, because there's nothing common binding you in a higher framework, and some people now think that this is exacerbated by social media. The idea that a group of people can demand something just because they're a group of people with a common identity tag or grievance, we see that a lot now. But on the other hand... let's go back to the RE curriculum to make it concrete. That's what they're really trying to grapple with, isn't it? You can't teach that many separate worldviews, so you're going to have to group them somehow. I think in any society you always have this tension. Everyone was always a unique individual, perhaps, but then there are authorities who want to help those unique individuals understand 'No, actually you're not X, Y, Z, you've got a common framework'. And they say, 'We're the orthodox manifestations'. 'We're telling you what true Hinduism is' or 'we're telling you what true humanism is'. And you always get the tension between the two, the ones who want to tell you what your identity is and the ones who say, 'No, I'm a unique individual!' Both of them are quite wrong really, aren't they? None of us are unique individuals.

AC

Well, we are and we aren't. I mean, we're all unique individuals, but part of clearly identifiable demographic chunks.

LW

Exactly. You've written a book on humanism, do you want to tell people what real humanism is like, Andrew?

AC

Well, we were very careful in that book, of course, to say it was an invitation to an open-ended conversation, which is the humanist tradition.

LW

You must have boundaries to what humanism is.

AC

Every broad church has walls, obviously, so of course, yes, there are boundaries.

LW

I think where that's gone in our society is into values talk, which is recent and coincides with this increase in diversity and non-religion. And because you can't say, as a school or whatever, 'Well, we have these Christian values... we have a motto and we can take for granted certain commonalities because we are all culturally Christian', you have to have values now, and they're used to set a boundary and to say that behaviour is not acceptable because it's not in conformity with our institutional values. I think that's why there's this somewhat desperate move to values now, because we've lost other ways of putting it.

AC

I have a slightly different perspective on that. I don't think it's desperate. I think it's very rational and measured. Some years ago I was part of the Citizenship Foundation when we were assisting primary schools in producing their school value statements, and the schools undertook this ongoing deliberative process involving the children, which was absolutely brilliant. It meant that this wasn't a top-down 'cut and paste' exercise, but was a process where people thought about the questions 'What sort of community do I want to be part of when I'm at school? Why am I here? What do I want from other people?' And this was an acknowledgement that beliefs can't bring us together but values can. Which is like what you were saying earlier about how we still have a sense of being a nation.

LW

Yes. That was why Gordon Brown put those 'Fundamental British Values' in place. It was particularly driven by Islamic radicalisation, wasn't it? He

164 Religion and Atheism in Dialogue

wanted to say 'As a nation, there are certain lines you cannot cross'. Do you know your five fundamental British values?

AC

Well, they're so ingrained in me that I couldn't make them explicit.

LW

Of course!

AC

Rule of law was one of them.

LW

Rule of law was one of them, democracy, toleration, individual liberty, mutual respect. They are things where, if you say 'No, I don't believe in democracy', you're not a British citizen. New Labour felt there was an absolute need to draw that line and say certain things are not acceptable in this country.

AC

To be fair to Gordon Brown, just before the general election he put together a commission to revise the statement and see whether it was still valid. So he was at least committed to permanent revision of these things, which is a sort of deliberative element.

LW

That's interesting, because they're enshrined now and there is a duty to promote them. And it's interesting that one of them is democracy, because schools aren't democratic, so they're quite at odds with a lot of the school values. I'm studying with some people how schools negotiate their values. Of course schools always had values, and they had discipline around those values, and I think our main question is: 'Is this any different?' Is it just a new label for what was always there, or is there actually something new about these values?

AC

It does depend how they're produced, whether they're co-produced, whether it's deliberative ....

Religion, Non-Religion and Values **165**

LW

But if you're doing that in a school, to make them really co-produced, you'd have to do it for every single year, wouldn't you? And that doesn't happen.

AC

Well, it could. I don't see any reason why it couldn't. My own feeling is that there was a lot of innovative and interesting practice that, like all sorts of things in 2010, just went dead when the money went away. I don't know if anyone is doing these sorts of school values exercises now, but in theory you could see it happening very easily, especially when a new year came into the school, that they could discuss these things and think about them, and if they had ideas, they could be taken into account.

LW

That's true. So you rather like the shift to values?

AC

I love the shift to values. It's very humanistic, isn't it? It is saying, look, here's a human community, one where people seriously consider their values, commit to them on an ongoing but dynamic basis, and they change. That's why the myth of the social contract is an important part of my view of society. So, to come back to dialogue, how could good dialogue do justice to this? How can good dialogue do justice to the diversity? I suppose it'd be about creating a common framework in the same way.

LW

Honouring and recognising and protecting the values we have. People don't remember how many unspoken laws we have, that govern everything, until someone like Trump upends them. That's his trick, really. We've always had a convention that we won't do x or y, because if we did, the whole system would fall over. Those common conventions are much more important than written stated laws and rules. They keep everything going. The fact that they're now being called into question and people are flouting them is dangerous. And so we need to recognise and secure them. Take politeness, the basic rules of courtesy. They're absolutely fundamental to a society. And the minute you start flouting them, and turning a blind eye to it and saying, 'That's some boring convention that doesn't apply to me', your loss is enormous, because they're common things that have held us together for so long,

166 Religion and Atheism in Dialogue

and it only takes a few 'big men' who are purely self-interested and us not defending them for things to go wobbly.

AC

What others are there?

LW

Apart from the rules of common courtesy? Around what you do and don't do in parliamentary democracies, there are all sorts of unwritten rules.

AC

I was thinking more in our social life, if this was a roundtable with people of lots of different religions and beliefs... I agree that there would be common courtesy. That would be a good one. I think truth would be one.

LW

There's a presumption that we all tell each other the truth.

AC

... As we see it. We might not agree about what's true, but there is an assumption that when we speak about what we think...

LW

Yes, we're not going to enter into this conversation and tell a whole pack of lies and see if we can get away with it. We could call it a good faith presumption.

AC

So politeness and truth. How do you feel about toleration? I'm a tolerance fan, but I know that some people find it quite mean-spirited. I think it's very grand-spirited, tolerance, but some people say, 'Well, tolerance, that's not enough, we must celebrate and respect...'

LW

I think I agree with you, because you can't celebrate and respect things you really don't, or don't yet, celebrate and respect – it's too much to demand. Truth goes by the board then, because you're being dishonest. But to say

'Well, you have a perfect right to your ridiculous beliefs, Andrew' is tolerant. [laughter]

AC

'Fill your boots with nonsense, I don't mind!'

LW

Exactly. I allow people their views and listen to them because I might be wrong. Sometimes you do listen to someone and think, 'Oh, actually, maybe I do see where you're coming from now, and that is interesting'. And so you suspend your own disbelief, don't you, to respectfully give them the benefit of the doubt and try and make sense of what they're saying. So that's a sort of tolerance?

AC

I think it seems a bit richer than tolerance...

LW

Empathetic listening, maybe?

AC

Yes. And you're coupling it, as I would, with a commitment to discussion, with an open mindedness. That's important.

LW

Yes, I do it for my job. I'm a sociologist, so I listen to lots of views, and I can believe anything, I'm very good at it while I'm in a group, such as a religious group. I find it all completely credible and quite exciting. As soon as I go home, I think 'Goodness, Linda, what were you thinking?' But I can suspend disbelief quite effectively.

AC

That's so interesting. That will be very alien to many people who are reading this book and who are participants in formal dialogue, because that is often, I believe, about your own personal authenticity and representing your view and not becoming an accidental participant in the views of others.

168 Religion and Atheism in Dialogue

LW

I'm not that wedded to my own views or my own identity. For good or ill, I don't hold on to it that tightly, I can suspend it quite easily. It kind of clamps back into place, I'm sure, at a certain point.

AC

You are someone, beyond being ethnographic.

LW

That's very nice of you to say so! [Laughter]

AC

There is a Linda in there!

LW

Thank you Andrew. I feel quite affirmed!

AC

I think diversity among the non-religious is slightly different from diversity among the religious. I don't think there is so much. That might be because of the analytical category I'm choosing to use, but of the 52% for whom we'll use the identity 'non-religious', 60% of them agree about where morality comes from, 60% of them agree about how they decide what is true, a huge majority of them agree about god, and so on. I find that we are quite a homogeneous category at that level. But of course, there are other ways in which they're more of a diverse category, no more or less diverse than the religious are, but nonetheless diverse.

LW

Well, the test is, if you met a non-religious person in the street, how much could you know about them? You couldn't know what they are politically.

AC

Well, you couldn't know where they were party-politically, but you could know their view on quite a few political and ethical questions.

LW

They're quite liberal, aren't they, in their values?

AC

They skew very liberal, yes.

LW

You'd know, of course, that most of them don't believe in gods – some do, more than you'd think, but not all. You wouldn't know if they pray or not, because quite a few pray. You wouldn't necessarily know about their practices. You wouldn't know their values apart from the liberal value of, 'It's up to me to choose how I live my life'. There's a common commitment to that basic liberal value as against the paternalist idea that someone else can tell me, some authority, or God.

AC

You'd know that their views are probably more liberal on questions of sexual orientation, but you wouldn't know their own personal sexual orientation.

LW

But non-religion is very good at replicating itself. Non-religious parents bring up non-religious children. Why do you think that is?

AC

I think that's because religions are just human culture, and so by definition, if they're not passed on in the normal culture-transmitting environment of the home, they won't...

LW

But non-religion is... it's passed on in the culture-transmitting environment of the home.

AC

I don't think non-religion is passed on. What we're really saying, when we say that non-religion is passed on, is that the children of non-religious parents

170 Religion and Atheism in Dialogue

don't become members of one of the religions that are available. But that is highly unlikely to happen anyway. The interesting question would be, 'How good are non-religious families at transmitting their values and beliefs, whatever they might be?'

LW

Do you therefore think that having non-religion studies as a field is mistaken?

AC

Yes, I do. That's one of the ancillary reasons why I like the 'religion and worldviews' approach to RE – it genuinely comprehends how human beings live their lives, make their values and their meaning, and so on. It takes the human being as the start. Non-religious.... well, even the word, it's obvious that the assumption is that there will be religions, people will be in those religions, and some people will be outside that space, the implication being that they have left it because their commitment has deteriorated somehow, generationally or personally, and they're separate and can be studied in that way. Of course, for some research questions, that is absolutely the right way to categorise, but for others, obviously not.

LW

And going back to diversity, I think we were agreeing that what happens in the classroom and in the RE space in this country has been important. You're in favour of religion and worldviews. Do you think that that will be important in shaping future diversity?

AC

I think it should be.

LW

How can it be? How can it do a good job in that way?

AC

I think it will humanise people's ideas about religions and traditions, because it will start with people's experience of them, what it means to them, rather than exoticise religions.

LW

But why not just let everyone do that in their own private lives?

AC

I don't think it will happen naturally. I don't think it does happen organically in societies. We need institutions to bring people together.

LW

So it's not just about getting clear on what my own worldview is. It's about getting clear on what yours is, as well.

AC

Absolutely. In order to be not just a citizen of a democracy, but a human animal in a diverse society – I think it's essential for both those things. And I think a good deal of personal fulfilment and growth can come out of it, too, of course. It's not just for social utility.

LW

Well, that is, I think, a good point to make in a book on diversity: that what we do in schools does have a place, that there is an active movement in this country to change how we do that, and that that's important.

19

"THE WONDER OF DIVERSITY"

A Gift to Global Ethics

Alan Race

> [The] practice of global ethics presupposes a prior assumption that regards reciprocating dialogue or conversation as an integral part of this practice. It is by means of open, honest, reasonable, and reciprocating, communications between people of different moral, religious, political, legal, and economic persuasions that the practices of global ethics takes place.[1]

The movement Médecins Sans Frontières assumes that the reliability of scientifically based medical practice is universally applicable. Being borderless in terms of reach it represents a form of global ethics: it is not bounded by local traditions and cultural assumptions. But there are forms of medical practice that, because of our culturally interconnected lives, are equally universally available, even if not universally accepted. Think Chinese acupuncture or Indian head massage. At root, suspicions between so-called Western Medicine and so-called Alternative Therapies are based not simply on physical or emotional effectiveness but also on cultural and religio-philosophical assumptions about the nature of human beings and their environments. This medical example of suspicion could be replicated across many human fields – economic, ecological, political, and so on. Sooner or later we enter the zone of diverse assumptions about the nature of reality, as highlighted by my epigraph with its suggested solution of "open, honest, reasonable, and reciprocating communications" if practical global ethics are to become more than an admirable aspiration.

If identity makes an impact at every level of our human interactions how can dialogue not be involved in seeking solutions to global problems? Central in the negotiation of challenges confronting would-be advocates of

DOI: 10.4324/9781003536185-22

"reciprocating communications" (dialogue) is to observe that we are creatures of both empathy and distancing in relation to those whose ways are not my ways. Empathy entails a sharing among human beings at existential levels of emotion (e.g., joy, fear, anxiety, love), and a mutual interest in discerning what constitutes a good and fulfilling life. These associations of empathy draw us into a common humanity and open up the possibility of seeing the world as others see it. But the opposite distancing tendency also operates: the effect of strangeness leads us to mistrust the outsider and to discriminate in the face of difference.

In interreligious dialogue we have learned that we can correct stereotypical impressions of one another by concentrated listening and by a historical interrogation of inherited prejudices. We have also learned that we can engender a sense of collaborative endeavour for social change by joining forces in the face of social ills, locally, nationally, and internationally. But for the religious mind, at its deepest level, the motivation for dialogue is necessarily theological, that is, it embodies an expectation that something of transcendent reality is both learned and hoped for through the encounter. In dialogue we learn about the religious lives of others and of their search for that truth which the religions ponder as ultimate mystery. But the question arises: how can we know when we have encountered something of "transcendent reality" in dialogue? Once we set aside the temptation to think that sheer difference between traditions automatically entails the rejection of the other (the exclusivistic attitude) we are then likely in dialogue to "measure" others by their closeness to our own tradition's outlook (the inclusivist attitude). In other words, we seek to interpret the other within terms dictated by the framework of our own faith. The actual experience of dialogue, however, tells us that this strategy does not fully face up to what is involved.

An illustration of this has been supplied by the American Jewish theologian and dialogue practitioner, Rabbi Marc Shapiro, in dialogue with Jain monks. Shapiro realized that his attempts to interpret non-dual Jain spirituality in terms of his own Jewish doctrine of the relational unity between the world and perceived transcendent reality were forlorn. "As this point dawned on me," he said, "I began to laugh ... I laughed as the idol of a false unity was toppled and the wonder of diversity was affirmed. I laughed with joy at our different paths and the fundamental pathlessness of Truth."[2] I have always been struck here by Shapiro's phrase "the wonder of diversity." Born of the experience of dialogue, the phenomenology of dialogical experience represents a new moment for the interpretation of religious thought and life.

The practices of interreligious dialogue span a spectrum oscillating between practical collaboration and dialectical wrestling over issues of theological and philosophical epistemologies of diversity. These ends of course are distinguished for ease of analysis, but they are implicated in one another.

174 Religion and Atheism in Dialogue

Practical collaborations might need no epistemological justification in the face of deep-rooted global problems such as unequal economic development, peace between nations, or the climate emergency. But the religions will want to appeal to their ethical traditions for guidance in efforts at collaboration, and at that prospect the new moment of dialogue will challenge the religions concerning compromise, openness to different perspectives, and the willingness to tread what Shapiro called "the pathlessness of Truth." Without some modelling underpinning "the wonder of diversity," the practical scope of collaboration could well remain forever precarious.

Is there anything from these wrestlings between religions in dialogue that might be transferable to the wider dialogue between Atheism/Secularism/Naturalism, and Religion? In many ways, the Interreligious and the Atheism/Religion dialogues represent two different arenas of dialogue, each with their particular forms, histories, and focussed challenges. Yet it might be that there could also be overlap, and it is this that I want to consider in this chapter. I shall embark on this by exploring what is termed Global Ethics, and which we could imagine falls part way between the practical and theoretical ends of the dialogue spectrum. In other words, it draws attention to practical challenges while proposing a central principled motif around which both religions and non-religious ethical traditions might coalesce. In this sense, Global Ethics is but one manifestation of the "wonder of diversity."

From an interreligious perspective perhaps the best-known version of a Global Ethic is the one that was adopted at the centenary celebration of the Parliament of the World's Religions,[3] held in Chicago in 1993, and largely crafted under the inspiration of the liberal Catholic theologian, Hans Küng (1928–2021), following a wide-ranging consultation with leading religious and philosophical thinkers from many traditions around the world. It begins from the basic diagnostic principle, that there can be no global order without a new Global Ethic. Küng called this Projekt Weltethos, and it entails that the envisioning of any global order fit for an interconnected world of diverse religions and beliefs requires grounding in fundamental values. There must be what the Chicago declaration called "a minimal *fundamental consensus* concerning binding *values*, irrevocable *standards*, and *fundamental* moral attitudes."[4] This ethic must be responsive to changing world circumstances and be in tune with an increasingly positive appreciation of ethical plurality. Moreover, faith communities cannot escape their particular burdens: "it is the communities of faith who bear a responsibility to demonstrate that such hopes, ideals, and standards can be guarded, grounded and lived."[5] But it should also be capable of being embraced by humanistic and non-religious belief systems.

The fundamental demand of the Parliament's Global Ethic is that every human being, regardless of age, sex, race, physical or mental ability, religion, or nationality, possesses an inalienable dignity and must be treated humanely. This is the so-called ethical Golden Rule. As the Chicago declaration states:

> There is a principle which is found and has persisted in many religious and ethical traditions of humankind for thousands of years: *What you do not wish done to yourself, do not do to others.* Or, in positive terms: *What you wish done to yourself, do to others!* This should be the irrevocable, unconditional norm for all areas of life, for families and communities, for races, nations, and religions.[6]

If the Golden Rule seems so generalized, so as to promise little of significance, its potential virtue is that it opens the door to the prospects of possible cross-cultural and cross-religious criteria for judging basic moral values.

The original Global Ethic in 1993 named four what it called Irrevocable Directives, or Commitments, that represent the beginnings of a practical application of the Golden Rule:

(a) Commitment to a culture of non-violence and respect for life.
(b) Commitment to a culture of solidarity and a just economic order.
(c) Commitment to a culture of tolerance and a life of truthfulness.
(d) Commitment to a culture of equal rights and partnership between men and women.

Since then a fifth directive was added in order to respond to the crises of Nature and Climate Emergency that have come to the foreground in more recent decades:

(e) Commitment to a culture of sustainability and care for the earth.

Although these Commitments seem rather abstract they nevertheless contain the seeds for generating radical ethical demands at concrete levels.

The goal of these Directives is the transformation of consciousness: "Earth cannot be changed for the better unless we achieve a transformation in the consciousness of individuals and in public life."[7] Not only do religious responses to global threats require sound analysis, based on multidisciplinary principles in the spheres of science, politics, economics, and so on, they also demand a change of heart in individuals and in public life. The adoption of a Global Ethic, while attempting to reflect ancient guidelines, nevertheless challenges the representatives of the world's ethical systems to develop their own ethical formulations in dialogue with other worldviews and in relation to the changing needs of the global future.[8]

What does dialogue involve within the framework of a Global Ethic? Consider the five Commitments providing for a substantial critique of much of

176 Religion and Atheism in Dialogue

the destructive effects of human behaviour: (a) is the basis for a critique of policies that promote the militarization of international relations; (b) intrinsically raises doubts about the long-term benefits of unbridled economic globalization and its capitalist engine; (c) promotes human respect, celebrates the differences between histories and cultures, and embraces questions of truth as a function of new relationships; (d) envisages a way of relating that refuses to lock men and women into prefigured roles and seeks to honour the full humanity of both genders, and is easily extended to include transgendered people and others of non-binary convictions; (e) binds peoples and cultures together in the search for a way of living respectful of the Earth and the call of a sustainable future.

The five Commitments of the Global Ethic are selective and more could be added. But they are symbolic of what a collaboratively shaped shared future might hold. Beyond their basic statement, each is hugely challenging not only in terms of the processes and hopes of dialogue but also in terms of what might be realistically possible. They propel the religions and ethical worldviews into patterns of relationship that are potentially transformative of the outlook of all of us. We do not know enough of what each of us thinks, let alone practises, in relation to each of these issues. However, one writer from the Chicago Parliament draws a simple conclusion:

> When people are given the opportunity to say how they wish to be treated, how they wish to live with other members of their societies, the vision of the good life that they describe often looks like the vision of the good life at the heart of the Global Ethic.[9]

But more than *learning about* our different approaches to basic ethical challenges envisaged by global ethic thinking, what would it be to share wisdom on "non-violence and respect for life" or "a just economic order" in this new framework? I submit that it would mean exploring each issue *about, with,* and *through* the other; in other words, exploring dialogically.[10]

While this example of global ethical thinking from the Parliament of the World's Religions has been religiously inspired its application is not limited to religious frameworks only. In this way it provides a platform for an Atheism-Religion dialogue based on mutual respect and foundations inherent in the value of dignity accorded to both the human world and its environmental contexts. Philosophies – religious or secular – will not always agree on the specifics of ethical judgements, nor will they need to, but the call of dialogue will mean that neither are they free to abdicate responsibility from commitment to truths that reflect "the wonder of diversity."

The idea of a Global Ethic as a basis for dialogues on many levels could be accused of a "totalizing" tendency, that is to say, imagining a unity between traditions when in fact none exists. From my perspective this criticism is wide of the mark. The Global Ethic observes diversity as a source of wonder. Traditions are different in terms of their origins and historical developments, but that does not mean that they are automatically incommensurate: they incorporate "a minimal *fundamental consensus* concerning binding *values*, irrevocable *standards*, and *fundamental* moral attitudes," a not impossible prospect. In fact, in a much less noticed study, Hans Küng traced the historical developmental trajectories of numerous religious traditions and showed how they are fully capable of convergence in terms of tracing a "common human ethic."[11] It turns out that Global Ethic thinking is not an abstract model guilty of imposing universal pretensions.

A further response to accusations that a Global Ethic represents an imposition of universal pretensions can be made by borrowing from a comparable discussion in the realm of human rights ethics, where the *Universal Declaration on Human Rights* is sometimes accused of being far from universal and at odds with many of the values that stem mainly from non-western cultures. In 1994, an impressive worldwide study project entitled *Religion and Human Rights* reported that many of the assumptions made concerning the incompatibility between universality and respect for cultural diversity in human rights tend to be exaggerated. The highly respected American scholar of Human Rights, Philosophy and Comparative Religion, Sumner Twiss (1944–2023), one of the editors of the report, commented that "human rights set aspirational norms, and no persuasive case has been made to show that human rights as a goal for all peoples is either illegitimate or unattainable."[12] This highly suggestive observation could be applied in the case of a Global Ethic, in so far as it seeks comparable aspirational norms and goals.

As part illustration of this conclusion, the *Religion and Human Rights* research noted a distinction between corrupt leaders and oppressed peoples in their appeals to culturally specific traditions. Corrupt leaders used local traditions "as a smoke-screen to deflect attention away from the abuses they perpetrate on their own citizens," while advocacy groups defending the poor "use elements of local culture and religion to translate human rights into cultural idioms so that they might be more effectively recognized and respected." Further, and most importantly: "the group found that many oppressed peoples – regardless of their cultural locations and differences – have little difficulty accepting the idea of universal human rights ..."[13] The tension between individual and collective rights, in so far as this may be cited as a reason for rejecting universal human rights, turns out to be a chimera. The often-heard accusation that the UN *Universal Declaration of Human Rights* represents a purely abstract idea, which is based on Western ideology and is not really applicable to other cultures, is simply incorrect. Again, as Twiss concludes: "No one tradition is the sole source of human rights values, and these values are not exclusively Western"; and, moreover, international human rights "represent a shared vision of moral and social values compatible with a variety of religious and cultural world-views – a unity within a diversity."[14] The wonder of diversity!

It is important not to claim universal values too quickly, for it is in the details of our particularist traditions, religious and non-religious, that the struggle to embody the five commitments of the Global Ethic will be most keenly felt. In dialogue we open up our treasury of wisdom to scrutiny from alternative sources of vision and human transformation. We open ourselves up to challenges from critical reasoning and the democratic spirit. And as dialogue is reliant on some sense of democratic openness in its assumptions and processes, democratic openness in turn confronts all traditions with the summons to abandon those elements in tradition that are inconsistent with it. For example, equality, human rights and responsibilities, the scientific search for truth in understanding the way the world works, and the goal of on-going transformation in what it is to be humanistic or religious, these pressures cumulatively exact a price to be paid for signing up with a Global Ethic!

From a philosophical perspective it is always epistemological concerns that put a brake on enthusiasm for universal ethics. Useful in this regard, however, is the distinction that was made by the Princeton social scientist, Michael Walzer (1935–), between what he called "thick" and "thin" morality. On the one hand, "thin morality" – or "minimal morality" – refers to "a whole set of elementary ethical standards, which include the fundamental right to life, to just treatment (including just treatment from the state), to physical and mental integrity."[15] Echoing the *Religion and Human Rights* study, it just seems to be the case that a hold on universal values does arise when human beings are faced with oppression or unjust treatment, irrespective of the context in which such universalism is articulated. These values may be limited to fundamental values such as justice and truth, but nonetheless they are capable of being harnessed as "a certain kind of universalism."[16] On the other hand, "thick morality" refers to the tradition-specific articulation of fundamental norms and principles, which may vary widely according to cultural history and religious commitment. Moreover, these norms and principles may even be in opposition or contrast, but this need not militate against agreement at the level of "thin morality." The opposition or contrast then becomes simply an invitation to dialogue in order to discover whether or not the disagreements are real or apparent.

In plural societies there is the need to allow freedom of expression and argument for all citizens, yet balance this with respect for the reasons that citizens give for thinking and acting in the ways that they do. This seems to me to be in line with what has been termed the post-secular outlook, advocated chiefly and controversially by the German philosopher and sociologist,

Jürgen Habermas (1929–), a philosophy that is resonant with the dialogical ethics I have been pressing. In Habermas's own words:

> The neutrality of state power vis-à-vis different worldviews, which guarantees equal individual liberties for all citizens, is incompatible with the political generalization of a secularized worldview. Secular citizens, in their role as citizens, may neither deny that religious worldviews are in principle capable of truth nor question the right of their devout fellow-citizens to couch their contributions to public discussions in religious language. A liberal political culture can even expect its secular citizens to take part in the efforts to translate relevant contributions from religious language into a publicly intelligible language.[17]

Habermas here is revising his former stance which supported a strong distinction between religion and public decision-making. If his revised view is adopted, however, does it mean that we must imagine a public square crowded with argument, a state of affairs which will be necessarily untidy and risky in terms of orderly debate, but where religious voices take their place alongside others in open exchange? In the best possible world, what might emerge from such an open exchange will be an outcome that is the fruit of listening and rational persuasion – rational, that is, in the desired sense of seeing the persuasive reasons for something, even if one disagreed with the comprehensive view of life lying behind them.

What seems to be needed is a model of participation in public democratic debate that allows for the particularities of religious and secularist voices, and which relies on seeking common ground while respecting differences, and balancing compromise where necessary with critical solidarity for the sake of a greater good. As we cannot know what that greater good might look like in advance such a model must surely be dialogical at heart if religions and beliefs are to develop their ethical democratic political relevance. Most of all, the model must involve comprehensive worldviews self-critically if they are to both overcome their historic mistrust of one another and learn the values of provisionality and humility that are necessary in the context of interpreting and negotiating plurality.[18]

So, for religion in public life to be healthy what seems needed is not so much an empty public square but what we might call a dialogically filled public square. We accept critical reasoning which means that we explain to one another the reasons we have for believing the things we do and why we want to act on them, whether we are confessionally secularist or religious. Why can we not come to mutually agreed decisions based on such mutual listening and mutuality of respect?

The public square should not be filled with theocratic religious voices or be left hostage to a liberal secularist absence of religious reasoning, but be

180 Religion and Atheism in Dialogue

occupied by a dialogical conversation where each values the other even as it might disagree with certain dimensions of them. Global Ethic thinking is not simply a matter of responding pragmatically to the threats and problems emerging within our interconnected world; it is also a function of a new way of being human across borders and boundaries.

Religion has not disappeared in the way that many voices predicted would happen in the modern period. During this same period we have also realized that pragmatism, which has served us well and is preferable to ideological or theocratic politics, too has limitations. Add to this the plurality that stems from globalization and the stage looks set for a change of direction. An ethically informed global ethos which upholds pluralism requires a dialogue built not simply on respect or hospitality, commendable as these values might be, but on an acceptance that affirms separate identities even as it might not approve of everything those belonging to any particular tradition want to pursue or promote.

Notes

1 Frederick Bird, Sumner B. Twiss, Kusumita Pedersen, Clark A. Miller, and Bruce Grelle, *The Practices of Global Ethics: Historical Backgrounds, Current Issues and Future Prospects* (Edinburgh: Edinburgh University Press, 2016), 19.

2 Rami Marc Shapiro, 'Moving the Fence: One Rabbi's View of Interreligious Dialogue', in M. Darrol Bryant and Frank Flinn, eds., *Inter-religious Dialogue: Voices From a New Frontier* (New York: Paragon House, 1989), 36.

3 For a brief overview, see https://parliamentofreligions.org/our-work/

4 Hans Küng and Karl-Josef Kuschel, eds., *A Global Ethic: The Declaration of the Parliament of the World's Religions* (London: SCM Press, 1993), 18.

5 Hans Küng and Karl-Josef Kuschel, eds., *A Global Ethic: The Declaration of the Parliament of the World's Religions* (London: SCM Press, 1993), 20.

6 Hans Küng and Karl-Josef Kuschel, eds., *A Global Ethic: The Declaration of the Parliament of the World's Religions* (London: SCM Press, 1993), 23f.

7 Hans Küng and Karl-Josef Kuschel, eds., *A Global Ethic: The Declaration of the Parliament of the World's Religions* (London: SCM Press, 1993), 34.

8 See Hans Küng, *A Global Ethic for Global Politics and Economics* (London: SCM Press, 1997). Also consult Note 1 above, *The Practices of Global Ethics*.

9 Myriam Renaud, 'The Global Ethic and the Fifth Directive', in *Interreligious Insight*, Vol. 17, No. 1, June 2019, 42–49.

10 For a theological exploration of this, see my 'Religious Experience in an Interfaith Context', in *Beyond Boundaries: Essays on Theology, Dialogue, and Religion in Honor of Perry Schmidt-Leukel* (Münster and New York: Waxmann, 2024), 21–32.

11 Hans Küng, *Tracing the Way: Spiritual Dimensions of the World's Religions* (London and New York: Continuum, 2002).

12 Sumner Twiss, 'Religion and Human Rights: a Comparative Perspective' in Sumner Twiss and Bruce Grelle, eds., *Explorations in Global Ethics: Comparative Religious Ethics & Interreligious Dialogue* (Boulder, Colorado: Westview Press, 1998), 158.

13 Sumner Twiss, 'Religion and Human Rights: a Comparative Perspective' in Sumner Twiss and Bruce Grelle, eds., *Explorations in Global Ethics: Comparative*

Religious Ethics & Interreligious Dialogue (Boulder, Colorado: Westview Press, 1998), 158–159.

14 Sumner Twiss, 'Religion and Human Rights: a Comparative Perspective' in Sumner Twiss and Bruce Grelle, eds., *Explorations in Global Ethics: Comparative Religious Ethics & Interreligious Dialogue* (Boulder, Colorado: Westview Press, 1998), 161.

15 Cited in Küng, *A Global Ethic for Global Politics and Economics*, 95.

16 Cited in Küng, *A Global Ethic for Global Politics and Economics*, 97.

17 Jürgen Habermas, 'A "post-secular" society – what does that mean?', in *Reset Dialogues on Civilizations*. https://www.resetdoc.org/story/a-post-secular-society-what-does-that-mean/, 2008.

18 Habermas's post-secularism has generated much interest, especially around the concept of "translation," whereby a shared ethical language, appropriate for practical decision-making processes in a pluralistic society, remains a necessity. A good example of dialogue on the issue can be found in the exchanges between Habermas and Charles Taylor, the Catholic sociologist, in Eduardo Mendieta and Jonathan VanAntwerpen, eds., *The Power of Religion in the Public Square* (New York: Columbia University Press, 2011), 64.

20

CATHOLICISM AND ATHEISM

Peter A. Huff

It has been said that "and" is the most Catholic word in the theological lexicon. At its deepest mythic level, the Catholic tradition, to take an analogy from music theory, is built upon the device of the two-note phrase: one and three, human and divine, virgin and mother, bread and body, scripture and tradition, Athens and Jerusalem, and on and on. The recurring pattern permeates the make-up of Catholic thought, art, liturgy, devotion, experience, and behavior. While *coincidentia oppositorum* is a venerable theme of Catholic mystical life, this broader persistent coupling is a signature of the Catholic mind itself. Despite innumerable instances in its ecclesiastical expressions of restriction and parochialism, when, as Newman might say, it has "worn its dark side outwards," Catholicity as a worldview is by its most fundamental impulse expansive and conjunctive.[1]

I speak of Catholicism or Catholicity not merely as a doctrinal system, ritual cult, or moral code, but rather as a vast and living cultural product that performs its essence in a discernable way. When in the second century, Ignatius of Antioch for the first time linked *katholiké* with *ekklesia*, he named what would become one of the tradition's most recognizable features: its near-unconscious inclination toward reconciliation or at least combination, almost libidinously absorbing ideas and practices from previous and competing worldviews.[2]

Since Ignatius's unparalleled grammatical move, Catholicism has made itself more and more *katholiké*. Newman's image of a rolling river has become the operative metaphor for this characteristic of the tradition.[3] Catholicism's dynamic relationship with multiple predecessors and various environments means that its intellectual and affective world deepens and widens as it lengthens, progressing through space and time. Reformation-era adversaries

DOI: 10.4324/9781003536185-23

were not far from the mark. Nor are contemporary critics of Catholicism's proclivity for supersessionism, cultural appropriation, and metaphysical avarice. At the very least, we may add Christian-pagan and Christian-Jewish to Catholicism's distinctive set of two-note phrases.

But when we analyze the score of Catholicism or listen to a performance of Catholicism, to continue our analogy, do we also detect a Christian-atheist motif? In other words, just as paganism and Judaism somehow exhibit presence and exercise agency within Catholic mythic structure, is atheism an element in the Catholic psyche too?

Newman's "and"

Newman gave us the phrase "Atheism and Catholicity."[4] The eminent Victorian lived in the age of the equally eminent Victorians Besant, Bradlaugh, Holyoake, and Huxley and was well acquainted with the varieties of atheism and agnosticism that manifested themselves in that first great age of public doubt and unbelief. His contribution to the perennial debate regarding proofs for God is well known. The unexpected phrase "If there be a God ...," appearing in *Apologia Pro Vita Sua*, *Grammar of Assent*, and *The Idea of a University*, testifies to a remarkably undaunted Christian mind willing to take seriously the modern atheist imagination and understand it principally in experiential terms.[5] Newman admitted that it "is indeed a great question whether Atheism is not as philosophically consistent with the phenomena of the physical world, taken by themselves, as the doctrine of a creative and governing Power."[6] He also knew the cogency of the problem of pain and the cognitive and emotional impact of God's apparent absence. He rejected "notional" views of both the affirmation of God and the denial of God and exposed the weaknesses of "smart" syllogisms and "paper" arguments.[7] His extensive intuitive repertoire included sensitivity to grammars of assent and dissent.

Upon further examination, though, Newman's "and" turns out to be more of an "or." He argued that "no medium, in true philosophy," exists between the two positions. A "perfectly consistent mind," he said, "under those circumstances in which it finds itself here below, must embrace either the one or the other."[8] Newman's implicit dialogue with atheism went very far, farther than most Christians could take it in the nineteenth century. He surveyed the fulfillment of all natural and revealed religion in Catholicism and observed that that great reality had an equally great antagonist labeled with its own capital-letter name. Arguably no other Christian thinker to date had accorded atheism so much *gravitas*.

Undiscerning readers might take Newman's "and" to be one way of expressing the decisive either/or of all time. But here we remember that even "or" is a conjunction. If there is truly no medium between "Catholicity"

184 Religion and Atheism in Dialogue

and "Atheism," then—emphasizing the implied spatial imagery of Newman's language—arguably the two phenomena touch. And if they touch, how and why does that contact happen and with what consequences? And what does this proximity or actual connection suggest about the relationship between Catholicism and atheism?

"We are atheists"

Newman's generation thought a good deal about Christianity and atheism. So does ours. The mental linking of the two worldviews, however, goes back to the beginning of Christianity and the discussion regarding the upstart faith among pagan observers, especially the discussion of what to call the new religion.

At first, Christianity had no name. According to the author of the book of Acts, the movement briefly acquired the moniker "Way" (see Acts 9:2, 19:23, 24:22), perhaps an *hommage* to a saying attributed to Jesus (John 14:4–6). About halfway through his narrative, the same author specifies the occasion when the disciples were "for the first time called Christians" (Acts 11:26). He does not, however, identify the source of *Christianŏs*, nor does he explain its psychological or sociological force. Was it a self-chosen term of affirmation or an epithet of derision imposed by outsiders? Many religious movements have adopted pejorative nicknames spawned in the context of uncivil contest. The scanty New Testament myths of origin are disappointing on this question. Documents of the second century demonstrate the full Christian adoption of "Christian." Ignatius, notable for *katholiké*, also gave us "Christianity" (*Christiānismós*).[9] In any event, the earliest names of the Christian tradition are shrouded in mystery.

This includes the name that stands out most: *atheos*. By the middle of the second century, *atheos* was a charge against and a name for Christianity. The pagan intellectuals and officials who endeavored to describe what they took to be a baffling and threatening new movement are well known: Caecilius, Libanius, Tacitus, Pliny the Younger, and others. Polemicists Crescens, Celsus, and Julian each employed the term *atheoi* to christen the growing body of Christian devotees.

The term was a commonplace in classical and Hellenistic literature and was routinely used as an instrument of censure. Individuals accused of *atheos* included Protagoras, Xenophanes, Anaxagoras, Prodicus, Euripides, Critias, Diagoras, Theodorus of Cyrene, Euphemerus, and, of course, Socrates. Epicurus and Clitomachus composed lists of notorious *atheoi*. The term appears once in the New Testament, where Gentile converts are designated as previously *atheoi* (Ephesians 2:12).[10] No record, though, indicates anyone adopting the word as self-identification.[11] Not until the self-styled Christian philosopher Justin Martyr, that is. In his First Apology, speaking on behalf of all Christians, Justin declared: "We confess that we are atheists [*atheoi*]."[12]

Early Christian writers rejected allegations of incest and cannibalism and leveraged indictments of misanthropy. The charge of *atheos*, however, triggered a variety of responses. Polycarp turned it into one of the cleverest theological retorts of all time.[13] Athenagoras sought to deflate the attack by pointing to the lack of theological unanimity among his pagan detractors.[14] Justin pled guilty. Although he followed his surprising confession with "but not with reference to the most true God," he never reversed or recanted his initial affirmation.[15] The lack of precision with which *atheos* was used in his day does not diminish the significance of his strategic acknowledgment, just as it does not nullify the confidence with which twenty-first-century atheists discover and claim ancient ancestors. None of us knows what it felt like in the second century to be charged with *atheos* or to admit it. Many modern historians have quested for the elusive first atheist. Few have reckoned seriously with the irony that the first self-professed atheist in the Western world may have been Christianity's first major apologist.[16]

"It seems that God does not exist"

Justin perceived *atheos* as in some sense a fitting name for his philosophy. He recognized something in *atheos* that registered with his emerging worldview, ratifying, at least in part, the hunch of Christianity's critics. Since then, theologians have acknowledged the logic and even comic appeal of his confession. They have also shielded readers by placing the translation of *atheoi* in inverted commas. Few have accepted Justin's statement as a *topos* for theological reflection. Stephen Bullivant urges his readers not to confuse Justin's provocative declaration with the death of God "fads" of the 1960s.[17] In his magisterial *Does God Exist?*, Hans Küng never mentions Justin or the fact that Christians and atheists once shared the same name.[18]

Despite theological anxiety and denial, much would reinforce Justin's inkling of a correspondence between Christianity and atheism as the fullness of Catholic Christianity developed. Classical Christian theism would never be what Newman called a "nude" proposition.[19] Christianity's thick biblical inheritance invested Catholic intellectual life with strains of iconoclasm and conspicuous and irreconcilable intuitions regarding *agnosto theo* (Acts 17:23), the coexistence of faith and unbelief (Mark 9:24), and *deus absconditus* (Isaiah 45:15), God's inaccessibility, inscrutability, and disturbing truancy and silence. The tradition's evolving spiritual life wrapped Catholic theism inescapably with haunting themes such as the "cloud of unknowing" and the "dark night of the soul."

These dimensions of life and imagination have been evident in firsthand accounts by generations of the tradition's saints and contemplatives, from late antiquity to the present. The private writings of Mother Teresa of Calcutta, to cite one example, reveal an interior life not unlike that experienced

186 Religion and Atheism in Dialogue

by individuals who have embraced certain types of atheism or agnosticism: "The place of God in my soul is blank ... There is no God in me."[20] Granting the possible distortion of mystic hyperbole, still we wonder, what on the experiential plane is the difference between a Christian's admission of "no God in me" and an atheist's assertion of "no God at all"?

Even the structures of Catholic discourse disclose the lingering influence of Justin's unexpected and, to some, discomforting awareness. Works by writers such as Augustine, Boethius, Gregory the Great, Anselm, Thomas à Kempis, Catherine of Sienna, Erasmus, and of course Justin himself give evidence of a propensity toward the dialogic form in the Catholic literary imagination. The interrogative format of catechisms, the "yes and no" of Abelard's signature work, the movement from *Videtur quod* ("It seems that") to *Sed contra* ("On the contrary") in Aquinas, the invention of the "devil's advocate" in the medieval university, all springing arguably from the lively collision of unvarnished ideas and emotions in Paul's correspondence, the prototype for so much of Christian literature, portray the Catholic search for meaning not as a mute quest of "the alone for the Alone" but as continuing and full-bodied conversation—a risky exchange involving real problems, candid inquiry, multiple voices, and the unknown of the reader's response. The tradition that perfected polyphony in choral music, exemplifying harmony's dependence upon dissonance, prepared for that achievement with centuries of contrapuntal work in the intellectual realm.

Some parties in these literary dialogues are admittedly foils. Justin's Trypho is a stain on the Christian conscience. Some dialogue partners exist for the sole purpose of stroking the principal speaker's ego. Others, though, contribute to reassessment of first principles or disregarded alternatives. In Anselm's *Cur deus homo*, junior monk Boso points out wrong-turns in his teacher's argumentation. In spite of its all-too-human failings, Catholic intellectual life, embedded in scripted and spirited dialogues, is at best a robust call-and-response enterprise, intrinsically communal and irrepressibly capacious in its desire to pursue nagging questions and face formidable objections.

Aquinas marshaled this mode to great effect in his *Summa Theologiae*, synthesizing pagan, biblical, Jewish, Christian, and Muslim arguments and endowing his work, as Josef Pieper observed, with "the character of a genuine conversation or dialogue, the character of reflective meditation, which makes no claim to possessing a definitive formulated answer."[21] The intellectual and literary commitment to this end is strikingly noticeable in Aquinas's analysis of the question of God's existence. The voice of the biblical "fool" (Psalms 14:1, 53:1) had long been lodged in the Christian mind. Aquinas began his "five ways," however, with the voice of another kind of figure: a reasonable skeptic or unbeliever who says, "It seems that God does not exist."[22]

Bertrand Russell criticized Aquinas for deciding on his truth before launching his philosophizing.[23] But Russell, brilliant thinker and communicator, stumbled as historian. Aquinas, far from merely repeating familiar answers, was a highly contested figure in his age, contributing to the process of articulating what would only later be considered orthodoxy. Peter Kreeft has ranked his approach "closer in spirit to agnosticism than to dogmatism."[24] Aquinas internalized an atheist or counter-theist perspective, gave it visibility and audibility, and couched it in the context of Catholic discourse—in this case, an exploration of "the nature and domain of sacred doctrine."[25] Anticipating Freud's success at the same technique, he was a master of vocalizing a contrary position in a non-defensive manner. Even though the reader has a rendezvous with what "everyone understands to be God" just a few paragraphs later, no one knows just how many students of the *Summa* for the last eight centuries have paused at the opening line of *Prima Pars*, Question 2, Article 3 and come to the conclusion that the problem of "evil in the world" is indeed the end of the inquiry.[26] The *Summa*, ceremoniously placed alongside the scriptures on the altar at the Council of Trent, intones recognizable notes of both belief and unbelief. Whatever the intent of the author, it speaks for and against God.

The Disappearance of God

So, for that matter, do the scriptures themselves. But unfortunately few works in the enormous field of biblical studies have investigated this feature of the biblical witness.

By contrast, a growing body of studies over the last half century or so has devoted great attention to the relationship between atheism and post-biblical Catholic thought. The Second Vatican Council identified atheism as "one of the most serious of contemporary phenomena" and called for dialogue with unbelievers.[27] Popes John XXIII and Paul VI endorsed dialogue in their encyclicals, and Paul, building on John's unprecedented initiatives in ecumenical and interreligious relations, established an equally unprecedented Vatican secretariat to oversee Catholic-atheist dialogue. Paul also commissioned the Jesuits to make the study of atheism a priority for their apostolate. A Cold War council and the church's first in an age of mass unbelief, Vatican II was obsessed with atheism, its causes, varieties, and future.[28]

The obsession created the conditions necessary for extraordinary achievements in the study of the history of Catholic thought, scholarship discovering the genesis of at least modern atheism in the very texture, style, and principles of Christian literature itself. Jesuit scholar Michael J. Buckley's *At the Origins of Modern Atheism* and *Denying and Disclosing God* have challenged all conventions in the history of atheism and Christianity, defining modern atheism as a product of Christian thought and identifying its sources in shifts within early modern Catholic intellectual life, especially what he deems its over-reliance upon natural theology, its minimizing of Christology

188 Religion and Atheism in Dialogue

and religious experience, and its reduction of theology to epistemology.[29] Gavin Hyman has traced the roots deeper into the Christian past, seeing modern atheism as a consequence of Duns Scotus's "univocal concept of Being," comparable to that of Averroës, which flattened the ontological distinction between God and humanity and bears some responsibility for the vacuous modern notion of a "higher being."[30] Representing an earlier generation, Paul Tillich judged Aquinas himself to be the Catholic font of atheism—the Aquinas who brought "God's existence down to the level of that of a stone or a star, and [made] atheism not only possible, but almost unavoidable."[31]

Each of these scholarly impulses has advanced the thesis that "the origins of modern atheism," as Hyman has put it, "are ultimately *theological*."[32] None of them, however, has pushed deeper into the Christian psyche and the earliest epochs of its evolution. None has made reference to ancient atheisms, Justin's curious confession, or the pagan intelligentsia's suspicion that Christianity and *atheos* were related. None wonders if the riddle behind Newman's "and" might be a feature of the Bible itself.

Two studies, both published thirty years ago, have taken this next step. Each argues that the overall effect of the sacred books, irrespective of both the theology alleged to be based on or continuous with them and the intent of their ancient authors and redactors, betrays the shape of a narrative arc almost imperceptibly moving from an active, articulate God to an inactive, unresponsive God. In *The Disappearance of God*, Jewish scholar Richard Elliott Friedman documents the "gradual diminishing apparent presence of the deity" in the Bible. Following the canonical order of the texts, he charts the stages of this process: the last person to receive a revelation from God (1 Samuel 3:21), the last person to perceive an appearance of God (1 Kings 11:9), the last appearance of the cloud and glory (1 Kings 8:10–11), the last public miracle (1 Kings 18), the last personal miracle (2 Kings 20:8–11).[33]

In *God: A Biography*, former Jesuit Jack Miles pursues a similar line of examination, only with greater intensity. Framed as a literary analysis of the Bible's complex and uncanny protagonist, the work uncovers a narrative that few Bible readers ever notice: the transition from divine action to divine speech to divine silence. Miles sketches a spectrum of divine realities — "presence, absent presence, present absence, absence"—and finds all in the biblical portrayals of God. More than another rehearsal of the theme of God's hidden face (Deut. 31:17–18), however, his work lays bare the Bible's "occultation" of God and the "long twilight" of scripture that sets in permanently after the book of Job.[34]

Both scholars concentrate on the Hebrew Bible. Friedman sees the "post-revelation world" established by the Bible's narrative structure as the metaphysical linchpin for rabbinic Judaism. The Torah verse "It is not in heaven" (Deut. 30:12), playing a pivotal role in the Talmud, represents the foundation for post-biblical Judaism, a religion of textual authority and authoritative

Catholicism and Atheism **189**

human interpreters who rely on skill, genius, and collegiality, not intervention from God.[35] Likewise, Miles sees a "secular spirit" emerging in the Bible. By the time of the wisdom literature and the post-exilic narratives, he says, "God's Bible" has replaced the "Bible's God" and humankind has become the protagonist.[36]

Conclusion

No work has extended this study of the biblical eclipse of God to the New Testament. Miles's *Christ*, published a half-dozen years after *God*, offers an additional glimpse into the fraught interiority of God, seeing the Incarnation as a resolution of God's dysfunctional relationship with the Jewish people, but it does not address the issue of a Christianity resembling *atheos* in pagan eyes.[37] Early Christians professed belief in God and eventually developed the doctrine of the incarnate Logos as their creed's cardinal article. The God they believed in and bequeathed to future generations, however, was a God whose significant presence was located in the past and only secretly in the life of Jesus. A sentence with "God" as subject followed by a present-tense action verb is a rarity in the gospels. Abba speaks, but his voice is confused with thunder (John 12:29). What is not rare is the image of a nascent religious community convinced of its authority to speak for God and its power to bind and loose on earth and in heaven accompanied by sporadic prophecies and private miracles—not unlike its Talmudic Jewish twin which found "It is not in heaven" paradigmatic of its worldview.

The dense Catholic tradition that Newman adopted and interpreted late in Christianity's second millennium was even better versed in cosmic binding and loosing and eminently accustomed to temporal vicars deciding and defining matters of eternal import. As forms of atheism slowly gained prominence and protection in his day, few imagined that such Catholicity and unbelief could be coupled by anything other than "or." No one conceived of something like atheism as part of the leaven of Catholic thought. Perhaps Newman's "and" was the result of an exquisitely trained theological ear, keenly attuned to the evolutionary course of his inherited tradition's mental life, detecting faint signals of what Buckley, Hyman, and even Miles would later identify as a fertile theism giving birth to atheism or a variant of theism strangely ill equipped to distinguish divine occultation from non-existence. Today's Catholic-atheist dialogue may be an echo of a perennial interior dialogue active at the deepest levels of the Catholic mind.

Notes

1 John Henry Newman, *An Essay in Aid of a Grammar of Assent* (Notre Dame, IN: University of Notre Dame Press, 1986), 305.

2 See Ignatius of Antioch, Epistle to the Smyrnaeans, 8. *Early Christian Writings*, trans. Maxwell Staniforth (London: Penguin Books, 1987), 103.

3 Newman, *An Essay on the Development of Christian Doctrine* (Notre Dame, IN: University of Notre Dame Press, 1989), 40.

4 Newman, *Apologia Pro Vita Sua* (New York: Image Books, 1956), 287.

5 Newman, *Apologia*, 320; *Grammar*, 335; *The Idea of a University* (New York: Holt, Rinehart, and Winston, 1964), 45.

6 Quoted in Anthony Kenny, *The Unknown God: Agnostic Essays* (London: Continuum, 2004), 170.

7 Newman, *Grammar*, 7, 309, 330.

8 Newman, *Apologia*, 287.

9 See Epistle to the Magnesians, 10 and Epistle to the Romans, 3. *Early Christian Writings*, 73, 86.

10 *Atheoi* appears in English translations as "without God" (following the Vulgate). Paul normally used *asĕbĕia*: "impiety" or "irreverence," often translated as "ungodliness." See Romans 1:18, 11:26; 2 Timothy 2:16; Titus 2:12.

11 See Jan N. Bremmer, "Atheism in Antiquity," *The Cambridge Companion to Atheism*, ed. Michael Martin (Cambridge: Cambridge University Press, 2007), 11–26. See also David Sedley, "From the Pre-Socratics to the Hellenistic Age," and Mark Edwards, "The First Millennium," *The Oxford Handbook of Atheism*, ed. Stephen Bullivant and Michael Ruse (Oxford: Oxford University Press, 2013), 139–151, 152–163.

12 Justin Martyr, First Apology, 6. *Ante-Nicene Fathers*, trans. Marcus Dods and George Reith, ed. Alexander Roberts, James Donaldson, and A. Cleveland Coxe (Buffalo, NY: Christian Literature, 1885), vol. 1. http://www.newadvent.org/fathers/0126.htm.

13 In his translation of The Martyrdom of Polycarp, Staniforth defuses the term "atheists" with "infidels." See *Early Christian Writings*, 126, 128.

14 Athenagorus, A Plea Regarding Christians, 4. *Early Christian Fathers*, trans. Cyril C. Richardson (New York: Collier, 1970), 303.

15 Justin, 6. *Early Christian Fathers*, 245.

16 See Michael J. Buckley, *At the Origins of Modern Atheism* (New Haven: Yale University Press, 1987), 4.

17 Stephen Bullivant, *Faith and Unbelief* (New York: Paulist Press, 2013), 3.

18 Hans Küng, *Does God Exist? An Answer for Today*, trans. Edward Quinn (New York: Doubleday, 1980).

19 Newman, *Grammar*, 389.

20 Mother Teresa, *Come Be My Light: The Private Writings of the "Saint of Calcutta,"* ed. Brian Kolodiejchuk (New York: Image, 2007), 210.

21 Josef Pieper, *The Silence of Saint Thomas*, trans. John Murray and Daniel O'Connor (Chicago: Henry Regnery, 1966), 84.

22 Aquinas, *Summa Theologiae*, Ia 2, 3. Translations are from *Basic Writings of Saint Thomas Aquinas*, ed. Anton C. Pegis (New York: Random House, 1945), 2 vols.

23 See Bertrand Russell, *The History of Western Philosophy* (New York: Simon and Schuster, 1972), 463.

24 Peter Kreeft, *A Shorter Summa* (San Francisco: Ignatius Press, 1993), 53.

25 Aquinas, Ia 1.

26 Aquinas, Ia 2, 3.

27 *Gaudium et Spes*, 19. See *Vatican II: The Essential Texts*, ed. Norman Tanner (New York: Image, 2012), 210.

28 See Peter Hebblethwaite, ed., *The Council Fathers and Atheism* (New York: Paulist Press, 1966).

29 See Buckley, *At the Origins* and *Denying and Disclosing God: The Ambiguous Progress of Modern Atheism* (New Haven: Yale University Press, 2004).
30 Gavin Hyman, *A Short History of Atheism* (London: I. B. Tauris, 2010), 71.
31 Quoted in Buckley, *Denying*, 50.
32 Hyman, 67.
33 Richard Elliott Friedman, *The Disappearance of God: A Divine Mystery* (Boston: Little, Brown, and Company, 1995), 20–26, 82.
34 Miles, *God: A Biography* (New York: Vintage, 1995), 11, 12, 253, 329.
35 Friedman, 122–126.
36 Miles, 292–292.
37 See Miles, *Christ: A Crisis in the Life of God* (New York: Vintage, 2001).

21

ATHEISM AND ESOTERISM

A Muslim Perspective

Reza Shah-Kazemi

In his famous diatribe against religious belief, *The God Delusion*, Richard Dawkins paints an ugly caricature of the God of the Old Testament, referring to Him as "the most unpleasant character in all fiction", and describing Him, among other things, as a "capriciously malevolent bully".[1] This statement serves as a useful starting-point for our chapter. One of the chief reasons for the prevalence of atheism in modern times is a crude anthropomorphic conception of God. Dawkins's depiction of God as a malevolent bully stems from a childish reading of the Old Testament, which arises out of, and in turn feeds into, a simplistic notion of an anthromorphic divinity: a flat, planimetric, and impoverished conception of ultimate reality, devoid of mystical depth, metaphysical subtlety, and mythical texture.[2] To conceive of God in exclusively anthropomorphic terms is to conjure up a reified projection of human subjectivity, a constructed image of some fabricated macrocosmic entity, an image denuded of the unfathomable mystery of divine immanence, subjectively; and bereft of the sublime ineffability of divine transcendence, objectively. This kind of literalist exegesis is, ironically, the basis both of religious fundamentalism and militant atheism, serving as a common epistemological premise linking the two apparently opposed mentalities, a common ground constructed out of rationalistic premises and reductionistic prejudices.

One could direct the likes of Dawkins to such exegetes as the Jewish Platonist, Philo of Alexandria (d. ca. 50 CE) who would be able to explain that the apparent emotions of God—His "anger", "revenge", etc.—are so many ways of alluding to the inner dramaturgy played out every day in the struggles of the soul in quest of deliverance from error and sin, the "punishments" of the anthropomorphic deity being understood as the remonstrances of the immanent intellect (*nous*). And Dawkins would also learn from Philo that

DOI: 10.4324/9781003536185-24

this subtle appreciation of scriptural imagery will only emerge in proportion to one's intellectual maturity, itself not so much the result of rational speculation but rather arising out of the creative synthesis of intellectual contemplation and spiritual praxis. Pierre Hadot, in his ground-breaking work, *Philosophy as a Way of Life*, refers to Philo's "spiritual exercises" in terms of so many philosophical "therapies" (reminding us that the Greek *therapeiai* "can also mean acts of worship", and that "this meaning would be entirely possible in Philo's mind"):

> Research (*zetesis*), thorough investigation (*skepsis*), reading (*anagnosis*), listening (*akroasis*), attention (*prosoche*), self-mastery (*enkrateia*), and indifference to indifferent things ... reading, meditations, therapies of the passions, remembrance of good things ... and the accomplishment of duties.[3]

However, modern atheists are unlikely to take seriously the claim that these spiritual, intellectual, and ethical disciplines generate in some mysterious way a radical enhancement, let alone epistemological transformation, of one's cognitive capacity, such as would allow one to conceive of the existence of God, or, more profoundly, to intuit the reality of the Absolute. Indeed, it is most improbable that any traditional theological exegeses will make atheists change their minds about the existence of "God", such as this word has been understood according to prevailing norms within both contemporary religious thought and atheistic discourse alike.

However, we believe that it is possible that an esoteric appreciation of the meaning of the Absolute, understood as at once transcending and comprising the Personal God, may give atheists cause to re-think the premises upon which they construct their arguments denying the existence of God. If we consider the esoteric perspectives of mystics such as Meister Eckhart, Ibn al-'Arabi, Shankara, Nagarjuna, etc., we might come to see that the negation of the existence of "God" is tantamount to an illogical negation of existence, *tout court.*

First, however, in the interests of "full disclosure" we have to explain how an ostensibly "Muslim" perspective can be substantiated by reference to sages, saints, and scriptures outside the framework of Islam, understanding the latter as one religion among others. In doing so, we will be touching on another of the great stumbling-blocks in the path of belief in God: the mutually exclusive truth-claims of the different religions.[4] The following Koranic verse, describing the Muslim *credo*, is one of the premises upon which we would posit the legitimacy of a supra-confessional epistemology, which is nonetheless rooted in Koranic discourse:

> The Messenger believes in that which has been revealed unto him from his Lord, and [so do] the believers. Every one believes in God and His angels

194 Religion and Atheism in Dialogue

and His scriptures and His Messengers—[saying:] we make no distinction between any of His Messengers ...

(K 2:285)

The Muslim who is sensitive to the universalist implication of the injunction not to make any distinction between any of the prophets of God will read in a different light those verses proclaiming that all of the prophets were sent by God with the identical message: "For every community (umma) there is a Messenger" (K 10:47).

The Koran makes explicit reference to several prophets, but the scope of prophetic guidance extends far beyond those mentioned, for "Verily We sent Messengers before you [Muhammad]; among them are those about whom We have told you, and those about whom We have not told you" (K 40:78). The following verses further substantiate the legitimacy of an epistemology that is both authentically rooted in the Koran—and thus properly "Islamic"—and radically open to all other scriptural revelations—and thus universalist, transcending the boundaries of "Islam" as conventionally conceived:

Truly We have revealed unto you as We have revealed to Noah and the prophets after him, as We revealed to Abraham and Ishmael and Isaac and the tribes, and Jesus and Job and Jonah and Aaron and Solomon, and as We bestowed upon David the Psalms;

And messengers We have mentioned to you before and messengers We have not mentioned to you; and God spoke directly to Moses;

Messengers giving good tidings and [also] warnings, so that mankind might have no argument against God after the messengers. God is ever Mighty, Wise.

(4: 163–165)

And We sent no Messenger before you but We inspired him [saying]: There is no God save Me, so worship Me.

(21: 25)

Naught is said unto you [Muḥammad] but what was said unto the Messengers before you.

(41: 43)

The universalist Muslim is therefore at liberty to turn to any of the revealed religions—and indeed any of the pre-religious shamanistic traditions[5]—for inspiration, seeing them all as modes of revelation of the self-same transcendent reality. At the same time, we can regard all religious dispensations as what the Buddhists call *upāyas*, "saving strategies": ways of subtly intimating, not exhaustively explicating, realities that infinitely transcend the

Atheism and Esoterism **195**

domains of human thought and language: "Glorified be God above what they describe" is a frequent refrain in the Koran.

Given the limitations of space in this volume, we will restrict ourselves to looking at two of the mystics mentioned above, Ibn al-ʿArabī and Meister Eckhart, in order to critique Dawkins's caricature of the anthropomorphic deity, and to show that, according to both of these spiritual masters, the very essence of human intelligence is constituted by innate knowledge of transcendent reality—or, in Eckhart's terms, intellectual perception of the "God beyond God", the "Godhead", the "Ground", the "Essence".

The first point to make regarding the inadequacy of the anthropomorphic conception of God is that all human conceptions of God are so many veils over the transcendent Essence of God. For the true nature of God, Eckhart tells us, "is to be without nature. To think of goodness or wisdom or power dissembles the essence and dims it in thought. The mere thought obscures essence".[6] All human thought inescapably falls short of the reality of the Essence, for this Essence transcends the "God" that can be conceived. Similarly, according to Ibn al-ʿArabī, this "God", the putatively divine counterpart of human thought, is in one respect a "creature", that is, a conception created in the form of the beliefs held concerning God. Toby Mayer explains: "In his typically outspoken formulation, the conceptual God is just a 'created God'". He is "the God created in dogmas (*al-Ḥaqq al-makhlūq fiʼl-iʿtiqādāt*). In the Islamic ethos, such a deity is ultimately a deception".[7]

How, then, to see through this "deception"? Ibn al-ʿArabī tells us that we do so by recognizing the manifestation or self-disclosure (*tajallī*) of God in and through all forms of belief, on the one hand; and by knowing that the human being cannot know the Essence of God, on the other. Ibn al-ʿArabī substantiates the first perspective with reference to a canonical saying of the Prophet, according to which God will appear to the believers on the day of Resurrection, declaring that He is their Lord. The believers not recognizing Him, seek refuge in God from Him; only when God "transforms" (*yataḥawwal*) Himself according to the forms of their beliefs do they recognize Him, and worship Him accordingly.[8] Ibn al-ʿArabī thus warns us:

> Beware of being bound up by a particular religion and rejecting others as unbelief! If you do that you will fail to obtain a great benefit. Nay, you will fail to obtain the true knowledge of reality. Try to make yourself a Prime Matter for all forms of religious belief. God is greater and wider than to be confined to one particular religion to the exclusion of others. For He says: "To whichever direction you turn, there surely is the Face of God".
>
> *(K 2: 115) (Sufism, 254)*

Like Eckhart, Ibn al-ʿArabī distinguishes between the "level" or "degree" (*martaba*) of divinity that is circumscribed within the dualistic ontological

196 Religion and Atheism in Dialogue

framework defined by cause and effect, creator and creature, etc., on the one hand; and the divine Essence (*al-dhāt*), on the other hand, the unconditional 'Self of the Real' (*nafs al-ḥaqq*), transcending all duality, and ultimately knowable only through the effacement of the veils or limitations placed upon consciousness by specifically human modes of cognition. The gnostic sage (*al-ʿarif bi'Llāh*) knows that God can only be known through the extinction (*fanāʾ*) of empirical individuality and all the limitations on consciousness implied thereby. Only when such limitations are deconstructed and rendered inoperative can consciousness *per se* subsist, that consciousness which, being devoid of specific content, can alone be identified with pure being, matrix of all possible contents of consciousness.

Instead of being conscious of some "thing" by which consciousness becomes conditioned and relativized, consciousness as such "subsists" (in the state called *al-baqāʾ baʿd al-fanāʾ*, "subsistence after annihilation"), that is, consciousness pure and simple. It is not a question of simply becoming conscious of being—for it is still the individual agent who is in play, a subject who remains distinct from the object, "being"; nor is it a question of simply being conscious—it is the individual subjectivity that is conscious, or has consciousness. Rather, it is about the perfect identity or union between being and consciousness. In the words of Frithjof Schuon: "to know that which is" means, in the final analysis "to be that which knows: the Self".[9] Consciousness and being are indistinguishably identified with each other.

Here, we should note that both Eckhart and Ibn al-ʿArabī are in complete agreement with the Vedantin ternary *Sat-Chit-Ananda*, "Being-Consciousness-Bliss" by which the ultimate reality, the absolute Self (*paramātman*) is designated in the Advaita school of Hinduism. The Vedantin formula is expressed by Ibn al-ʿArabī as follows: "Being is the finding of the Real in ecstasy"; and by Meister Eckhart in his assertion that the "content" of the divine Word that is mystically "spoken" by God in the depths of the heart is "immeasurable power, infinite wisdom, and infinite sweetness"; likewise, Eckhart speaks of his ultimate state of unitive realization in terms of the same three transcendent values, undifferentiated though they be in the Absolute: "I was bare being and the knower of myself in the enjoyment of truth".[10]

Eckhart would surely have resonated with Ibn al-ʿArabī's simple description of the ultimate attainment of gnosis (*maʿrifa*): "The final end and ultimate return of the gnostics … is that the Real is identical with them, while they do not exist".[11] We find Eckhart saying, on the one hand, as regards the "non-existent" dimension of the gnostic: "All creatures are pure nothing. I do not say that they are a little something, or anything at all, but that they are pure nothing".[12] And, on the other hand, as regards the identification of the gnostic with the oneness of reality: "One is the negation of the negation and a denial of the denial. All creatures have a negation in themselves: one negates by not being the other ... but God negates the negation: He is one and negates all else, for outside of God, nothing is".[13]

Let us now return to Dawkins's caricature of the personal God. Eckhart tells us that "God, inasmuch as He is 'God', is not the supreme goal of creatures". That is: the divinity that can be conceived by the creature as its Creator is not the Absolute, it is not transcendent Reality; this "god" cannot constitute the "supreme goal" of the creature because there is something in the creature that is uncreated, and seeks only what is at one with its own uncreatable substance, and that is the intellect: "There is a power in the soul.... If the whole soul were like it, she would be uncreated and uncreatable, but this is not so. In its other part it has a regard for and a dependence on time, and there it touches on creation and is created. To this power, *the intellect*, nothing is distant or external" (emphasis added).[14]

The stunning implication of this uncreated and uncreatable power of the intellect—which Eckhart has evidently verified experientially, hence his prayer at the end of this sermon for his congregation "to come to this experience"—is spelt out in the following extraordinary statement: "If a fly had reason and could intellectually plumb the eternal abysm of God's being out of which it came, we would have to say that God, with all that makes Him 'God' would be unable to fulfill and satisfy that fly!"[15] If the fly possessed an intellect, it would be capable of discerning the "eternal abysm" out of which God, qua Creator, arose. This is because the uncreated intellect can conceive of its own uncreated Essence, the absolute unicity of which perforce transcends the level of being proper to the Creator, who is relativized by its very creation of creatures; in other words, the Creator cannot be absolute, cannot be identified in every respect with the Absolute whence it, *qua* first of all relativities, emerges into being. The creature can worship the Creator, but this relationship remains, precisely, a *relation*-ship, that is: an expression circumscribed by *relativity*, whose dualistic ontological framework is transcended by the unicity of the Absolute.

For Ibn al-ʿArabī, likewise, the relationship between Creator and creature is ontologically dualistic, and cannot attain to the unicity of ultimate reality. The creature praises God, according to Ibn alʿArabī, "with a praise worthy of God, *accident for accident*" (emphasis added).[16] Since there is no common measure between the creature and the One, the worship performed by the creature cannot but "relate" to the relative divinity, the personal God, the Creator, the Lord. Ibn al-ʿArabī highlights this principle by means of an esoteric interpretation of the Koranic injunction: the servant who hopes to meet his Lord should not "associate (any) one with his Lord's worship" (18: 119). The literal meaning of the verse relates to the prohibition of *shirk* or associating false deities with the true God, but Ibn al-ʿArabī interprets the "one" in question here as being the One, who "is not worshipped in respect of His Unity, since Unity contradicts the existence of the worshipper". What is

198 Religion and Atheism in Dialogue

worshipped is only the Lord, "so connect yourself to Him and make yourself lowly before Him, and do not associate Unity with Lordship in worship.... For Unity does not know you and will not accept you".[17]

At this point we observe that Dawkins and his fellow atheists may well share some common ground with Eckhart and Ibn al-'Arabī: they affirm that the Personal God is not absolute. The negation of relativity in question here might be seen to be akin to the negation expressed in the first half of the Muslim testimony of faith: *lā ilāha*, "no divinity". However, the second half of the testimony, *illā'Llāh*, "only the Divinity", which is the affirmation of the pure Absolute, is what the atheists cannot accept. The baby (the Absolute) is thrown out with the bathwater (the relative). Denial of the ultimate reality of the Personal God entails denial of ultimate reality per se. As a consequence of the denial of any reality that transcends the level of existence proportional to ordinary modes of human cognition, it becomes impossible for atheists to conceive of the ways—at once mysterious and marvelous—in which the Absolute as it were makes itself relative, revealing itself as the Personal God, or does not so reveal Itself, as in the case of Buddhism.[18]

In terms of the Buddhist *upāya*, perception of the relativity of the Creator-God is a "categorical imperative"; the need to transcend the level of being upon which the Creator-God is situated is expressed forcefully in the Zen statement: "If you see the Buddha, slay him!"[19] The question may be asked here: what is the relationship between "slaying" the form of the relative, in order to realize the supra-formal essence of the Absolute, on the one hand, and the perception of the relative form *qua* real expression of the Absolute, on the other? Eckhart gives us an answer:

> The least creaturely image that takes place in you is as big as God. How is that? It deprives you of the whole of God. As soon as the image comes in, God has to leave with all His Godhead.... Go right out of yourself for God's sake, and God will go right out of Himself for your sake! When these two have gone out what is left is one and simple. In this One the Father bears His Son in the inmost source.[20]

To appreciate the metaphysical significance of Eckhart's statement here, we can profitably turn to the famous incident narrated in St John's Gospel (20: 17). When Mary Magdalen tried to embrace the resurrected body of Jesus, she is told by him: "Do not cling to Me, for I have not yet ascended to My Father; but go to My brethren and say to them, 'I am ascending to My Father and your Father, and to My God and your God'".[21] The Son—the form assumed by formless—will be revealed as a reality—a relative one, but real nonetheless—insofar as its essence is grasped as being one with absolute reality, the "Father". On the basis of the fundamental intuition of the Absolute—of necessary as opposed to possible being, of a reality that cannot not be—the forms by which the Absolute enters into relativity are perceived as veils, at once enshrouding and revealing the Absolute. The form—the Personal God—is thus real by virtue of its identity with the supra-personal Essence: "I and the Father are one" (John, 10:30); and also unreal, to the extent that it is distinct from the Essence: "Why callest thou me good? There is none good but one, that is, God" (Matthew, 19:17).

It is precisely because of the presence of the pure Absolute in the depths of the heart—in the uncreated intellect, in Eckhart's terms—that the individual is capable of discerning between itself as a relative reality and "God" as absolute reality: it is by virtue of divine immanence that divine transcendence is conceivable. If the intellect is capable of conceiving of the transcendent Essence, it must be because the intellect is not other than it. If God be defined as Creator in relation to creatures, it is perforce subordinate to the Essence, the Godhead. This perspective might be seen as the metaphysical logic implicit in the classical ontological proof of God: whereas for St. Anselm, the reality of God is as it were proven by the human capacity for conceiving of God, Eckhart would have us see that the relativity of God *qua* Creator is proven by our intellectual capacity to conceive of the uncreated Essence of God. This intellectual capacity, in turn, derives from the uncreated essence of the intellect, which is the ontological foundation, and not simply the logical premise, upon which spiritual realization of the Essence of the One is conceivable and attainable.

We conclude this essay with the following passage from Frithjof Schuon's *In the Face of the Absolute*. It distills the essence of the metaphysical distinction made by the mystics studied in this essay—the distinction between the relativity of the Personal God and the absoluity of the Essence of God; and at the same time it helps us to understand why the Absolute, in its self-disclosure as so many "Faces" of the Personal God turned towards particular religious communities, cannot but manifest apparently contradictory and mutually exclusive features. The atheistic arguments founded upon these apparent contradictions, together with the literalist readings of scripture by anthromorphically inclined theologians, are forestalled by the intuitive vision elicited by Schuon's metaphysical exposition:

> From the strictly human point of view … "God" could not be the Absolute as such, for the Absolute has no interlocutor; we may, however, say that God is the hypostatic Face turned towards the human world, or towards a particular human world; in other words, God is Divinity which personalizes itself in view of man and insofar as it more or less takes on the countenance of a particular humanity. Another question: what does this personalized Divinity, this God become partner or interlocutor, or this Divine Face turned towards man "want" or "desire"? The most concise answer seems to us to be the following: if the Divine Essence, being infinite,

200 Religion and Atheism in Dialogue

tends to manifest itself by projecting its innumerable potentialities into the finite, the Divine Face, for its part, operates this projection and then—at a more relative level—projects within this first projection a principle of coordination, among other things a Law intended to regulate the human world and above all to regulate this miniature world that is the individual. This Face is thus like a sheaf of rays with diverse functions; a Face which, although it issues from the same Divine Order, does not amount to a single subjectivity with a moral intention; thus it is vain to seek behind the infinitely diverse combinations of the veil of *Māyā* an anthropomorphic and humanly graspable personality.[22]

Notes

1 Richard Dawkins, *The God Delusion* (Boston, MA: Houghton Mifflin Harcourt, 2008), 31.
2 We use the word "mythical" not in the pejorative sense, but in the sense well expressed by Karen Armstrong: "A myth is true because it is effective, not because it gives us factual information. If it works, if it forces us to change our hearts and minds [metanoia], gives us new hope, and compels us to live more fully, it is a valid myth. Mythology will only transform us if we follow its directives. A myth is essentially a guide; it tells us what we must do in order to live more richly. If we do not apply it to our own situation and make the myth a reality in our own lives, it will remain as incomprehensible and remote as the rules of a board game, which often seem confusing and boring until we start to play". Karen Armstrong, *A Short History of Myth* (Edinburgh: Canongate, 2005), 10.
3 Pierre Hadot, *Philosophy as a Way of Life: Spiritual Exercises from Socrates to Foucault*, ed. Arnold I. Davidson; trans. Michael Chase, (Oxford: Blackwell, 1995), 84.
4 See the works of Frithjof Schuon, particularly his *The Transcendent Unity of Religions*, trans. Peter Townsend, (London: Faber and Faber, 1953), for a compelling demonstration of the essential unity of the religions underlying their formal incompatibility.
5 See our *The Other in the Light of the One: The Universality of the Qur'an and Interfaith Dialogue*, (Cambridge: Islamic Texts Society, 2006), for discussion of these and kindred themes.
6 *Meister Eckhart: Sermons & Treatises*, trans. and ed. M. O'C. Walshe (Longmead: Element Books, 1987), vol. 2, 32.
7 Toby Mayer, 'Theology and Sufism' in *The Cambridge Companion to Classical Islamic Theology*, ed. Tim Winter (Cambridge: Cambridge University Press, 2008), 257.
8 See for discussion, William Chittick, *The Sufi Path of Knowledge: Ibn al-ʿArabī's Metaphysics of Imagination* (Albany: State University of New York Press, 1989), 38, 100, 336–338.
9 Frithjof Schuon, *Gnosis: Divine Wisdom*, trans. G. E. H. Palmer (London: John Murray, 1957), 88.
10 See our *Paths to Transcendence: According to Shankara, Ibn Arabi and Meister Eckhart* (Bloomington: World Wisdom Books, 2006), chapter 4, 'The Realisation of Transcendence: Essential Elements of Commonality', 193–211.
11 Quoted in Chittick, *Sufi Path*, op. cit., 375.
12 *Meister Eckhart*, op. cit., vol. I, note C.

13 *Meister Eckhart*, vol II, 339.
14 *Meister Eckhart*, vol. I, 190.
15 *Meister Eckhart*, vol. II, 271.
16 Chittick, *Sufi Path*, op. cit., 367.
17 Chittick, *Sufi Path*, 244.
18 See our *Common Ground between Islam and Buddhism* (Louisville: Fons Vitae, 2012), where we propose ways in which Buddhism can be appreciated as non-theistic rather than atheistic; the arguments of this book were endorsed both by the Dalai Lama (in his Foreword to the book) and by Buddhist scholars such as Robert Tenzin Thurman and Jack Cornfield. See Frithjof Schuon, *Treasures of Buddhism*, trs. Mark Perry & Jean-Pierre Lafouge; ed. Harry Oldmeadow, (Bloomington: World Wisdom Books, 2018) for the key insights on which our book was based.
19 A saying first uttered apparently by Linji Yixuan, a 9th century Chinese Buddhist patriarch of Zen (Ch'an). See *Hoofprint of the Ox: Principles of the Chan Buddhist Path as Taught by a Modern Chinese Master*, Master Sheng-yen & Dan Stevenson (New York: Oxford University Press, 2001), 119.
20 *Meister Eckhart*, op. cit., vol I, 118.
21 See for discussion of the profound teaching in question here, James S. Cutsinger, "Disagreeing to Agree: A Christian Response to *A Common Word*" (www. cutsinger.net/scholarship/articles.shtml). Cutsinger argues that Christians and Muslims can disagree on the level of theology in order to agree on the plane of metaphysics. This argument is based upon the teachings of Frithjof Schuon, whose perspective on this question is summed up in the formula: conform to holy separation at the base in order to realize holy union at the summit. See Frithjof Schuon, *Logic and Transcendence—A New Translation with Selected Letters*, ed. James S. Cutsinger (Bloomington: World Wisdom Books, 2009), 195.
22 Frithjof Schuon, *In the Face of the Absolute* (Bloomington: World Wisdom Books, 2014).

22

FAITH, SEXUALITY AND GENDER

Navigating Difficult Conversations

Christopher Lynch

> When talking of minority sexualities and gender identities, I typically refer in this essay to 'LGBT+' people. 'LGBT' refers to lesbians, gay men, bisexual people and trans people. I use '+' to include people who might not neatly fit into traditional categories of sex, gender identity or sexuality. I also use the term 'queer' to capture the same communities as denoted by 'LGBT+', and therefore 'queerphobia' to mean prejudice towards or discrimination against any LGBT+ individuals or communities. Hopefully this makes what I say clear whilst avoiding stopping to clarify my terms as I go which felt distracting.

Constructive dialogue can sometimes be difficult. There are some areas in which it can be excruciatingly difficult. In what follows I set out why the area of faith, sexuality and gender is especially challenging. I show why this is such a painful area to navigate, and then go on to say that even in such circumstances, better conversation is possible. More than that: it is necessary.

Acknowledging past and present: tensions and antagonisms

The relationship between religion on the one hand, and minority sexualities and gender identities on the other, is often experienced by LGBT+ people as tense, hostile, even incompatible. Religious communities, traditions and leaders have done real and lasting harm towards LGBT+ people. Some harms are historical, many with aftereffects reaching into today; others are happening, both in the United Kingdom and across the world, right now. Personally, I

DOI: 10.4324/9781003536185-25

have been forced to endure overwhelming shame from an early age, much (though not all) of it springing from explicitly religious condemnation of my sexuality. I have worked in schools and seen first-hand the horrific damage done in the name of religion to children and young people. Kids are made to feel dirty, sick, wrong or unlovable. They can experience disabling insecurity as they fail to see any sense of the future for themselves. Working within the charity sector, I have supported queer people desperate to come to the United Kingdom to escape exorcisms, beatings and death threats just for being who they are. I have also known friends, students and strangers take their own lives because of forces masquerading as religious robbing them of any hope or self-worth. This seems to be the majority account of how religion typically lands with LGBT+ people.[1] Sadly, the evidence base for such an account is compelling.

The Catholic Church, the largest denomination of the world's largest religion, has long spoken in favour of many anti-gay laws, instructs gay people to be chaste, and still refuses to recognise same-sex marriages in Catholic liturgy on the same footing as heterosexual ones.[2] The Church of England enjoys oversized political power within our state legislature, where bishops have been amongst the most persistent opponents of equality for LGBT+ people.[3] Many British Muslims are deeply uncomfortable with homosexuality; few recognise trans identities as valid.[4] In both the United Kingdom and across the world, queer people are threatened with torture, imprisonment or death. In 21st-century Britain, overwhelmingly religious crowds have protested to tell schools that simply teaching that gay people exist is wrong. The broadcast media are saturated with commentators 'debating' almost every aspect of trans people's lives – many of the most hostile commentators appeal to a religious standpoint. Religion has played a significant role in many places for at least the best part of a millennium in supporting queerphobia and is often one of the most openly hostile voices against LGBT+ people worldwide today. The fruits of this hostility are plain to see and undeniable in their depth and breadth: the closet, the queer suicide, the anti-trans hysteria, the murderous laws enacted in Uganda and Iran and far too many other countries.[5]

Consider, instead, non-religion. Without the queerphobic baggage attached to many religious traditions, prominent atheists are often vocal supporters of LGBT+ rights and freedoms. The loud and controversial leaders of the New Atheist movement of the past 20 years explicitly highlighted the queerphobia of religions and defended a non-religious championing of LGB people's rights (although some of the most famous New Atheists have made comments seen by many as transphobic).[6] The message for queer people is often plain: where religion is, queerphobia tends to follow.

204 Religion and Atheism in Dialogue

Humanism – a better option?

The commonest non-religious worldview today is probably humanism.[7] The word 'humanist' has come to mean someone whose beliefs and values have the following core features:

1 Human beings are a natural species whose capacities evolved over time.
2 The world is a natural place, best understood using reason and science.
3 This is the one life we know we have and so any happiness for ourselves or anyone else can only be pursued or realised in this life.
4 Humans should employ reason and empathy in making moral decisions, based on the welfare of humans, other animals and the planet.
5 By recognising our shared humanity, we can work for a better world where human rights and freedoms are enhanced, compatible with the rights and freedoms of others.[8]

The humanist approach to life has existed across different times and cultures and is shared by millions of people today. You can be a humanist having never heard the word 'humanist'. What matters is not subscribing to a set of doctrinal commitments or conditions. For many people, 'humanism' is a term that people come to later in life if at all, often after many years of believing and living out the beliefs and values I have listed.

These core features I have listed could make humanism a favourable life-stance for LGBT+ people. The rational component of humanism, embodied chiefly in features 1 and 2, highlights a concern for evidence and the dispassionate pursuit of knowledge by observation and empirical testing. When humanists look at the evidence, amongst humans and other animals, they encounter an abundance of examples of same-sex activities, pair bonding and, in the case of humans at least, lasting and even lifelong romantic union. Likewise, humanists will see that diverse gender identities have been described in societies as wide-ranging as the ancient Canaanites, Indian hijra communities and Native American two-spirit cultures. LGBT+ people's lives and loves are therefore natural and a brute fact as much as anything else is. They pose no problem or question distinct from any other natural phenomena.

The moral component, encapsulated in features 3 to 5, explains how many humanists approach LGBT+ people's equality and rights. If being trans, or participating in a consensual non-heterosexual relationship or sex act, harms no-one else, then it is not morally wrong. After all, we have one life in which to live out our projects and relationships. This gives a profound urgency and preciousness to the life we are living now. There had better, therefore, be a powerful reason to ever inhibit or limit someone's actions. For humanists, this reason is elegantly simple: do what you want, provided you act within the rights and freedoms of others.[9] Sex and relationships are

Faith, Sexuality and Gender **205**

a central part for many humans of a well-lived life, providing interpersonal fulfilment and a sense of connection that can be a cherished source of meaning in people's lives. Being able to live freely without others suppressing your identity is an important avenue for freedom and self-actualisation. By applying empathy and considering what best maximises happiness or flourishing, humanists see nothing to condemn and everything to celebrate in people living out their lives in a consensual and fulfilling way based on their sexuality or gender identity. This is precisely what humanists have long advocated and campaigned for, and many humanist individuals and organisations today remain at the forefront of the struggle for LGBT+ equality and liberation worldwide.[10]

The truth isn't always simple

The antagonistic picture of religion and LGBT+ rights I have painted so far captures much, but not all. Before I note two complications, I want to emphasise something fundamental: the reality of genuine and deep disagreement between non-religious and religious believers. Take humanism as an example. Many humanists' starting points for thinking and acting aren't just different from those of religious believers, but antithetical. Most religious believers posit a supernatural dimension in which God or gods exist(s); humanists do not. Most humanists think meaning and purpose emerge from finding fulfilment in this life; religious believers typically assert an external standard of absolute purpose in life tied to what happens after bodily death. These are deep disagreements, and they matter. Some people may not be prepared to fully (or even partially) concede ground on some of their core beliefs. However, as I argue later, this depth of disagreement should not impede the possibility of genuine dialogue and of shared action for a better world.

With that statement made, let's turn to two complications of the picture I have been painting, both of which challenge the notion that religion and queerphobia are as straightforwardly intertwined as might be assumed. I mention both here as I think they both contain some truth and are important to acknowledge.

First, many people of faith see religion as compatible with LGBT+ equality. Most scriptural texts hardly mention queer identities, but where they do, it isn't conclusive that they explicitly condemn LGBT+ people's lives and loves. Political and social forces have often co-opted cherry-picked religious quotes and weaponised them, sometimes with catastrophic success, against LGBT+ communities. We know that Jesus never mentioned homosexuality. We also know that where Jewish and Christian texts discuss homosexuality it is within a context that relegates homosexuality to one mundane sin amongst hundreds or ends up condemning all sorts of acts that we take to be morally neutral or even good. Similarly, there is lively disagreement amongst

206 Religion and Atheism in Dialogue

Muslims about where theological condemnation of LGBT+ ends and political and personal biases and bigotries begin.

There are many exemplary voices defending LGBT+ rights in religious spaces, ranging from Ruth Hunt (former CEO of Stonewall and a practising Catholic) and Waheed Ali (Muslim member of the House of the Lords) to scholars like John Boswell and clerics like Seong Yang. 'Organised religion' – that is, the institutions and networks of communities formally categorised by sets of rules and united under a common affiliation – might sometimes be queerphobic, but religious texts are mostly inconclusive regarding matters of sexuality or gender identity. Moreover, testimonies abound of religious believers and communities welcoming LGBT+ individuals. God is love, such people sometimes say, whilst others state that judgement should be left to the divine rather than to fallible human beings. The claim that wherever religion goes, queerphobia follows is a hasty generalisation. And this is clearly true. Not all religious people are anti-LGBT+, and a good number of religious believers are champions of equality.

Second, religion is not and never has been the sole cause of queerphobia. There are examples of hostility to LGBT+ people and their rights which are not religious in nature. Section 28 was a nasty piece of governmental legislation; it was not a religious injunction.[11] The voices today seeking to deny trans people access to certain spaces are not always religious, and the banners under which they march are often wholly secular. Throughout history, humans have pursued power, they have been tribal and they have made use of convenient bandwagons to entrench and reinforce these tendencies. Religion has sometimes been a tool used to put down other human beings, but arguably this is a sad distortion of religious teachings of peace and it says more about the darker sides of humanity than about the essential character of any religion. Again, there is some truth to this. Not all queerphobic people and organisations are religious, and some of the most strongly antagonistic voices are secular.

Temptations to avoid

There can be a temptation to over-emphasise the two complications I have described. Some well-meaning people point always and only to examples of religious believers supporting LGBT+ rights and they strategically ignore the evidence of religious damage. But this is a mistake. Burying our heads in the sand may at times feel like the most viable option. However, it can also be dangerously dismissive, robbing those at the sharp end of religious queerphobia of their lived experiences and their voices. We have both an intellectual and moral obligation to acknowledge where real harm has been done and that, in far too many cases, religion has damaged LGBT+ people. Until we acknowledge these painful facts and acknowledge the reality of deep disagreement, we kid ourselves if we think we are doing anything more than exercising wilful ignorance. Genuine dialogue is possible and desirable, but it must be open-eyed and look squarely at the evidence.

It is wonderful that many areas of inclusive and loving practice exist where LGBT+ people are not just tolerated but accepted and welcomed within faith communities. It is also important and right that we signpost instances of Christian history where LGBT+ people were recognised and loved, and that we teach children about Islamic poetry that depicted same-sex relationships and about the Mahabharata stories of sex-changing deities. We should remind ourselves, too, that forces other than religion have played their part in fanning the flames of queerphobia. But we cannot ignore that religion has frequently had a uniquely nefarious part to play.

Some 'religious' condemnation of LGBT+ people can be traced to politicised interpretations of scripture. It can be more a reflection of culture than theology. Still, there are the hard realities of religious texts where no amount of theological interpretation will totally remove the sting for many LGBT+ people. The Qur'an warns that sex with a same-sex partner 'exceeds all bounds' and warrants hellfire.[12] The Bible might not single out homosexuality as uniquely detestable, but it is an abomination nonetheless.[13] In a world where religious slogans are the final words heard by young people targeted for 'conversion' therapy or by gay men being thrown off buildings, it is simply not good enough to dismiss all religious queerphobia as 'merely cultural' or as an unfortunate misunderstanding of God's word.[14]

Ground rules for better conversations

Given these deep disagreements and both awkward and painful facts, where do we go from here? How can we have better conversations about gender identity and sexual orientation? There are many people of sincere intent and good faith who passionately want to create a world that is safe for everyone whilst also respecting different people's opinions. Some might say this is impossible. On the contrary, better dialogue is possible. Moreover, it is necessary, because without it we fall into ever greater mutual suspicion and fragmentation. We can and should resist a moral and political instability that spells disaster for everyone and guarantees the safety and security of no-one.

Some non-negotiables should be agreed as ground rules for informed and respectful dialogue to get going. These should be ground rules in principle acceptable to anyone, so not exclusive to any worldview, religious or otherwise. They should be as uncontroversial as possible – it may be impossible to please everyone, but these should be rules that have enough content that they can be useful in framing dialogue, whilst not being so value-laden that

208 Religion and Atheism in Dialogue

they privilege the dialogue too much in a particular direction. Perhaps a good place to start is the following:

1 Be fact-sensitive. Lived experience matters.
2 Be harm-sensitive. Where possible, harm should be minimised and safe-guarding ensured.
3 Seek shared values, not shared beliefs.

Let's start with fact-sensitivity. Conversations must be informed by the best available evidence. There will be times when this will be lived experience. Testimonies of LGBT+ people bruised at the hands of religion should be heard and acknowledged, not skipped over in misplaced pursuit of 'politeness' or 'sensitivity'. Likewise, people of faith must be listened to, whether they are working tirelessly for greater LGBT+ inclusion within their faith communities or whether they have profound anxieties around where LGBT+ matters and religious teachings meet. We get nowhere if we ignore the facts and evidence on all sides.

Just as evidence matters, so does avoiding unnecessary (further) harm. This might be achieved in part as a by-product of fact-sensitivity, giving due credence to people's experiences and feelings and avoiding ostracism or gas-lighting. It is important to listen in a way that assumes positive intent, but this openness should never be an excuse for enabling the violation of dignity. Where legal frameworks or safeguarding policies exist, these must be followed. The Equality Act of 2010 protects religion or belief as well as sex, sexuality and gender reassignment.[15] Imperfect though legislation might be, laws can be vital in spaces of contested rights-talk as tools to protect and to affirm the principle of equal dignity. People can believe whatever they like, but where these beliefs turn into degradations or violations of others' rights, safeguarding responsibility must come in.

Finally, we should focus on shared values, not shared beliefs. I have already mentioned the idea of starting points. Non-religious people have different, and sometimes antithetical, starting points in their thinking and action from many religious believers. It helps no-one to deny this. However, any look at history or at contemporary societies like the United Kingdom shows us that holding antithetical beliefs need not mean holding antithetical values. Every day, people of multiple faiths and none gather in schools, workplaces, and many other settings and work together. The COVID-19 pandemic brought neighbours and strangers together regardless of their disparate or even contradictory beliefs and approaches to the world. These examples might seem mundane, but widened out on a macro-level, they represent the importance and obviousness of this fact: people can share common values across difference. Whilst the routes taken to arrive at these values may be unalike, even strikingly so, the shared point at which people arrive is often nevertheless the same – or, at least, it is similar enough to make both dialogue and shared action possible. Seeking to change people's beliefs is counter-productive, morally dubious and illiberal. Values are a much more promising target to aim at.

Conclusion

I have shown that many LGBT+ people experience religion as harmful. I have also shown that religious and non-religious people often differ radically in their worldviews. I have made the case that both these facts must be acknowledged if we are to have meaningful conversations with one another to find shared values and share the same society. Throughout, I have tried to listen, with empathy and good faith, to a range of voices whilst setting out certain ground rules that must be accepted if better conversations around religion, gender identities and sexual orientations are to proceed. The facts of religious queerphobia and of deep disagreement cannot and should not be ignored, but they need not close off urgent conversations around sexuality and gender identity.

These conversations might be difficult and painful. They might take a long time. But the only way to get to the other side with anything like a sustainable and meaningful outcome is to put in the deep, sensitive and laborious work that actual listening requires. Not only is better quality of public conversation possible and desirable: in a complex and interconnected world beset by crises on all levels, it is necessary. We can do better for everyone and work towards a future world where we stare brute facts in the face, listen to all well-intended participants, and where the failures of past and present need no longer continue. I hope that my contribution here is a step towards such better conversations.

Notes

1 See, for example: Chapter 6: Religion | Pew Research Center, last accessed 28/05/2024; LGBT people are 'being made homeless due to religion' – BBC News, last accessed 28/05/2024; https://humanists.uk/2023/05/05/most-lgbt-people-are-non-religious-census-2021/, last accessed 28/05/2024.
2 https://www.usccb.org/sites/default/files/flipbooks/catechism/568/, last accessed 28/05/2024.
3 https://www.theguardian.com/world/2023/jan/18/church-of-england-bishops-refuse-to-back-gay-marriage, last accessed 28/05/2024.
4 https://edition.cnn.com/2016/05/11/europe/britain-muslims-survey/index.html, last accessed 28/05/2024; https://www.advocatesforyouth.org/wp-content/uploads/2019/05/Im-Muslim-My-Gender-Doesnt-Fit-Me.pdf, last accessed 28/05/2024.
5 https://www.humandignitytrust.org/lgbt-the-law/map-of-criminalisation/?type_filter_submitted=&type_filter%5B%5D=crim_lgbt&type_filter%5B%5D=death_pen_applies, last accessed 28/05/2024.

210 Religion and Atheism in Dialogue

6 For supporting LGB rights, see, for example: https://www.theguardian.com/books/2018/mar/20/richard-dawkins-to-give-away-copies-of-the-god-delusion-in-islamic-countries, last accessed 28/05/2024; for Richard Dawkins' interventions regarding trans people: https://www.thepinknews.com/2021/05/20/richard-dawkins-humanist-of-the-year-american-association-trans-twitter, last accessed 28/05/2024.

7 https://understandinghumanism.org.uk/what-is-humanism/how-many-humanists-are-there/, last accessed 28/05/2024.

8 https://understandinghumanism.org.uk/what-is-humanism/, last accessed 28/05/2024.

9 https://andrewcopson.com/2022/11/a-humanist-perspective-on-freedom-of-thought-conscience-and-religion-or-belief/, last accessed 28/05/2024.

10 See, for example: https://humanists.international/2015/06/iheu-defends-importance-of-free-expression-for-lgbt-people/, last accessed 28/05/2024; https://humanists.international/2016/03/iheu-calls-on-un-to-reinforce-human-rights-mechanisms-protecting-lgbti-people-and-srhr/, last accessed 28/05/2024; https://humanists.international/2023/07/at-un-humanists-condemn-ghanas-anti-lgbti-bill-and-discrimination-in-the-country/, last accessed 28/05/2024.

11 However, many religious organisations supported Section 28 and some have even called for its reinstatement. See, for example: Section 28 was a shameful piece of legislation prompted by fake news | National Secular Society (secularism.org.uk), last accessed 28/05/2024; Section 28 – The Christian Institute, last accessed 28/05/2024.

12 26:165-166, *The Qur'an*, (London: Oxford University Press, 2005).

13 *Leviticus 18:22, The Bible (NIV)*, (Grand Rapids, MI: Zonderan, 2005).

14 See, for example: Microsoft Word – 2020–12–15 Conversion Therapy Research Report_AJ edited(clean) (4).docx (coventry.ac.uk), last accessed 28/05/2024; conversion-therapy-ban-legislating-to-protect-the-mental-health-of-the-lgbtqia-community-december-2022.pdf (mind.org.uk), last accessed 28/05/2024; Failure to deliver ban on conversion practices is disastrous for the UK – University of Birmingham, last accessed 28/05/2024; Small kids made to look on as ISIS throws 'gay' man off building and stone him to death | PinkNews (thepinknews.com), last accessed 28/05/2024.

15 https://www.legislation.gov.uk/ukpga/2010/15/contents, last accessed 28/05/2024.

23

GENDER, ISLAM AND DIALOGUE

A Muslim Feminist Perspective on Navigating 'Hard-to-Have' Conversations

Sariya Cheruvallil-Contractor

Islam and Gender is one of those debates that is consistently fraught. We are bombarded with information (and misinformation) via traditional and new media, in our studies and via our families and social networks. We are told of the travails of Muslim women in Afghanistan, Iran and elsewhere, who are forced into all sorts of dehumanising situations. We are told of various bans on Muslim women's sartorial choices – is this the righteous West looking out for the rights of a vulnerable group or is it a State imposition on women's sartorial choices?

This article focuses on Islam. Why? Because in terms of numbers, it is a *deen* or way of life that has around 4 million adherents in the United Kingdom, as per the 2021 national census, or 6.5% of its total population, and around 2 billion people or 24% of the global population. A minoritised group in Britain, but also a global majority. Islam holds meaning for a large number of people, who draw upon it to make life choices and decisions. But their experiences of Islam are not homogeneous *at all*. Indeed, Islam is diverse, decentred and lived differently, shaped by diverse Muslims' ethnicity, gender, where they live, class and how much *or how little* they believe. Beyond statistics, Muslims are increasingly more visible in Britain's urban centres. Furthermore, the ugly blot of terrorism has meant that ordinary Muslims face scrutiny of their choices and their lives, scrutiny that impedes dialogue.

This piece draws on empirical data from conversations with Muslim women. Why? In his exploration of how Islam is characterised in the Western mind, Richardson identifies perspectives of Islam as a religion that systematically discriminates against women as one of seven narratives that determine how it is perceived.[1] There is almost a societal expectation that ordinary people take sides on the matter of Islam and gender – either that Islam is a

DOI: 10.4324/9781003536185-26

212 Religion and Atheism in Dialogue

misogynist faith that discriminates against women or that such perceptions of Islam are an Islamophobic misrepresentation of an egalitarian faith. Such dichotomous thinking has many problems. It positions Islam as a monolith. Second, it impedes dialogue. How are we to engage with each other, *to understand*, if we occupy different moral high grounds? 'Never the twain shall meet'.

Third, when one side is trying to 'save' Muslim women and the other trying to 'defend' their honour, constructive dialogue becomes particularly difficult, as my co-contributor to this volume Christopher Lynch, identifies in his piece on 'Faith, Gender and Sexuality'. This makes me wonder about the enduring lack of female Muslim voices in such debates. Does *she* want to be saved or defended? I argue that this debate needs to be led by Muslim women who experience the 'Islam and gender' debate every day, and in ways that are *not* provocative, but which are mundane, ordinary and perhaps a little boring. The mundanity opens up spaces for dialogue – dialogue that Lynch identifies as being important and necessary. We need these spaces of authentic voice and diversity to build resilient, safe and secure societies, where we all respect our differences and not just tolerate them. This article hopes to make a contribution to dialogue around Islam and gender, with a view to building respect around women's diverse choices.

Who am I to be writing this reflective piece?

I write as a scholar who has studied Islam and diverse Muslim lived experience for two decades. My research stems from my unique vantage point.

I write as a believing Muslim woman, whose faith is visible. I wear a *hijab* every day and a *burkini* when I go swimming. I remember feeling personally affected by the French *burkini* ban. I love swimming in England. My local swimming pool has a banner about what people can wear in the pool, which includes an image of a *burkini!* But I was concerned I might never swim in France. As a convert to Islam, I have viewed it from the outside and now from the inside. I remember as a young woman, being extremely critical of Islam's treatment of its women, telling a friend that they cover their women in black *chadors*. Today I wear a *hijab*, grateful that I am judged for my scholarship and not the shape of my body. As a scholar and a public intellectual, I am transparent about my faith, my choices as a Muslim woman to wear a *hijab* and how it and other aspects of my faith determine my everyday life, including my scholarship. Yet I am a Muslim woman who demands rights and respect for women, which makes me a feminist.

So, I also write as a feminist. My 'version' of feminism strives for rights and respect for all, irrespective of gender and not just for women. In their struggles for equality for women, early feminists interrogated existing literary and scientific sources of knowledge that they realised were created by and for dominant social groups and which were biased towards these groups. In their striving to reclaim knowledge for women, feminists build approaches that can be used to advance the cause of any marginalised group who are under-represented in traditional discourses of knowledge. Jane Flax describes feminism thus:

> Feminist philosophy thus represents the return of the oppressed, of the exposure of particular social roots of all apparently abstract and universal knowledge.
>
> *(p. 249)*[2]

My feminism also derives from foundational Islamic texts. As a Muslim woman and feminist, I am able to reconcile many aspects of feminism with my Islamic faith. The Quran sets out separate roles for men and women, but also enshrines equality and respect for both. Indeed the Quran address men and women equally:

> For Muslim men and women, for believing men and women, for devout men and women, for true men and women, for men and women who are patient and constant, for men and women who humble themselves, for men and women who give in charity, for men and women who fast (and deny themselves), for men and women who guard their chastity, and for men and women who engage much in Allah's praise – for them has Allah prepared forgiveness and great reward.
>
> *(Holy Quran, Chapter 33, Verse 35)*[3]

Is it possible that my Islamic faith and my feminism can have shared objectives? I believe they do. I also know that both my faith and my feminism have been mischaracterised in unhelpful ways that impede wider societal dialogue. But let's start at the 'beginning'.

A 'beginning': thinking about the past

Writing in 2012, I started my first book on Muslim women in Britain with the following paragraph.

> In a perceived clash of civilisations,[4] Islam and Muslims have been portrayed as the different other who needed to be civilised by western culture and education. The Muslim woman signified the backwardness of Islamic society and her emancipation was essential.[5] In contemporary western society, there are concerns about 'Islamism' – an interpretation of Islam with allegedly violent undertones. There are also concerns about the assertion of identity among many young Muslims.[6] Young British Muslim women

are a topic for public and media debate in the UK[7] and the resurgence of the *hijab* in western societies adds to modern suspicions of the other. Unfortunately, in some Muslim societies, patriarchy can cause the stereotypes to be true by denying Muslim women their social and personal rights. [....] I take the standpoint that in all of the debates mentioned above, the Muslim woman's version of events – her story – is neither told nor heard. Due to various sociological and historical conditions the Muslim woman has been marginalised from the processes that produced, recorded and disseminated histories of Muslim women. [...] I seek to reinstate her as a storyteller who tells her own story.[8]

Although this writing is over a decade old, the significance of reinstating the Muslim woman to tell her version of life, faith and citizenship in Britain remains. Throughout history, her 'Muslimness', perceived as a monolithic construct, has been sufficient for society to inscribe meanings upon her, a process in which she has had limited say and which seldom takes into consideration diversities among Muslim women. From the 1700s onwards, male colonialists described her as exotic and sensuous even though 18th century *female* writer Lady Mary Wortley Montague reports that these men may never have had access to Muslim women.[9] Partly as a response to the colonial rulers, patriarchy superimposed male honour upon the Muslim woman's body which then had to be protected from the 'corrupt world', so she was covered in the *chador aur char deewari* – the veil and the four walls, her domestic sphere. The proto-feminist pitied her, and wanted to rescue her from her 'inferior' culture.[10] Modernity considered her religion archaic and that faith made her backward. The Muslim woman was the damsel in distress locked up in her cage waiting to be rescued by whoever was narrating the story – be it the orientalist, the colonialist, the feminist or the patriarch.

This historic polemic endures in contemporary British society and beyond. In the nineties, Hiro in his contextualisation of immigration and race relations described 'ill-informed objections to the treatment of women in Islam' and 'ignorance and stereotyping about women's role in Islam [which] verged on being racist' (p. 190).[11] Contemporary rhetoric about banning various pieces of clothing that a Muslim woman may choose to wear – *hijabs* or head scarves, *niqabs* or face veils, long loose dress whatever they are called, in different countries, Turkey, France, Britain and others, all echo similar sentiments of either cloistered lives or of individuals who are anti-modern and anti-west. Allawi sums up: 'whenever gender issues are discussed, Islam's treatment of women becomes the other, unacceptable, alternative' (p. 187).[12]

Thus, the Muslim woman has become a visual signifier of the prevalence of faith and of difference in a deeply secular society. Her choices face scrutiny that they do not deserve. Concurrently she is to be feared, while also being vulnerable. In our immediate memories, successive British leaders described pejoratively her sartorial choices as marks of segregation (Tony Blair)[13]; questioned her abilities to speak English and to integrate in British society (David Cameron)[14]; and equated her to a letter box (Boris Johnson).[15] That this has come from men who once led the British nation is indicative of a groundswell of suspicion and stereotyping. To me and to all British Muslim women, this is disheartening.

But only one side of the debate

In 2012,[16] I quoted various statistics from the World Economic Forum,[17] from Social Trends[18] and from the Indian government[19] to demonstrate that Muslim women indeed lagged behind in various social indicators – employment, education and even in accessing health care. I wrote about my brilliant Muslim friend in high school. She had wanted to become a cardiologist, but was married off instead. Was this what she wanted? I didn't know and cannot ask her now.

In the 13 years since that book was published, some of the statistics seem to have moved on. The World Economic Forum insists that social and economic empowerment of Muslim women across the Muslim world will transform their countries, with working Muslim women constituting a trillion dollar market.[20] So, the narrative seems to be changing. Within this last decade, women in Saudi can drive and work. During my recent 2023 pilgrimage to the Holy cities Mecca and Medina in Saudi Arabia, it was amazing to see Saudi women running restaurants, serving fast food, policing pilgrims and checking passports at the airport. This change is visible all over the Muslim World, with Afghanistan perhaps being the only exception. Even here our perceptions must be contextualised. While there is no excuse for the ill treatment of women, this is a country and people who have been ravaged by multiple wars for more than a century.

My study of Islam, my lived experience and the lived experiences of many Muslim women, indicate a different story – of Muslim women who practise their faith in secular society, balancing the two. There are Muslim women who are denied their rights but there is also evidence of Muslim women who enjoy them[21] and of Muslim women who are using their agency to garner rights for other women.[22] These Muslim women are under-represented and misrepresented by stereotypes that portray them as either the 'different exotic other' or the 'oppressed and subjugated victim'.[23]

What does the Muslim woman say about all this?

My first book, published in 2012, was a feminist giving of voice to Muslim women, to reinstate them as storytellers who tell their own story.[24] This piece would be amiss if I did not include their voices. I start with Khalilah,[25]

216 Religion and Atheism in Dialogue

who wonders why she and other Muslim women like her are perceived as so different:

> I just think singling us out also makes us feel very different from women as a category. Like when you say Muslim women it's like we're not women but a different species – we don't feel, we don't cry, we don't laugh, we don't moan, we don't feel unhappy. You know when somebody says you're a Muslim woman, I feel like I have to take a step back and say 'I am a Muslim woman I must behave like this. I must behave like that'. [...] Why do I have to do that, just because somebody expects me to do that? Why do I have to be completely alien from womankind altogether?

> *I am a woman.* I feel everything another woman would feel. The only thing that makes me different from them [other women] is that I chose Islam [...]. And this doesn't change me being a woman [...]. I was born a woman. I feel like a woman. I talk like a woman. Everything else about me is woman-like. I don't think it should make such a drastic difference that I am Muslim woman. And sometimes I struggle with that because people don't want to see you as a human being or as a woman. They just want to see you as, 'who are you?'; 'where are you from?'; 'do you come in peace?' – that kind of thing.

Samina agrees with Khalilah:

> I think in day-to-day life we are no different. I think there are certain challenges in terms of equal pay and equality in the home which I think are across the board. But because of our appearance and the hijab, we are seen as the 'other'. I acknowledge that the differences between a non-Muslim woman and Muslim woman are not much and the day-to-day challenges are the same. But I don't think that a non-Muslim woman believes that.

This disunity/disjunction within the sisterhood is something that feminists have grappled with for a long time. Some of these differences are due to societal power relations that position some women (and men), to be more authoritative than others.[26] This may be because class privileges have given one set of women better education and more authority,[27] or it could be because of politically infused indigenous-migrant relationships. It may also be caused by stereotypical understandings of Muslim women that deem her and her choices to be inferior and hence incapable of being able to participate in the sisterhood, making her different from 'other' women.

Other participants were at a different end of this 'woman' dichotomy, for them Islam was sufficient to differentiate them from other women. Their 'Muslim-ness' gave women rules and regulations that they chose to follow, they wore hijabs, did not drink alcohol and some of them limited their inter-actions with unrelated men. Norazian describes this sentiment:

> Yes definitely because I follow Islam and we do have restrictions like we can't drink, we can't mix freely with men. I am 100% different from non-Muslim women. I am a Muslim and I know the rules of being a Muslim.

Difference is important, it makes us who we are, but we need spaces of encounter with the 'different' other where we can find and use shared values, experiences, struggles and journeys. Dialogue to me is not about removing difference but aims to understand difference and to become part of the shared realities of individuals who we perceive to be different.

For many women (and men of all identities) this is an ongoing debate that requires self-reflection. When I first interviewed Samreen, a volunteer teach-ing assistant, she said that as a Muslim she was distinct from other women. A year later, she became a mother to a baby girl. She asked to be interviewed again. She had changed her mind about the similarities and differences among women and was keen to set the record straight:

> Of course we are [similar]. When women have babies, many want to leave their jobs and careers because they want to spend time with their children. When I walk through town in the afternoon, I see more women than men and all with their babies. But I think you must take cognizance of the fact that Muslim women are different on one point. I feel that 50% we are the same and 50% we are different. And out of this second 50%, 25% is legitimate difference but the other 25% has been made to *seem* different [Samreen's emphasis]. You cannot base opinions of Muslim women on the actions of a few, just as we Muslim women cannot judge all non-Muslim women by the actions of a few women. I cannot judge all western women because some drink excessively. I have seen many who are highly educated, well-dressed and who have strong values by which they live their life.
>
> *(My translation)*

Samreen had found a shared space – the centre of the town she lived in. Here she also found values and experiences that she shared with the other moth-ers. This encounter and uncovering of shared experience was transformatory for Samreen.

Building bridges in hierarchised society

To conclude, to foster respect in diverse society, we need to think together, with each other and across our differences. Years of societal discourse have taught us to emphasise what makes us different – ethnicities, beliefs, values, choices and so on. Without devaluing these differences or diminishing them in any way, I argue for a permeable membrane between different communities, a space where Muslim women may tell their stories to others who are not Muslim, and where these stories are heard and understood. I suggest that in these spaces we *all* reserve judgement, at least as we listen. In my book on Muslim women, I posed a rhetorical question: what meaning will Muslim women's narratives have for audiences who subscribe to different value-systems?

- Will the patriarchal listener reject women's narratives as unauthentic 'feminist' interpretations?
- Will the feminist listener reject them because they are Islamic?
- Will the secular listener reject religious authority?
- And will the naïve listener simply be flummoxed?

I still do not know the answers to these questions, but in the decade that has passed, I have come to recognise the importance of listening without judging, of empathy, and of recognising our own biases in perceiving the world around us. Perception and reception of the 'different other', whoever they may be, underpin dialogue activities in plural society. The term 'different other' is used in feminist scholarship to delineate how dominant social voices do not just construct culturally differentiated actors within society as different but also 'other' them as alien, foreign and somehow less worthy (of equality, respect and/or rights).[28] Society is hierarchised, which means that certain groups are 'minoritised' and the voices and views of dominant groups are privileged. Recognising societal hierarchies, dominant and minoritised voices is key, if we are to make sense of why debates around Islam and gender remain enduringly polemic.

As a final thought, it we are to overcome the polemic (and overcome we must), we need to be able to think beyond our own worldviews and to recognise that there are ways of being that are different to our own, but which are equally valid. I suggest three pathways for dialogue irrespective of any standpoint we may take and no matter how unbridgeable these stances may seem:

1 I agree with Lynch (in this volume) that while constructive dialogue is difficult, it is possible and indeed it is *necessary* if we are to build resilient futures for our diverse communities. We all need to recognise this necessity.
2 We all need to be reflective of our positions within societal hierarchies, positions of privilege or of minoritisation, and how these determine our views, ideas and perceptions of the different other.
3 Finally, I suggest bravery, not necessarily to confront external provocateurs, but to reflect on and challenge our own deeply held beliefs and ideas, in this case within debates of Islam and gender.

Notes

1 Robin Richardson, "Islam' and 'the West' – competing narratives in the UK media". Lecture at *Respect for Religious Diversity: Fighting Islamophobia* Conference, 2007, European Youth Centre, Budapest, April 2007. Retrieved 1st April 2007.

2 Jane Flax, 'Political Philosophy and the Patriarchal Unconscious: A Psychoanalytic Perspective on Epistemology and Metaphysics' in Harding, Sandra & Hintikka. Merril (eds) *Discovering Reality – Feminist Perspectives on Epistemology, Metaphysics, Methodology and Philosophy of Science*, 2nd edition (London: D. Reidel Publishing Company, 1983), 245–282.

3 *Holy Quran*. Translation and Commentary by Yusuf Ali, Abdullah. 'The Meaning of the Holy Qur'an' (first published 1938) Retrieved 26th April 2010, https://www.usc.edu/schools/college/crcc/engagement/resources/texts/muslim/quran/.

4 Samuel P. Huntington, 'The Clash of Civilizations?', in *Foreign Affairs* Vol. 22, No. 3 (1993), pp. 22–49.

5 Mohja Kahf, *Western Representation of the Muslim Woman - From Termagant to Odalisque*. (Austin: University of Texas Press, 1983); Katherine Bullock. *Rethinking Muslim Women and the Veil – Challenging Historical & Modern Stereotypes.* (Herndon: IIIT, 2003).

6 Sophie Bowlby and Sally Liod-Evans. '"You Seem Very Westernised to Me": Place, Identity and Othering on Muslim Workers in the UK Labour Market' in Hopkins, Peter & Gale, Richard (eds), *Muslims in Britain: Race, Place and Identities* (Edinburgh: Edinburgh University Press 2009), 37–54.

7 Claire Dwyer & Bindi Shah, 'Rethinking the identities of young British Pakistani Muslim women: educational experiences and aspirations' in Hopkins, Peter & Gale, Richard (eds), *Muslims in Britain: Race, Place and Identities* (Edinburgh: EUP 2009), 55–73.

8 Sariya Cheruvallil-Contractor, *Muslim Women in Britain: Demystifying the Muslimah* (London: Routledge, 2012).

9 Montagu, Lady Mary. *The Letters and Works of Lady Mary Worthley Montagu* (1716–1717), Edited by Lord Wharncliffe (London: Richard Bently, 1837).

10 Reina Lewis, Reina, *Gendering Orientalism – Race, Femininity and Representation* (London: Routledge, 1996).

11 Dilip Hiro. *Black British White British: A History of Race Relations in Britain*, expanded and update edition (London: Paladin, 1991).

12 Ali Allawi *The Crisis of Islamic Civilization* (London: Yale University Press, 2009).

13 https://www.nytimes.com/2006/10/18/world/europe/18britain.html.

14 https://www.bbc.co.uk/news/uk-35345903.

15 https://www.bbc.co.uk/news/uk-politics-45083275.

16 Sariya Cheruvallil-Contractor, *Muslim Women in Britain: Demystifying the Muslimah* (London: Routledge, 2012)

17 World Economic Forum (2005), *Women's Empowerment: Measuring the Global Gender Gap* Retrieved 25th July 2007 https://www.weforum.org/pdf/Global_Competitiveness_Reports/Reports/gender_gap.pdf.

18 Social Trends (No. 36, 2006 edition) Retrieved 15th August 2007 https://www.statistics.gov.uk/downloads/theme_social/Social_Trends36/Social_Trends_36.pdf.

19 Rajinder Sachar, *Social, Economic and Educational Status of the Muslim Community of India – A Report*. 2006 Retrieved 12 June 2007 https://minorityaffairs.gov.in/newsite/sachar/sachar_comm.pdf.

20 https://www.weforum.org/stories/2018/05/muslim-women-trillion-dollar-market-saadia-zahidi/.

220 Religion and Atheism in Dialogue

21 See Leila Ahmed, *Women and Gender in Islam – Historical Roots of a Modern Debate* (London: Yale University Press 1992).
22 See Aisha Bewley. *Islam: The Empowering of Women* (London: Ta-Ha Publishers, 1999); Lamya Al Farūqi. *Women, Muslim Society and Islam* (Indianapolis: American Trust Publications, 1991)
23 Yvonne Haddad, Jane Smith & Kathleen Moore, *Muslim Women in America – The Challenge of Islamic Identity Today* (New York: Oxford University Press, 2006); Sandra Wilson, 'Being British and Feeling Muslim - Challenges to Police Understanding' in *Muslim Education Quarterly*, 2003 Vol 20, (1 & 2), 5–12.
24 Sariya Cheruvallil-Contractor, *Muslim Women in Britain: Demystifying the Muslimah* (London: Routledge, 2012).
25 Pseudonym.
26 bell hooks, *Talking Back: Thinking Feminist - Thinking Black* (London: Sheba Feminist Publishers, 1989).
27 Robin Morgan, 'Introduction' in Morgan, Robin (ed) *The Sisterhood is Powerful – An Anthology of Writings from the Women's Liberation Movement* (New York: Random House, 1970), xiii–xli.
28 See Uma Narayan and Sandra Harding. 'Introduction. Border crossings: Multicultural and postcolonial feminist challenges to philosophy' (Part I), 1988 *Hypatia* 13(2): 1–6.

PART IV

Conclusion

24

DOING DIFFERENCE DIFFERENTLY

Anthony J. Carroll and Richard Norman

Beyond the Divide was the sub-title of our earlier book *Religion and Atheism*, published in 2017. That sub-title reflected a recognition of the growing diversity of religion and belief in this country and in many other societies, and in particular, as one dimension of that diversity, the increasing numbers of people who describe themselves as 'not religious' or as having 'no religion'. It reflected also the further diversity within the category of the 'non-religious', including those who would say they are humanists, atheists or agnostics but also those who see themselves as 'spiritual but not religious', and the considerable complexity within those descriptions. As Brian Pearce said in his Foreword to the book, 'The notion of there being two coherent and unified categories of the "religious" and the "non-religious", separated by a deep ditch, is difficult to sustain in such a complex terrain'. He suggested that

> In an increasingly plural society we can only gain from having a better understanding of one another, including the beliefs and values which shape our attitudes and hopes. We need to think together, as well as work together, to achieve this.[1]

The sub-title of the present volume is *Doing Difference Differently*. The phrase was suggested by John Saxbee, and it marks the fact that some of us have indeed been thinking together and working together. After the publication of the earlier book, a number of the contributors began meeting to explore further our agreements and disagreements, our similarities and differences. With the coming of the Covid-19 lockdown, we moved to arranging online conversations, and our discussions have continued in this form. The loss of the physical mode of meeting has necessarily limited the range

DOI: 10.4324/9781003536185-28

224 Religion and Atheism in Dialogue

of qualities that face-to-face encounters allow: physical presence, informal conversations, a cup of tea and a sandwich, and generally more spontaneous interaction. It has however had the advantage of allowing more frequent exchanges to occur and permitting participation across great distances without the accompanying costs and environmental impact which result from face-to-face meetings. It has also allowed for a wider range of topics to be explored as each participant has been able to contribute from their own interests and perspectives. New people to the group have been able to participate in these online conversations, and members of the group for whom travel would be difficult have been able to continue their participation. All in all, the online forum has been a valuable means of fostering further dialogue. Since the beginning of 2020 we have had nineteen online meetings. Their frequency has enabled the participants to get to know one another better and thereby become more aware of the personal experiences which inform one another's thinking.

With the present book, we are endeavouring to take the process further. As editors we have invited contributions not only from those who participated in the online conversations but also from other people, with the aim of widening further the range of perspectives involved in the dialogue. In this concluding chapter we reflect on what we have learned from that whole history of engagement, and we offer our own personal thoughts on what, in our experience, makes for good dialogue.

What have we learned from the dialogues?

Perhaps the most important thing we have learned is that it is indeed possible to 'do difference differently'. Historically, at least, religious and non-religious people have often 'done difference' poorly. The early modern Reformations, both Protestant and Catholic, created a legacy of internal divisions within the Christian world, with those differences understood as 'disobedience', 'heresy' or simply 'error'. This carried over into a deep intolerance and persecution of atheists and critics of religion. Until relatively recent times, in this country, those who disavowed any religious belief faced legal penalties or at least social ostracism. And today, in many parts of the world, both religious minorities and non-believers face persecution and the threat of death. The historical legacy of intolerance means that 'doing difference differently' still has a very long way to go.

In more tolerant societies, ideas still persist that the rejection of religion must leave a void in people's lives, or that it must leave non-believers without any moral compass. Too many atheists have, for their part, engaged in sweeping generalisations about the religion they reject, viewing all religious belief as crude superstition which should be swept aside by science and the enlightenment which it brings. They have paid too little attention to the great diversity not just between religions but between the different ways in which religious commitments are understood and lived. They have failed to do justice to the complex and nuanced ways in which thinking believers, such as those who explore what is sometimes called a 'progressive Christianity', seek to articulate their commitments and to take on board all that can be learned from the sciences.

Our starting point in our dialogues has been that religious believers and the non-religious are each saying things which are important, that we currently lack an adequate language in which to articulate them, and that the process of dialogue, of seeking to explain ourselves to one another, can help us to forge the language we need. In part, then, this is a process of looking for areas of agreement 'beyond the divide', but as Julian Baggini and Fiona Ellis both note in their chapters, this is not to suggest that we should hold out a vain hope of absolute convergence. Rather, we should aim to obtain greater clarity on our differences, and thereby foster a better understanding of the extent of the common ground that we do share with one another.

What, more specifically, have we learned? Our initial discussions, like Part I of this book, focused on the most obvious point of contention between us. What exactly is meant by this word 'God' when it is used to describe what religious believers typically believe in and atheists reject? Are there ways of clarifying it which can make it more plausible for the non-religious, and might this at least blur the dividing line and make it less stark?

The paper by Brian Pearce which forms Chapter 1 of this book exemplifies the clarifications which many religious believers, including many of the participants in our discussions, would wish to make. The God in which they believe is, they say, not 'a being' in the sense of an extra item of furniture added to the inventory of the world by theists but not by atheists. Nor is God a 'supernatural' being in the sense of occupying a separate realm, distinct from the natural world, in a 'double-decker universe'. Rather, talk of 'God' serves to articulate a way of seeing and relating to reality as a whole, to 'Being' as such rather than *simply* 'a being' on a list of items. In seeking to correct these misconceptions, responding to the criticisms of the sceptics, religious believers could perhaps be seen as continuing the tradition of what is called 'apophatic theology', 'negative' theology which emphasises the importance of negative statements, statements about what God is *not*, as a route to understanding.

At the same time, these clarifications may serve to disabuse the non-religious of simplistic assumptions about what religious believers believe. They may foster a recognition that religious commitment is not only, and indeed not primarily, a matter of holding certain intellectual beliefs. It is not the acceptance of a scientific hypothesis which can be refuted simply by proper attention to the scientific evidence. An over-simple atheism may give insufficient attention to the place which belief in God has in the whole life of the believer, and the way in which it gets its meaning from that. In these ways, then, dialogue may help to achieve greater clarity about the God that theists and atheists do or do not believe in.

A better understanding, however, is not necessarily an absolute convergence. As was recognised in the note circulated by Brian Pearce and reproduced at the end of Part I, our discussions had led him to the conclusion that if we are looking for language with which to identify common ground, we would do well to set to one side distinctively theistic terminology. The common ground is best located at the level of shared human experience. This may well include responses of awe, wonder and reverence towards the world that we share. Such responses are often described as experiences of 'transcendence'. Several of our discussions were about how to understand this word, and the chapters by Baggini, Ellis and Brierley explore some of the ways in which it is used by theists (including panentheists) and by the non-religious. As emerges from those discussions, perhaps the fundamental difference between the theist and the atheist is that the former but not the latter will typically use *personal* language to describe those deep experiences. They will use second-person as well as third-person language. The reality to which they respond is for them a 'you' and not just an 'it'. In our discussions Robin Gill used the carefully chosen phrase 'a sense of personal presence'. And the second-person language, however fumbling and hesitant it may be, creates the space for responses not just of awe and wonder, but of prayer and worship. As Andrew Steane put it in one of our discussions, the non-religious may feel a sense of gratitude to be alive and to be in the world, but theism gives you 'permission to be grateful' because there is one *to whom* you can be grateful. (Robin Gill makes the same point.) The atheists among us may understand the appeal of such a perspective, but it still marks a real difference.

If we are looking for common ground between the religious and the non-religious, then, we are more likely to find it in our shared human experience of a shared world – in the 'immanent', as Julian Baggini suggests, rather than the 'transcendent'. For our own dialogues, exploration of the full range of the human condition has become central, reaching towards a better understanding of the human person and of human flourishing. This has involved what John Cottingham described as a 'practical turn' in our discussions, focusing less on what we believe and more on what we *do*, on how, as religious or non-religious, we live our lives.

Most obviously, this involves looking at the *values* which we share. Some of our conversations on this theme, looking especially at Christian and humanist understandings of morality and altruism, are recorded in John Saxbee's chapter. These discussions recognised challenges for both perspectives. There are questions for theists about whether simplistic appeals to scriptural authority are liable to provide spurious justifications for 'man's inhumanity to man'. There are questions for atheists about whether the insistence on a purely human foundation for moral values is a sufficient bulwark against a relativistic acceptance that 'anything goes'. But we can come together in affirming basic 'values which we share because we are all part of the same interdependent human community' (Saxbee p. 64).

Discussion of our shared human experience has included also conversations about what may or may not be described as 'spiritual' experiences. Jeremy Rodell's chapter notes the hesitation many humanists feel about employing that label, but also the difficulty of finding a better word. These may be experiences relating to our profound inner life, or responses to the natural world around us, such as the experience of being overwhelmed by the immensity of the night sky filled with stars, which gives us a sense of connectedness with something larger than ourselves. The chapters by Jeremy Rodell, David Scott and John Cottingham reflect our conversations about different ways of understanding such experiences, including the differences between religious and humanist interpretations, but they start from the common ground of recognising the importance of deeply meaningful experiences of these kinds. As Rodell says, 'They are part of our shared humanity'.

The 'practical turn' in our discussions has led us also to look at 'practices' in a more specific sense, to consider the rituals and observances which are central to the religious life and to ask whether there is a need for secular equivalents in some form. The chapters by Michael McGhee, George Guiver and Liz Slade have grown out of these discussions. McGhee looks at 'spiritual practices' which help to address the consciousness of moral failure, and at their relevance both for religious believers and for humanists, such as the practice of meditation from which the humanist as well as the believer 'may emerge with a sense of wonder and a compassion for the world' (p. 105). Ritual, Guiver suggests, is everywhere in our lives, and reflects a deep human need to make sense of the world not just through our beliefs but through the activities which we share as members of a community and participants in a culture. Slade picks up the problem that, as Guiver puts it, 'our society is ritually depleted', and reflects on her work as a Unitarian in devising practices such as secular pilgrimages. As she says, the non-religious are likely to see traditional religious practices as bound up with unhealthy power structures, but there is also much to learn from them.

A fourth dimension of shared human experience considered in our discussions has been the shared legacy of forms of human knowledge. That includes the knowledge derived from the sciences, a precious common ground which is, as Andrew Steane and Raymond Tallis emphasise from their Christian and humanist standpoints respectively, not a private possession of those who reject a religious outlook and who see science as their weapon with which to demolish it. At the same time, as they also both agree, in embracing science we should reject 'scientism', 'the assumption that science, more precisely natural science, is the sole or ultimate source of truth about the fundamental nature of things, including ourselves' (Tallis p. 124). For a fuller understanding we need to draw on the humanities, including literature, history, art, jurisprudence, philosophy etc., which 'each also have their own valid discourse and contribution' (Steane p. 152). Joanna Kavenna develops this point about the arts, and especially the indispensability of creative literature as a shared treasury. The language of poets and novelists challenges fixed categories, and the forms which it imposes on formlessness are always provisional and incomplete. This takes us back to the emphasis, in the dialogue between Gill and Norman, on the importance of metaphor and analogy to articulate our deepest experience, both religious and non-religious.

It would be foolish to generalise hastily from our own experience of dialogue. All the participants shared a narrow demographic niche, socially and culturally, making productive conversations relatively easy. The contributions in Part III of this book, invited from people who had not participated in the preceding dialogues, are a recognition of the need to widen the conversation: to look at the bigger social picture, to bring in new perspectives including other religious traditions, and to tackle more difficult subjects, including ones where feelings can sometimes run high.

Three themes emerge from these chapters. The conversation between Andrew Copson and Linda Woodhead, and the chapter by Alan Race, locate our own discussions in a wider context. The dialogue between Copson and Woodhead explores the major cultural and religious shifts which have taken place in Britain since the 1980s, with the growth of pluralism and of nonreligion, and the move, especially in education, to shared values rather than a common religion or shared beliefs as the basis for social cohesion. Race charts parallel developments at a global level, where the idea of a 'Global Ethic' of universal values has emerged out of interreligious dialogue and can, he suggests, be transferable to the wider dialogue between atheism and religion.

A second theme is the engagement with atheism within particular religious traditions. Peter Huff, writing from a Catholic perspective, traces the history of a dialogue with atheism as 'part of the leaven of Catholic thought'. Reza Shah-Kazemi criticises contemporary atheists for employing a crudely anthropomorphic conception of God, and he contrasts this with the mystical tradition in Islam which has much in common with Christian, Hindu and Buddhist mysticism. In contrast with other chapters, his critical stance towards atheism is strong and uncompromising, but we could see this as another example of how engagement with atheism can be the 'leaven' to stimulate a deeper theism.

The third theme to emerge from Part III is the need to engage in difficult conversations, especially on issues of sexuality and gender, which can be deeply divisive. Christopher Lynch writes that if such conversations are to be fruitful, there must be an honest acknowledgement of the pain experienced by gay people in consequence of how they have been treated and regarded, including by religious communities and leaders. As Sariya Cheruvallil-Contractor also emphasises in her chapter on gender and Islam, it is essential to listen to people's own lived experience, to listen directly and with empathy, making space for them to speak for themselves without prejudging or stereotyping. She and Lynch both insist that, despite the fraught character of the debates, better conversations are nevertheless possible. Lynch recommends that they should focus on shared values, not shared beliefs. This returns us to the outcome of the conversation between Copson and Woodhead and the chapter by Race. And indeed, perhaps the most important thing to come out of all our conversations is the common ground to be found in the values which we share, grounded in our shared humanity.

These chapters, then, and our own experience of dialogue, suggest that it is at least possible for religious and non-religious people to achieve a better understanding of the differences between us, and to find some common ground where we can dwell together. In conclusion, therefore, we offer some reflections on how we can best talk to one another.

What makes for good dialogue?

An important part of the answer is *humility*. An attitude of humility makes for good dialogue because it fosters an enquiring mind, because it recognises, in a Socratic manner, that it does not know the whole story and so is keen to learn from others about parts of the story which may be unknown territory.

At the same time, and in appropriate balance with humility, we need *honesty*. While recognising that we are not in sole possession of the truth, we need to be open about what we do believe, and be willing, in a respectful manner, to make the case for it. We need humility in order to learn from one another, but without honesty there will be nothing to learn. We cannot make progress towards greater understanding if we simply fudge the differences between us.

Honesty about one's own views and commitments requires, in turn, honesty about those of one's interlocutor. We need to do full justice to what the other really thinks. A sound rule is the principle of *charity*: when engaging with views with which we disagree, we should always look for the best case that can be made for them, and engage with that, not with a caricature or a 'straw man'. This depends on the empathy which Christopher Lynch highlights as an essential component of often difficult conversations about sexuality, listening to the other person's experience, in good faith, and seeking where possible to put a positive construction on it.

Good dialogue also requires a certain degree of *tenacity*, a commitment to follow the argument wherever it goes. It should not be dogmatic, but it should be courageous. As Sariya Cheruvallil-Contractor suggests, we should summon up the bravery to reflect on and challenge our own deeply held beliefs and ideas. We need to leave familiar shores and go on the unknown journey of the understanding. In this journey nobody knows where they are headed and that is part of the joy of it.

Such tenacity encourages *creativity* as participants attempt to reach for expressions that others can resonate with. It fosters growth in the linguistic competence of the members of the group, to speak 'beyond the divide'. It is not enough to settle for familiar safe ground. It is not helpful to attempt to 'grab the default position' – assuming one's own settled views as the starting point for discussion and putting the onus on others to come up with reasons for dissenting from them.[2] It is this creativity which makes the activity particularly enjoyable and enriching for those involved. Through such learning processes, members find that some ways of articulating issues are cumbersome and unhelpful, and are stimulated to innovation.

In conclusion, we have found that a dialogue is a good one when it leaves its participants with a sense that they have learnt something and that they need to go away and think more about it. This 'thinking more about it' is an indication that the dialogues we are involved in are part and parcel of an enquiry into the mysteries of life, which no one group ever exhausts.

Notes

1 *Religion and Atheism: Beyond the Divide*, ed. Anthony Carroll and Richard Norman (Routledge, 2017), xvi–xvii.
2 The phrase was coined by Anthony Kenny in his *What I Believe* (London and New York: Continuum, 2006), Chapter 3 'Why I am Not an Atheist', 21.

INDEX

absolutes 134, 141, 198–9
accountability 59–65
agape 59
akrasia 99–100
Allawi, Ali 214
altruism 57–66
analogy 37–8, 41–2, 45, 228
anthropomorphism 41, 45, 192, 195
Aquinas, Thomas 40–3, 186–7
Arnold, Jonathan 45–7
art, the arts 133, 142, 152, 228
Augustine 92, 94
Averroes (Ibn Rushd) 40–2
awe 11, 15–18, 22–3, 53, 226

Barfield, Owen 141
Barr, William 103
belief 91, 98, 106, 225
binaries 141–2
biologism 125–6
Blackmore, Susan 74
Blake, William 104, 141
Boethius 84, 92
Borges, Jorge Luis 138–9
brain 125, 148–9
Brooke, Rupert 135
Buckley, Michael J. 187
Buddhism 73, 100, 103, 194, 198
Bullivant, Stephen 185

Catholicism 182–91, 228
Christianity 4–5, 47, 49, 62–4, 75, 88, 97, 111, 113–4, 145–6, 157–8, 184–5, 203, 205–7
Clayton, Philip 26–7
common ground 10–11, 12–19, 25, 33–4, 38–9, 52–3, 61–3, 87, 98, 103, 105, 108, 130, 146, 152–3, 179, 226–9
community 110–1, 117–20
Comte-Sponville, André 70, 79
Connelly, Peter 67
consciousness 70, 74, 92, 125, 196
corporate life 110–1
Cottingham, John 62
culture 111–4
culture wars 97
Cupitt, Don 21–2

Dalai Lama 69, 75
Darwin, Charles 123–5
Dawkins, Richard 43, 47, 192
democracy 146
dialogue xii–xiii, 11, 19, 161, 167, 172–80, 186–9, 207–9, 212, 218, 224–5, 229–30
diversity 160–2, 168, 170–1, 173, 177, 228
divine command ethics 58
Duffy, Bobby 158, 160

232 Index

Einstein, Albert 72
Eliot, T. S. 100–2, 133, 137–8
Emerson, Ralph Waldo 121
empathy 60–4, 209, 229
Enlightenment 145–6
evolutionary theory 125

faith 61, 65–6
Faraday, Michael 124
feminism 212–3
Feynman, Richard 126
Fiddes, Paul, 29
Flax, Jane 213
formlessness 133, 139, 141, 228
Francis, Pope 43–4
freedom, free will 126, 148–50
Friedman, Richard Elliott 188

Galileo Galilei 123–4, 129
Gaudier-Brzeska, Henri 135
gay rights 202–10
gender 202–20, 228–9
gender identities 202–10
gender roles 211–20
Gipps, Richard 91
Global Ethic 174–8, 228
God: anthropomorphic view of 41, 45,
    192, 195; as 'Being itself' 6–7, 28,
    34–5, 45; how term to be understood
    4–9, 25–30, 33–6, 40–5, 49, 225;
    interventionist view of 7–8; as
    omnipresent 7–8, 27; panentheist
    concept of, 7–8, 26–30; as personal
    8–9, 29, 35–8, 145, 226
Golden Rule 175
Good Samaritan 18–19
Goodenough, Ursula 88, 90
gratitude 39, 49, 53, 226
Graves, Robert 137
Griffin, David 26

Habermas, Jürgen 97, 178–9
Hadot, Pierre 193
Hardy, Alister 73
Hardy, Thomas 47–8
Harris, Sam 71, 74
Hawking, Steven 151–2
Heidegger, Martin 20–1, 24
Heaney, Seamus 69
Higgs, Peter 47
Hinduism 74, 196
Hinton, James 44
Hiro, Dilip 214

homosexuality 202–10
Hopkins, Gerard Manley 88
human nature 57–66
human rights 177–8
humanism 47, 49, 57–66, 75–6, 97–8,
    109, 111, 124, 130, 145, 204–5
humanities 152
Hume, David 60–1
humility 18–19, 22–3, 229
Hutcheson, Francis 102
Huxley, Thomas 123–4
Hyman, Gavin 188

Ibn al-'Arabī 195–8
Ibn Rushd *see* Averroes
immanence 16–19, 23–4, 26
interfaith dialogue 172–81, 193–200,
    228
Islam 40–2, 192–201, 203, 206–7,
    211–20, 228–9

James, William 134
Jesus 18–19, 64, 146, 198
Judaism 40–2, 44, 145–6, 161, 188
Justin Martyr 184–5

Keats, John 38
Kelvin, Lord 127
Kim, Chin-Tai 20
Koran *see* Quran
Krause, Karl 26
Kreeft, Peter 187
Küng, Hans 174, 177, 185

Ladyman, James 126
language 133–42
Lash, Nicholas 21
Lawrence, D. H. 136
Leavis, F. R. 101
Levinas, Emmanuel 29
Lewis, Wyndham 134–5
LGBT+ rights 202–10
Lightman, Alan 13, 17
literature 133–42, 152, 228
love 18, 29
Lucas, John 149

Maimonides, Moses (Musa ibn
    Maymun) 40–2
Mandela, Nelson 61
Maslow, Abraham 72–3
Mason, Marilyn, 69
materialism 5–6

Index **233**

Mayer, Toby 195
Maxwell, James Clerk 124
McGhee, Michael 75
measurement 127–30
meditation 74, 105, 107, 119, 227
Meister Eckhart 195–8
Menocal, Maria Rosa 40
metaphor 38, 133, 141, 228
Metzinger, Thomas 74–5
Miles, Jack 188–9
miracles 8
Mirrlees, Hope 136
models, scientific 147
moral authority 57–66, 97, 103–4
moral failure 98–100, 227
morality 57–66, 97–105
Morrison, Toni 133
Mother Teresa 185–6
Mulhall, Stephen 13
Musa ibn Maymun *see* Maimonides, Moses
music 37, 45–6
mysticism 195–9, 228

natural law ethics 58
naturalism 6, 14, 17, 22, 28
near-death experience 73
Nelson, Maggie 141–2
Newman, John Henry 182–4
Newton, Isaac 124
Nietzsche, Friedrich 134

Oldfield, Elizabeth 75
Owen, Wilfred 135

panentheism 7, 26–30, 34–5, 75
Pascal, Blaise 81–3, 92
Penrose, Roger 149
Philo 192–3
physics 126–7, 146–53
Pieper, Josef 186
pilgrimages 120–1, 227
Pittenger, Norman 25, 30
polarity 141
practices 106–7, 227; *see also* spiritual practices
prayer 49, 107

quantum theory 126–7, 146–50
Quran 193–5, 213

reductionism 5–6, 148–9, 153
Rees, Christina 67

relativity 127, 136, 146–7, 198
religious education 161
resonance 36–7, 45–8
Richardson, Robin 211
Rilke, Rainer Maria 102
rituals 108–9, 115–22, 227
Roberts, Alice 68
Robinson, John 13, 22, 28
Ross, Donald 126
Rovelli, Carlo 126
Rowson, Jonathan 74
Russell, Bertrand 186–7

schools 161, 163–5
Schuon, Frithjof 196, 199
science 5, 123–32, 144–53, 227
science and religion 123–4, 144–5, 227
scientism 5, 124–30, 227
secularization 157–9
Sedgwick, Eve 134
separation of church and state 145
sexuality 202–10, 228
Shapiro, Marc 173
Shelley, Percy Bysshe 38
social change 157, 228
social cohesion 159–61, 228
Soskice, Janet 42–4
Spencer, Nick 124
Spinoza, Baruch 23, 93, 100
spiritual experience 67–96, 119, 227
spiritual practices 101, 104–5, 122, 227
spirituality 10, 67–76, 87–90, 93, 98, 119, 122, 158
Steane, Andrew 43
Sunday Assembly 117–19
supernatural 7, 73, 75, 88, 91–2, 225

Tallis, Raymond 27, 47, 82–3, 92
Thoreau, Henry David 121
Thomson, William 127
Tillich, Paul 13, 22, 27, 188
Todorov, Tzvetan 130
tolerance 166–7
transcendence 7, 12–19, 20–4, 26, 34–5, 71–3, 80, 89, 195–9, 226
Twiss, Sumner 177

Unitarianism 116

values 9–10, 60–5, 103–4, 152–3, 163–7, 174–8, 208–9, 226–7, 229

234 Index

Walzer, Michael 178
Webster, David 68
Weil, Simone 29
Weinberg, Steven 130
Wilberforce, Samuel 123–4
Williams, Rowan 13, 65
Wolfe, Judith 88
women's rights 211–20

Woolf, Virginia 120–1, 134, 137–8
Wordsworth, William 50, 88–9, 93
World War I 134–5
Wright, C. 149

Yeats, W. B. 135–6

Zarum, Raphael 44

9781032881027